A Dictionary
of the English Bible
and its Origins

A Dictionary
of the English Bible
and its Origins

Alec Gilmore

FITZROY DEARBORN PUBLISHERS
LONDON • CHICAGO

Copyright © 2000 Sheffield Academic Press

First published in 2000 in paperback by
Sheffield Academic Press Ltd
Mansion House
19 Kingfield Road
Sheffield S11 9AS
England

This edition first published in 2001 by
Fitzroy Dearborn Publishers
310 Regent Street
London W1B 3AX
UK

and

919 North Michigan Avenue
Chicago, Illinois 60611
USA

Typeset by Sheffield Academic Press

and

Printed on acid-free paper in Great Britain
by Antony Rowe
Chippenham, Wiltshire

British Library Cataloguing in Publication Data. A catalogue record
for this book is available from the British Library

A Cataloging-in-Publication record for this book is available
from the Library of Congress

ISBN 1-57958-323-7 Fitzroy Dearborn

Cover photographs
The Cathach Psalter, folio 14 © Royal Irish Academy, Ireland
King James Bible, 1611, first edition © Adam Woeger
The Beginning of the Gospel of St. Matthew © The British Library
Contemporary English Version © American Bible Society 1991, 1992, 1995
Into the Light edition/Anglicisations © British & Foreign Bible Society 1997
The Beginning of the Gospel of St. John © The British Library

CONTENTS

Introduction   7
Abbreviations   11

Dictionary Entries   13

Bibliography   189

Introduction

Why a Dictionary?

Several factors have contributed to this book. One is the good biblical tradition of British nonconformity in which I grew up, with a sound emphasis on the importance of biblical scholarship and a firm rejection of anything approaching bibliolatry or fundamentalism, both of which I associated with people who had either got on the wrong bus or not been sharp enough to alight in time and strike off in a different direction. So it was something of a shock to discover highly intelligent beings preparing themselves for Christian ministry and seeking to explain, let alone defend, many of the issues which for me had never been a problem.

A second factor was a fascination with biblical languages, biblical texts, textual transmission and the growth of the canon which I wanted to share with everybody else. I thought that if only people knew how it all came together they would handle it differently, enrich their understanding and avoid many a heartache. But how? Most people were not going to learn Greek, never mind Hebrew. 'Text and Canon' sounded just about the dullest topic you could imagine. Somehow they needed the fruit of scholarship to arouse their interest.

A third factor was the discovery that once the light began to shine many of them did want to know more. Some were the product of very conservative environments from which they longed intellectually to escape. Some were in congregations finding new light and interpretation and wondering whether they could safely believe what they were being told. Some were Bible students who wanted to distract me from what I was trying to say and force me back to first principles.

A fourth factor undoubtedly was a change of climate. In Britain, unlike the USA, from the launching of the Revised Standard Version shortly after the war new translations caught on. J.B. Phillips, William Barclay, Ronald Knox and a few others saw to that. Not with everybody, of course. There was, and still is, a significant rearguard movement, though nowadays, apart from a tiny if vociferous minority, it amounts to little more than a choice between the New International Version, the *Revised English Bible* and the *Good News Bible*. So where did all these new translations come from? People began to argue which was the best, which the most reliable, and how they could decide which one to use.

Why Another Dictionary?

The story has of course been told before, many times. But it is usually told in two parts, as the bibliography amply demonstrates. The first part deals with original manuscripts, their production, compilation and recognition, and tends to be left to a fairly limited number of specialists. The other part is the story of the English Bible, from Tyndale to the *New Revised English Bible*. This Dictionary brings the two together so as to see the story whole.

Furthermore, instead of simply telling the story, it offers a work of reference. Students coming to the subject for the first time and finding themselves confronted with a mass of technical terms can find them alphabetically. The curious, wondering what part Coverdale played in Bible translation and where he fits into the scheme of things, or travellers wondering whether there is anything of interest in Alcalá or Soncino can check it out before they go. Readers confronted with more translations than they know what to do with can find potted summaries to help them to make their own assessments. And those with time on their hands can work their way through the cross-references and make their own connections.

Explanations

It is not of course complete. It is of necessity selective, and scholars and readers with a knowledge of the territory will want to challenge the selection of topics, and in some cases the explanations given and the information presented. Nor is it a final and definitive tool. On many of the issues there is considerable difference of opinion among professionals and it was never my intention even to reflect them all, never mind address them. What I have tried to do is to avoid error, acknowledge variety, cover what seemed essential to an understanding of the issues and encourage readers to use it with an open mind and then pursue more detailed and varied study in other places.

The biographical notes, for example, are not intended to be composite biographies. Many of the people included, particularly scholars of recent vintage, have many more credits and achievements, including some relating to the Bible, than have been listed. What I have tried to do is to note their contribution to the origins and development of the English Bible, adding only such other details as were readily available to put that contribution in context.

Text in boxes is of two kinds. In some cases it is anecdotal, legendary, relevant but peripheral. In other cases it provides examples of the way in which variant readings occur in manuscripts and therefore affect translations and interpretations. Since it was not my intention to analyse and classify the various translations no attempt has been made to list the differences in the English versions, but where it was helpful differences between two or three translations, mainly AV and NRSV, have been noted. Readers who wish to pursue the study further can readily do so by consulting other translations for themselves.

Appreciation

To the discerning and undiscerning alike it will be obvious that none of this is the fruit of my own research. My debt to others is considerable and I make no hesitation in acknowledging it in general terms. I am indeed grateful for all the careful and painstaking work done by others and for making my task of compilation so much easier.

The bibliography is intended primarily to acknowledge my sources, particularly one or two on which I have drawn fairly heavily, and if occasionally their writers can hear themselves speaking this is less my reluctance to paraphrase and more my concern to achieve accuracy of content by using the writings of those who have worked at it so much longer and more deeply than I and to make the fruit of their scholarship available to others who may never find their specialist works. I trust any who may feel that they have been 'used' will accept this explanation in a work where regular identification of sources and frequent footnotes would have been inappropriate. I am indebted to the *Cambridge Bible Handbook* (Cambridge: Cambridge University Press, 1997), for the 'Early Curiosities' (p. 35) and to Edwin Robertson, *Taking the Word to the World* (Cambridge: Nelson, 1996), pp. 58-59, for Eugene Nida's African experience with translation (p. 123).

At the same time I have included a number of reliable, more popular and inexpensive works for further reading, most of which are marked with an asterisk. These are intended for people coming to the subject for the first time who want to explore the subject further, and in a more coherent form, but more or less at the same level, and for those who wish to go one stage further.

My other debts are: to Sheffield Academic Press for their initial encouragement and for trusting me with the venture as well as for many helpful suggestions in the course of production; to Richard Coggins, a friend of many years who has given freely of his time, knowledge, wisdom and experience, sometimes to prevent me from making mistakes, sometimes to point me in the right direction for further information and sometimes with straight positive suggestions for improvement; to Edwin Robertson, another long-standing friend whose own writings on the English Bible have contributed so much to the subject and who read through the manuscript and also made a number of suggestions for improvement; to Gerard Norton for technical help with the entries on Codex Aleppo, Codex Leningrad, Codex Petersburg, *Biblia hebraica* and the Hebrew University Bible Project; to Sarah Dobson, Librarian at the Athenaeum; to Christina Mackwell, Senior Assistant Librarian at Lambeth Palace; to several members of the library staff at Sussex University; to the Bible Societies and many others who have responded to my enquiries for details, particularly in the biographical entries. Without all this help the book could not have been what it is. For the errors and the failures, as one always says, the responsibility is mine.

My hope is that readers will find it interesting and enjoyable as well as useful, that it will enrich their appreciation of the Bible, and that it will stimulate them to pursue the subject in more detail for themselves.

Alec Gilmore
North Lancing

ABBREVIATIONS

ABS	American Bible Society
ASV	American Standard Version
AV	Authorized Version
b.	born
BCE	Before the Common Era
c.	*circa*
CE	Common Era
d.	died
DSS	Dead Sea Scrolls
fl	*floret*
Heb.	Hebrew
JB	Jerusalem Bible
KJV	King James Version
lit.	literally
LXX	Septuagint
ms.	manuscript
MT	Masoretic Text
NASB	New American Standard Bible
NEB	New English Bible
NIV	New International Version
NKJV	New King James Version
no.	number
NRSV	New Revised Standard Version
NT	New Testament
OT	Old Testament
pl.	plural
prelims	preliminaries
REB	Revised English Bible
rev.	revised
RSV	Revised Standard Version
RV	Revised Version
UBS	United Bible Societies
v.	verse

A

Abbott, Thomas Kingsmill (1829–1913). A biblical scholar, originally trained in mathematics, who held successively the chairs of Moral Philosophy, Biblical Greek and Hebrew in the University of Dublin, and who worked with W.H. Ferrar* in the discovery of Family 13*.

Abbott, Walter Matthew (1923–). A Jesuit who wrote an article in *America* (an American Roman Catholic journal) in October 1959, shortly after the publication of the RSV*, entitled, 'The Bible is a Bond', pointing out that a common translation of the Bible 'would be a great achievement in the history of Christianity' and reporting that a group of British Roman Catholic scholars had examined the RSV and found that with no more than 20 changes it could be completely acceptable to Catholics. Robert M. Grant of Chicago University, and President of the American Society of Biblical Literature and Exegesis, responded by saying that it would be 'hard to over-estimate' the 'unifying force' of such an agreed version among Christians. Further progress awaited the Second Vatican Council*, 1962–65, after which Abbott received the imprimatur for his book on the Council and was appointed personal assistant to Cardinal Bea to implement the Council's proposals for Bible Study with a view to closer cooperation between the Roman Catholic Church and the Bible Societies*. From 1967 to 1978 he was Director of the Office for Common Bible Work at the Vatican and one result was The Common Bible*, 1973.

Additions. Scribes by tradition, particularly when copying* the OT, copied only, and precisely, the text, with no amendments, alterations, additions or cuts. Anything other than the text required a marginal note. The most common additions are glosses*, corrections*, harmonizations*, variant readings* and scribal changes*, both intentional and accidental. They may be remarks, notes on content, sectional headings, interlinear or marginal corrections and interpolations*, though it is not always clear whether some interpolations took place during the literary growth of a book or in the later stages as a result of transmission. Scribal changes, however, did occur and were of many kinds. Some scribes were not averse to adding words where they felt something was missing. Some made additions or changes, possibly due to familiarity with the text being copied, possibly having already encountered it in other forms in other mss. or translations, possibly because that was how it appeared in the liturgy of their church. (See Additions, p. 14.)

Adulterous Bible, 1631. Another name for the Wicked Bible*.

Additions

Examples of additions are more obvious in some translations than others. They are not always apparent in English but sometimes help to explain differences between different English renderings.

The addition of one letter to the Hebrew תשמני (*tšmny*) ('thou hast delivered me') could give another word תשמרני (*tšmrny*) ('thou hast kept me'). Could this explain the difference between 2 Sam. 22.44 and the parallel Ps. 18.43, reflected in some English translations.

The addition of one letter in Isa. 63.2 could have changed the more meaningful לבושך (*lbušk*) ('Why is *thy* garment red?') to ללבושך (*llbušk*) ('Why is *to* thy garment red?').

The addition of one letter to the Greek εὐδοκία ('peace, goodwill toward men') in Lk. 2.14 could give εὐδοκίας ('peace among those whom he favours') and so explain differences in translation (see NRSV*) and interpretation and leave us wondering which Luke wrote.

Some mss. add 'openly' in Mt. 6.4, 6, some add 'to repentance' in Mt. 9.13 (perhaps following Lk. 5.32), some add 'the scribes' in Mt. 27.41, while one actually changes Mt. 12.36 altogether by adding, 'will render account for every good word they do not utter'.

Some mss. omit the words, 'And Philip said, "If thou believest with all thine heart, thou mayest." And he answered and said, "I believe that Jesus Christ is the Son of God" ' (Acts 8.37), leading some scholars to question whether they were added from some familiar liturgy which candidates for baptism were expected to utter.

Col. 1.23 describes Paul as a 'diakonos' ('servant', 'minister'). Later mss. call him 'a herald and apostle', and some 'herald and apostle and minister'. Did later scribes feel the need to enhance his status?

Aelfric (c. 953–c. 1020). Abbot of Eynsham, Oxfordshire, who became Archbishop of Canterbury and produced the West Saxon Gospels*.

Agnus Dei, An, 1601. One of the smallest Thumb Bibles*, 1.25 × 1 inches, containing 128 pages, each with 6 lines of text, a running title and a catchword. The text is a rhyming account of the life of Jesus by John Weever (1576–1632).

Agrapha. Lit. 'unwritten things'. As many as 256 sayings attributed to Jesus but lying outside the four canonical gospels have been identified by scholars. Sometimes referred to as 'unknown' (or non-canonical) sayings. Some occur in other parts of the New Testament but most are found in apocryphal gospels* and other non-canonical sources. Their connection with the historical Jesus is uncertain and scholars are divided as to

Some Unknown Sayings of Jesus

1. As you are found, so you will be led away [sc. to judgment] (Syriac *Book of Steps*).

2. Ask for the great things, and God will add to you what is small (Clement of Alexandria*, *Stromatas* 1.24.158).

3. Be competent [approved] money-changers! (Clementine, *Homilies* 2.51; 3.50; 8.20).

4. On the same day he [Jesus] saw a man working on the sabbath. He said to him, 'Man, if you know what you are doing, you are blessed; but if you do not know, you are accursed and a transgressor of the law! (Lk. 6.5 in *Codex Bezae**).

5. He who is near me is near the fire; he who is far from me is far from the kingdom (*Gospel of Thomas*).

6. [He who today] stands far off will tomorrow be [near to you] (Oxyrhynchus*).

7. And only then shall you be glad, when you look on your brother with love (*Gospel of the Hebrews*).

8. The kingdom is like a wise fisherman who cast his net into the sea; he drew it up from the sea full of small fish; among them he found a large [and] good fish; that wise fisherman threw all the small fish down into the sea; he chose the large fish without regret (*Gospel of Thomas*).

9. How is it then with you? For you are here in the temple. Are you then clean?... Woe to you blind who see not! You have washed yourself in water that is poured forth, in which dogs and swine lie night and day, and washed and scoured your outer skin, which harlots and flute girls also anoint, bathe, scour, and beautify to arouse desire in men, but inwardly they are filled with scorpions and with [all manner of ev]il. But I and [my disciples], of whom you say that we have not [bathed, have bath]ed ourselves in the liv[ing and clean] water, which comes down from [the father in heaven] (Oxyrhynchus*).

10. Lift the stone and you will find me, cleave the wood and I am there (Oxyrhynchus*).

11. They that are with me have not understood me (*Acts of Peter*).

their value. One argues that no more than 18 are authentic and another says not more than 10 are to be taken seriously and of those probably no more than 4 or 5 are likely to be authentic. (See Some Unknown Sayings of Jesus, p. 15 and Apocryphal Gospels, p. 21).

Ainsworth, Henry (1571–1622). A Hebrew scholar, educated at Eton and Caius College, Cambridge, who fled to Holland where he became minister of a separatist English congregation in Amsterdam, 1593–1622. He translated the Pentateuch*, the Psalms and the Canticles. His renderings were often too literal to be good English but the Pilgrim Fathers took his version of the Psalter with them to America.

Akibah, Rabbi (d. 132 CE). A Jewish scholar whose contribution to the restoration of Judaism after the fall of the Temple in 70 CE was to fix the Hebrew consonantal text. He was martyred in the second Jewish revolt (132–35 CE).

Alcalá, Spain. First Greek New Testament printed here (then known as Complutum) under the direction of Cardinal Ximenes* in 1514, after which it became part of the Complutensian Polyglot*.

Alcuin (735–804). A biblical scholar who lived at York* and was invited by the Emperor Charlemagne to visit France and to prepare a revised and corrected edition of the Latin Bible. French texts of the Vulgate* being corrupt as a result of frequent copying, Alcuin sent to York for more reliable mss. He finished the work in 801 and presented a copy of the restored text to Charlemagne on Christmas Day. He then carefully supervised subsequent copying.

Aldhelm (d. 709). First Bishop of Sherborne, Dorset, who translated Psalms into Old English, thus providing one of the first examples of Bible translation into English. He also had a gift for music, and legend has it that when people did not care for his sermons he used to sing his message dressed like a minstrel and standing on a bridge over which people had to pass.

Aleppo, Syria. Home of a Jewish community that kept Codex Aleppo* for centuries.

Alexander, Alexander (d. c. 1807). Member (and apparently founder) of an English family of printers and translators going by the Hebrew name of Ben Judah-Loeb. One of the earliest Jewish translators of the Pentateuch* into English, 1785. Pioneer of the Hebrew Press in London and a printer of Hebrew and English works for many years, including an edition of the Ashkenazi prayer book with English translation, followed by a Haggadah (a book of Jewish moral theological interpretation) in two editions and many other liturgical works.

Alexandria, Egypt. Capital city of Egypt in the third century BCE, a centre for both Semitism and Hellenism, and headquarters of commerce and literature in the East following the conquests of Alexander the Great. Traditionally the city where the LXX* originated, also in the third century BCE, in response to the needs of a significant colony of Jews in a Greek environment. Centre for the literary activities of the early church and home to the well-known Catechetical School, first under Clement* and Origen* and later Athanasius* and Cyril of Jerusalem*.

Alexandrian Text. An early text-type, identified by Westcott* and Hort*, dating from the third century, and found in a small group of varied authorities, all from Egypt, of minor importance and not always distinctly recognizable, but at one time regarded by many scholars as the best and most reliable. Most readily recognized in Codex Ephraemi*, the Coptic Versions*, and the quotations of the Alexandrian Fathers, Clement*, Origen*, Dionysius, Didymus and Cyril. Once thought to be a fourth-century recension, papyri (especially $\mathfrak{P}^{66}$ and $\mathfrak{P}^{75}$) now show it to go back to a second-century archetype. Shorter than some other text-types, with few grammatical and stylistic revisions, and noted for its correctness of grammar and syntax, style and polished language.

Alford, Henry (1810–71). Dean of Canterbury who produced a magnificent edition of the Greek NT with copious notes and worked, like Lachmann*, to move away from an excessive reverence to the Textus Receptus* in order to discover a more authentic one. One of five clergymen who worked with Ernest Hawkins* to produce the Authorised Version of St John's Gospel, revised by Five Clergymen*, 1857, and similar revisions of some of the epistles. In 1869 he issued a revision of the NT in the AV* and hoped his work would lead to the setting up of a Royal Commission to revise the AV. In 1870 the Convocation of Canterbury set in motion such a revision which later appeared as the RV*.

Alfred the Great (848–901). More literary than most kings and one of the earliest English translators of the Bible. Towards the end of his life he published a code of laws introduced by English versions of the Ten Commandments, followed by further extracts from Exodus 21–23. Thought to have been engaged in a version of the Psalms when he died but no copy has survived. The British Library holds a ms. called King Alfred's Psalter, giving the Psalms in Latin with an English translation between the lines, but it is really from a later time than Alfred.

Allen, William (1532–94). Fellow of Oriel College, Oxford, who refused to accept the Elizabethan Settlement and went to Flanders, where in 1568 he founded the English College at Douay* for the maintenance of the Roman Catholic cause and especially for the benefit of refugees who wanted to train for the priesthood. In 1578, when the college moved to Rheims*, Allen left Flanders for Rome, where he founded another English College and became a Cardinal. In 1593 the earlier College returned to Douay, but whilst it was at Rheims, Gregory Martin* translated the Douay-Rheims Bible* into English for the benefit of the Roman Catholics.

Allestry, Richard (1619–81). One of three Oxford dons responsible for a Paraphrase on the Epistles of St Paul*, 1675.

American Bible Society. Founded in 1816 to translate, promote and distribute the Bible in areas where USA missionaries were serving. Their decision not to include the Apocrypha* caused much controversy, dating from the Council of Trent* and the publication of the KJV* but changed in the mid-1960s, as a result of which there is today considerable cooperation between Roman Catholics and Protestants in Bible translation. Member of the United Bible Societies*.

American Standard Version, 1901. An American response to an invitation to share in the translation of the RV*, carried out by the American Revision Committee, set up in 1871, who reviewed the RV text as it became available and suggested amendments to make it more suitable for the American market, resulting in a verbal equivalence* translation, not including the Apocrypha*, and published by Thomas Nelson and Son, Nashville.

The American Revision Committee consisted of 32 members, representing nine different churches (Baptist, Congregationalist, Friends, Methodist, Presbyterian, Protestant-Episcopal, Reformed, Lutheran and Unitarian), with Philip Schaff* of Union Theological Seminary as President, William Green of Princeton Theological Seminary as Chairman for the OT and Theodore Woolsey* of Yale University as Chairman for the NT.

Terms were agreed by 1875. The British agreed to the Americans adding an appendix to the British edition, setting out the readings and alterations which the British translators rejected, and America agreed not to publish their own edition for 14 years.

As with the RV the underlying Greek text for the NT is Codex Sinaiticus* and Codex Vaticanus*, reflecting the work of scholars like Tischendorf*, Westcott* and Hort*. There is little influence from papyrus* mss. because most of them had not then been discovered.

Major differences included 'Jehovah' in place of 'Lord' or 'God', the improvement of marginal notes and paragraphing, a greater consistency of translation where Hebrew and Greek words had the same meaning, avoidance of some bad and outlandish Hebraisms, and the abandonment of certain archaisms of vocabulary and diction.

Amplified Bible, 1958 (NT), 1964 (complete). A verbal equivalence* translation based on Westcott* and Hort's* Greek text in the NT and the Masoretic Text* in the OT, produced by a committee of 12 editors working on behalf of the Lockman Foundation in California. 'Amplified' in the sense that it explores a range of meaning for each word, thus adding words to the text and including alternative translations to bring out the meaning instead of making better use of the margin or footnotes. More a commentary than a translation. Published by Zondervan, Grand Rapids.

Andrewes, Lancelot (1555–1626). One of the translators of the AV*, responsible for the panel which translated Genesis to 2 Kings. Born in London, 1 of 13 children, described as a brilliant child of 'honest and religious' parents, probably with Puritan leanings. Educated at Cambridge, well-grounded in Latin and Greek, with a lifelong passion for languages and subsequently competent in Hebrew, Aramaic, Syriac, Arabic and 15 modern languages. Appointed Dean of Westminster, 1601, Bishop of Chichester, 1605, and Bishop of Ely, 1609. Present at the Hampton Court Conference*, 1604.

Annotated Paragraph Bible, 1838. A publication of the Religious Tract Society, celebrating the 300th anniversary of the placing of a copy of the English Bible in every parish church.

Antiochan Text. See Syrian Text.

Antwerp, Belgium. Gave its name to the Antwerp Polyglot*, 1569–72.

Once thought the most likely place for the publication of the first English edition of the whole Bible, probably Coverdale's*, but Cologne* is now thought to be more likely.

Home of the printer, Daniel Bomberg*, and probably where the first edition of Matthew's Bible* was printed and published by Richard Grafton*, as well as a later edition of Tyndale's Translation* and some of the translations of George Joye*.

Home of John Rogers*, who was serving as chaplain to the Merchant Adventurers, and where he first met William Tyndale*.

Tyndale* was kidnapped here prior to his imprisonment at Vilvorde* in May 1535. Antwerp was a free city, but the surrounding territory belonged to Charles V, Holy Roman Emperor. Tyndale's enemies could take no action against him in

Antwerp, but they could charge him with heresy in the Emperor's domains.

Antwerp Polyglot, 1569–72. Eight volumes in Hebrew, Latin, Greek, and Syriac with a Latin translation. Mainly an expansion of the Complutensian Polyglot*.

Apocrypha. A collection of sacred texts, covering roughly the period between the end of the OT and the beginning of the NT, not included in the Hebrew canon but accepted by the hellenistic Jews and taken over by the church as part of the LXX*, plus 2 (4) Esdras, extant only in Latin and oriental versions. The texts fall into three categories:

> *narrative:* historical (e.g. Maccabees) and legendary (e.g. Tobit and Judith).
> *prophetic* (e.g. Baruch).
> *didactic* (e.g. Ecclesiasticus).

Allusions in the NT to books of the Apocrypha are few though the early church Fathers seem to have treated them as on a level with the Hebrew Bible*. Greek and Latin Bibles interspersed them among the canonical books. Protestant practice was either to omit them altogether or to print them as a single unit between the two Testaments.

The word 'apocrypha' comes from the Greek, meaning 'hidden' or 'concealed', and was applied to certain texts possibly because they were intended to be kept from the public on account of the doctrines and wisdom they contained, or perhaps because, appearing as they did in days of persecution, it was both judicious and necessary to 'hide', 'conceal' or 'code' the meaning. Over the years, however, Protestants and Catholics used the word differently.

Protestants use it to describe those books which are not included in the Hebrew canon. Catholics describe as 'deutero-canonical' those which were subsequently recognized and authorized

at the Council of Trent*, 1546, reserving 'Apocrypha' for a further collection of texts not included in the Vulgate* or the LXX*, for which Protestants use the word 'Pseudepigrapha'*. This division, and the fact that Protestants and Catholics have been fairly consistent in their use of apocryphal texts, has, however, led to the widespread impression that the Apocrypha exists as a single collection and appears in one, two or (if we include the Pseudepigrapha) three forms. This is not the case. Apocryphal books originated in different places, at different times, in different languages, and with different literary forms; they also have different relationships with the Hebrew Bible, some like 1 and 2 Maccabees starting there, others like Daniel 13–14 being added and at least one (the Song of the Three Young Men in Dan. 3) being inserted. Furthermore, early Greek Bibles varied in the number of apocryphal books they contained.

Early translators into English adopted different attitudes to the Apocrypha. Wycliffe* repeated Jerome's* statement that the Hebrew canon alone was of divine authority, but then included the Apocrypha. Tyndale* omitted it except for those passages used in the liturgical epistles. Coverdale* put it as a single unit between the two Testaments, except for Baruch which he put beside Jeremiah. Matthew's Bible*, reprinted Coverdale's Apocrypha, adding the Prayer of Manasseh.

Controversy in England started when the Council of Trent, 1545–63* accepted it, grew, with its inclusion in first editions of the AV*, intensified, in 1615 when Archbishop Abbot forbade anyone to issue the Bible without it on pain of one year's imprisonment, and reached something of a climax when Protestants who (along with the Jews) regarded those books as inferior, rejected them and printed a version without it following the

Calvinist Synod of Dort, 1618. In 1644 the Long Parliament, much under Puritan influence, decreed that only the canonical books should be read in church, and three years later the *Westminster Confession of Faith* classified the contents of the Apocrypha as human writings, a policy which prevailed in the Church of Scotland and (on the whole) among the Free Churches. The Church of England thereafter accepted the books 'for example of life and instruction of manners' but not 'to establish any doctrine'.

Most Protestants today take a more liberal view and, thanks to a change of policy by the British and Foreign Bible Society* and the American Bible Society* in 1964 and 1966 respectively, both of which had previously refused to print the Apocrypha, 1 in 3 out of 500 UBS* Bible translation projects in 1989 had Roman Catholic participation. As a result differences between Catholic and Protestant Bibles today are less sharp, though the one still tends to include the books in the body of the OT whereas the other keeps them in a separate section between OT and NT. Catholics and Protestants, however, have always agreed on the main corpus of the canon* and even among Catholics the apocryphal books have never been as highly regarded as the rest. Hence, what we have is not so much controversy as agreement at the centre with some diversity at the margins.

At the time of the RV* special committees were set up (1879–84) to handle a revised translation of the apocryphal books resulting in the RV of the Apocrypha, 1894. In 1913 a group of scholars, led by R.H. Charles, produced two large volumes, *The Apocrypha and Pseudepigrapha of the Old Testament*, in English, in the case of the Apocrypha mostly but not entirely following the translations in the RV in volume 1, and in 1938 Edgar J. Goodspeed* published *The Apocrypha: An American Translation*, in modern English. In 1952, on the initiative of the Protestant Episcopal Church, the National Council

---

Books of the Apocrypha

When the NRSV and the NEB list books of the Apocrypha they list 15, which might almost be described as the Protestant Apocrypha. None of these is in the Hebrew Bible. All are in Latin mss. of the Bible and all except 2 Esdras are in copies of the Septuagint.

They are:

1 and 2 Esdras	Baruch
Tobit	Letter of Jeremiah
Judith	The Prayer of Azariah and the
Additions to the Book of Esther	Song of the Three Young Men
Wisdom of Solomon	Daniel and Susanna
Ecclesiasticus (also called Wisdom	Daniel, Bel and the Snake
of Jesus son of Sirach, or ben	The Prayer of Manasseh
Sirach)	1 and 2 Maccabees

Roman Catholics regard 1 and 2 Esdras and the Prayer of Manasseh as apocryphal.

The Orthodox Churches, at the Synod of Jerusalem, 1692, declared Tobit, Judith, Wisdom of Solomon, Ecclesiaticus, Daniel and Susanna, Daniel, Bel and the Snake, and 1 and 2 Maccabees as canonical.

of Churches of Christ in the USA authorized a further revision of the Apocrypha which resulted in *The Revised Standard Version of the Apocrypha*, 1957, the work of ten scholars on the same principles as those for the RSV*, with Luther A. Weigle* as chairman and Bruce Metzger* as secretary. A further revision appeared with the NEB*. (See Apocryphal Books, p. 20.)

Apocryphal Gospels. A number of writings dating from the same period as the four gospels (and later), preserving many sayings of Jesus (agrapha*) and stories about him which circulated, first orally and then in written form, in various churches and cities in the first century but which did not acquire a sufficiently wide circulation or credibility to find a place in the NT. Many, of uncertain date and origin and often only in fragmentary form, came to light in the period of archaeological exploration beginning at the end of the nineteenth century, especially at Oxyrhynchus* and Nag Hammadi*, and have some value as a reflection of early Christianity and the literary world in which the writings of the NT took their shape. Besides 'Gospels' (according to Peter, Philip, Thomas*, Hebrews, Egyptians, etc.) there are also 'Acts' (of John, Andrew, Paul, etc.), 'Epistles' (of the Apostles, and to the Laodiceans), and various 'Apocalypses'. (See Apocryphal Gospels, p. 22.)

Aquila (second century). A disciple of Rabbi Akibah* and a convert to Judaism (c. 125 CE) who made a translation of the OT from Hebrew into Greek, which subsequently became the official Greek version of the Old Testament for Jews living in Palestine. A very literal translation, almost a recension* or revision of the LXX*, using the proto-masoretic text*, and reproducing in Greek not only the sense but also the idiom, grammar and even the etymology, sometimes to the point of obscurity. Thought by some

to be the Onkelos Targum*. Valuable because its literalism enables us to translate back into Hebrew and so check other translations but it has survived only in fragments. Irenaeus* refers to it c. 177. Found in Origen's Hexaplar*.

Arabic Versions. Origins of Arabic versions of the Bible are uncertain. They probably date from the seventh century since prior to that the language of Christians in Arabia was Syriac, but the oldest texts are ninth century or later.

Aramaic Language. One of the Semitic languages*, closely related to Hebrew, originating among the Arameans of North Syria, with inscriptions going back to the ninth century BCE and spoken from then until the present day. Increasingly the everyday language of the Jews when it replaced Hebrew after the Babylonian exile in the sixth century, and the spoken language of Jesus and his contemporaries. Forty fragmentary Samaritan business documents on papyrus*, found in a cave nine miles north of Jericho in 1962, illustrate the Palestinian Aramaic script c. 375–35 BCE and provide the oldest mss. yet to appear in Palestine, providing an important link in the history of the square Aramaic script between Elephantine* and the DSS*. ('Square' refers to the actual shape of the letters, rather like English capitals. The alternative, or cursive script, looks more like English longhand.)

Arbuthnot, Alexander (d. 1585). An Edinburgh* printer who obtained permission to print the first Bibles in Scotland in 1575 and the following year was granted exclusive rights of printing and selling for ten years. In 1579 he published the first English Bible to be printed in Scotland, a Scottish edition of the Geneva Bible*, 1579, after which he was appointed king's printer, licensed to print, sell and import psalm books, prayers and catechisms for seven years.

Apocryphal Gospels

Sixteen of the more generally acceptable non-canonical gospels from the first and second centuries:

Sayings

*Gospel of Thomas**
A collection of traditional wisdom sayings, parables, prophecies and proverbs attributed to Jesus and dated c. 200 CE. Widely read and quoted in the early church. Found at Oxyrhynchus.

Dialogue of the Saviour
A fragmentary document purporting to preserve the sayings of Jesus in conversation with Judas, Matthew and Mariam and dating possibly from the second half of the first century. Discovered in 1945 at Nag Hammadi.

Gospel of the Egyptians
Sayings, strongly ascetic, attributed to Jesus in quotations from Clement of Alexandria, dated towards the end of the second century.

*Oxyrhynchus Papyrus 840**
A single sheet of parchment containing the end of a conversation between Jesus and his disciples and a controversy between Jesus and a Pharisaic chief priest in the temple at Jerusalem, found in 1905 and dating from the fourth or possibly the fifth century.

Apocryphon of James
A teaching dialogue between Jesus and Peter and James, dating from the second century.

Stories

Secret Gospel of Mark
Contained in a letter of Clement of Alexandria at the end of the second century but dating from the beginning. The view that it might be an early and fuller edition of Mark's Gospel (Mark's original text no longer being available to us) has now been universally abandoned.

Egerton Papyrus 2
Three pages of sayings of Jesus, his miracles and stories of controversy, dating from the first half of the second century.

Apocryphal Gospels (continued)

Gospel of Peter
A gospel fragment containing a passion narrative, an epiphany story, a story of the empty tomb and the beginning of a resurrection story, dating from c. 200 CE.

Gospel according to the Hebrews
A Jewish-Christian document containing traditions of the pre-existence of Jesus, his coming into the world, his baptism and temptation, some of his sayings and a resurrection appearance, dating from the early second century.

Acts of John
A literary romance about the activities of John, dating somewhere between the end of the first and the middle of the third centuries.

Gospel of the Nazaraeans
An expanded version of Matthew's Gospel, possibly from western Syria, and dating from the end of the second century.

Gospel of the Ebionites
A gospel harmony in quotations from the writings of Epiphanius (c. 390) and dating from the middle of the second century.

Book of James
An infancy gospel describing the birth and dedication of Mary and the birth of Jesus, dating from the middle of the second century.

Infancy Gospel of Thomas
Novel miracle stories purporting to have been wrought by Jesus before his twelfth birthday, dating from the middle to end of the second century.

Epistle of the Apostles
A polemical document describing a special revelation of Jesus to his apostles justifying their position as against that of their opponents in the church, dating from the end of the second century.

Acts of Pilate
A Christian apologetic to introduce readers to the claims of the Christian community, containing detailed accounts of the trial and crucifixion, dating from the late second or early third centuries and later incorporated into the *Gospel of Nicodemus*.

Aristeas, Letter of. A letter written in the third century BCE, in Egypt, to his brother Philocrates, describing the origins of the LXX*.

Armenian Version. Eusebius reports that the church was established in Armenia by 250 and Armenia claims to be the first kingdom to adopt Christianity as its official religion. One of the most beautiful and accurate Bible translations, sometimes called the 'Queen of the Versions'. Except for the Vulgate* more mss. of this version are extant than any other early version, well over a thousand having been identified (many in Russian libraries), covering all or part of the NT, the earliest version apparently having undergone a revision prior to the eighth century.

Translated from the Syriac by Patriarch Sahug* and Mesropius* on the basis of the Greek (alongside the liturgy), as an attempt to assert the national language and as a reaction to the use of the Syriac in Armenian worship. Proverbs was the first book to be translated, followed by the gospels and the remainder of the OT which was completed by 415. It contains certain books which elsewhere were regarded as apocrypha*, including the Testaments of the Twelve Patriarchs and a third Letter to the Corinthians.

Arundel, Thomas (1353–1414). Archbishop of Canterbury responsible for the Constitutions of Oxford*.

Athanasius (c. 296–373). Bishop of Alexandria*. Followed Origen* in saying that Christians should have all the 22 books which the Jews had in their canon and promulgated a list of NT books in his Easter Letter, 367, the first example of such a list which includes precisely the books included today. For this reason it provides one of the early hints that the NT was increasingly being recognized as a canon of sacred scripture, and Athanasius was probably the first to use the term 'canon' in this connection. He also included some other recommended writings for catechumens. Though very similar in content to the list provided at the same time by Eusebius*. Athanasius's list seems to have much firmer edges and that of Eusebius more flexibility.

Augustine (c. 354–430). Bishop of Hippo and one of the early church Fathers. Objected to Jerome's* omission of the apocryphal books from the Vulgate* on the grounds that the LXX* and the Old Latin* texts had always included them and Christian leaders and teachers had regularly cited them as scripture. Jerome subsequently translated them but called them 'apocrypha'* and distinguished them from the books in the Hebrew Bible*, thus according them a 'lower' status, but since they appeared in the Latin Bible most people made no distinction and the whole Greek canon became the official Bible of the Western church until the Reformation. Augustine's canon consisted of 44 OT books, including each of the 12 minor prophets plus Wisdom of Solomon, Ecclesiasticus, Tobias, Esther, Judith, Maccabees, the additions to Daniel and Esther, with Baruch and the Epistle of Jeremiah as part of Jeremiah.

Authentic New Testament, 1955. A translation made by the Jewish scholar, Hugh J. Schonfield*, who, fearing that the word 'authentic' in the title might be misunderstood, went out of his way to explain that he intended a translation that broke with convention and tradition and was 'authentic in accent and atmosphere'. He did not wish to suggest that no other translation was genuine or reliable.

Mark's Gospel comes first, traditional verse* and chapter* divisions are ignored, there is some re-arrangement of passages within books and the whole has more the appearance of a modern book than sacred writings. Whilst agreeing that the official versions of the church need to convey religious language at its best, Schonfield says the original NT records have a diversity of style, many colloquialisms, an absence of literary grace and sometimes an infelicity of expression, which he is trying to convey in a translation that is both vivid and forceful. Useful introduction and notes supply much helpful information on the Jewish references in the NT documents.

Authorized Version of St John's Gospel, revised by Five Clergymen, 1857. A revision initiated by Ernest Hawkins* which paved the way for similar revisions of some of the epistles.

Authorized Version, 1611. Often known as the King James Version (KJV), particularly in America. Prepared in the England of Shakespeare's time and containing some of the best English prose and poetry. Most popular of all English versions until the latter part of the twentieth century when more modern translations took over for many, though by no means all, readers.

The result of a proposal made by John Reynolds* at the Hampton Court Conference*, 1604. Existing chapter* and verse* divisions were to be retained, with new headings for chapters. Old ecclesiastical words were to be kept and names were to be as close as possible to those in common use rather than transliterations of the Hebrew or Greek. Words not in the original but needed to complete the sense were to be printed in italics. No marginal notes save to explain Greek or Hebrew words and to draw attention to parallel passages.

The work of 54 scholars working in 6 panels (3 for the OT, 2 for the NT and 1 for the Apocrypha), 2 meeting in Westminster, 2 in Cambridge and 2 in Oxford, with authority to call on other specialists as they wished. How they were appointed is not known, possibly in consultation with the universities. Westminster was responsible for Genesis to Kings and Romans to Jude, Cambridge for Chronicles to Ecclesiastes and the Apocrypha*, and Oxford for Isaiah to Malachi, the gospels, Acts and Revelation.

The plan was for every translator to translate the same chapters, the whole panel then deciding which should stand, after which each book would go to the other two panels for comment, any differences being settled by a general meeting of the senior scholars in each panel. What appears to have happened was that 12 scholars (2 from each panel) received the whole, after which Miles Smith* (who wrote the Preface) and Bishop Thomas Bilson* put the finishing touches to it and saw it through the press. The work began in 1607, was completed in two years and nine months, and was printed in London by Robert Barker, the king's printer. Despite its name it was never formally 'authorized' by anybody.

The Bishops' Bible* was to serve as the basis but Tyndale*, Matthew*, Coverdale*, the Great Bible* or the Geneva Bible* were to be followed when they were nearer the original. Approximately 80 per cent of the words in the NT come from Tyndale. They also used the Douay-Rheims Bible*, the Antwerp Polyglot*, with a fresh Latin version of the Hebrew text by Arias Montanus, and Tremellius's Bible (1579). For the Greek NT they worked mainly from Stephanus* and Codex Bezae* though without any sure principles of textual criticism* to guide them.

After the title page the first edition contained a fulsome dedication to James I*, a defence of vernacular Bibles, an explanation of the methods used, various tables, a map of Canaan, a table of contents, chapter and headline summaries, numbered verses, paragraph signs, marginal notes (philological only) and cross references.

The inclusion of the Apocrypha* caused many tensions, particularly following the Council of Trent* and the decisions of the British and Foreign Bible Society* and the American Bible Society* not to issue Bibles containing it which meant that in practice it was rarely printed from the eighteenth century. Change came slowly and not until the Second Vatican Council* and a change of policy in the Bible Societies in the mid-sixties.

Three folio editions,16 x 10.5 inches, appeared in quick succession in 1611, the first being called The He-Bible*. Heavy punctuation marks were inserted to help reading in public. There were many misprints, one of which has continued to today: 'Strain *at* a gnat' should read 'strain *out* a gnat' (Mt. 23.24). Other misprints were soon corrected, like 'he slew two lions like ["for lionlike"] men' (2 Sam. 23.20), 'the dogs liked ("for licked") his blood' (1 Kgs 22.38) and 'printers ["for princes"] have persecuted me without a cause' (Ps. 119.161), but three in particular led to the Wicked Bible*, the Vinegar Bible* and the Murderer's Bible*.

It immediately superseded the Bishops' Bible for use in churches, but for private use it had strong competition in the Geneva Bible and the two versions vied with each other for half a century before the AV won. In that time there were several editions: one in 1613 had 400 variations from the first. In 1629 there was a more serious revision to take account of certain criticisms, followed by a minor revision in 1638 and yet another in 1653, called for by the Long Parliament. The more important changes occurred, however, in the eighteenth century when spellings, punctuation and expressions were all modernized, some by Thomas Price* of Cambridge and Benjamin Blayney* of Oxford, two great modernisers of the diction of the version from what it was in the seventeenth century. In 1701 dates were introduced into the margin based on the calculations of Archbishop Ussher.

Its strength lay in the richness of the language and the vitality of English poetry, probably best appreciated when read aloud. Its weaknesses were the translators' limited knowledge of ancient languages and of more recently discovered and reliable manuscripts, the growth of textual criticism*, and the way in which many English words have changed their meaning, some no longer even in use.

Autograph. The original copy of a manuscript. No autograph of any biblical book is extant. The nearest we have is the John Fragment* but this and other papyrus* fragments dating from the first two centuries are evidence for the way the NT was being copied and circulated in the early Christian world.

B

Babylonian Recension. See Recension.

Ballantine, William G. (1848–1937). Member of the YMCA College in Springfield, Massachusetts. Translator of the Riverside New Testament*, 1901, one of the few translators who referred to other modern translations, particularly Moffatt*, Weymouth* and Goodspeed*. He saw the task of a translator as being like a plate-glass window ('through which the man who does not read Greek will see in English just what he would see if he did read Greek') and like a pianist ('playing on the piano what was written for the violin').

Barclay, William (1907–78). Scottish theologian and minister of the Church of Scotland, educated at Glasgow and Marburg, and Professor of Divinity and Biblical Criticism in the University of Glasgow. Widely read popularizer and broadcaster. Creator and editor of the Daily Study Bible*, which won international acclaim and was published in many languages. In 1969 he published his own two-volume translation of the NT, *The Gospels and the Acts of the Apostles* and *The Letters and the Revelation*, together with a 45-page essay on translating the New Testament.

Barker, Robert (d. 1645). The king's printer, specially licensed 'to print all statutes and libels' for life, and 'all books in Latin, Greek and Hebrew'. His most important publication was the first edition of the AV*, including the Wicked Bible*.

Barrow, John (1810–80). Principal of St Edmund Hall, Oxford, and one of five clergymen who worked with Ernest Hawkins* to produce the Authorized Version of St John's Gospel, revised by Five Clergymen*, 1857, and similar revisions of some of the epistles.

Basel, Switzerland. The first NT with the Greek and Latin side by side, 1516, the work of Erasmus*, and subsequent editions, were printed here.

Basic English Bible. See Bible in Basic English.

Bauer, Georg Lorenz (1750–1806). A late-eighteenth-century scholar and one of the first to talk about reconstructing the Hebrew text in its pre-masoretic form by making comparisons with other biblical material and the ancient versions so as to get closer to the text as it left the hands of the authors. Other scholars who had expressed similar views had gone unnoticed but Bauer's work was the inspiration for de Lagarde* who took his ideas and applied them to the whole Bible.

Baxter, Richard (1615–91). Leading Puritan divine who published *New Testament with a paraphrase and notes*, 1685, at the time of the Restoration of Charles II.

Becke, Edmund (fl. 1550). Ordained 1551, supervised editions of the Bible with annotations, 1549 and 1551, and edited Bishop Becke's Bible*.

Bede (672–735). A monk of Jarrow* who translated several parts of the NT into English from the Vulgate*. Legend has it that when he lay dying on the eve of Ascension Day he was still busily translating John's Gospel. One account says he had got as far as Jn 6.9. Another says that on the morning of Ascension Day he had only one chapter still to translate which he did during the day and died that night. Unfortunately his translation has not survived.

***Belgica*, 1561.** A statement by the Reformed Churches, following their *Confessio Gallicana**, 1559, in which Articles 4 and 5 set out a canon of the OT, excluding the apocryphal* books included by Roman Catholics at the Council of Trent*.

Belsham, Thomas (1750–1829). Unitarian minister in Worcester and Professor of Divinity at Daventry and Hackney College, London. Editor of William Newcome's* translation of the NT to achieve the Unitarian Version*.

Ben Asher. The most famous family of the Masoretes* who worked on the Hebrew text for six generations, the last of whom, Aaron, perfected the Ben Asher vocalization* system, a major branch of the Tiberian system, most popularly used for the Hebrew OT and first used in Codex Aleppo*. The resultant text is known as a Ben Asher text.

Ben Sira, Jeshua (second century BCE). Author of Ecclesiasticus whose writings throw some light on the nature of the Hebrew Bible c. 180 BCE, in that he reflects the order of books in the Torah* and the Prophets*, knows the 'minor prophets' as 'The Twelve' and is aware of some of the Writings*, though not Ecclesiastes, Esther or Daniel.

Bengel, Johann Albrecht (1687–1752). A NT scholar who opened a new chapter in the history of textual criticism*. A man of deep faith and personal piety who studied at Tübingen, had charge of an orphan home at Halle, taught at a Lutheran Preparatory School for ministers and became Superintendent of the Evangelical Church of Württemberg.

As a student he was disturbed to discover the large number of variant readings* in mss. of the NT and decided to procure all editions, as a result of which he came to the conclusion that there were not as many real variations as at first appeared. Bengel was the first to move away from the Textus Receptus*, the first to argue that variants were to be weighed, not counted, and the first therefore to classify mss. into 'families' according to their importance and not simply according to their number, thus establishing the principle that a lot of mss. from a late date may be much less reliable than one ms. from an early date.

He divided mss. into two groups:

> African, including the ancient authorities coming mainly from Egypt and North Africa.
> Asian, including the great mass of later mss. containing the Byzantine* or Textus Receptus*, a clarification later extended by J.S. Semler*.

He published an edition of the Greek NT in Tübingen in 1734, based on the Textus Receptus and not printing any reading which had not already been published, indicating in the margin his estimate of the value of the variants in five different categories: the original reading, possible improvements, just as good, less good, and so bad as to be rejected. After his death his son-in-law published an enlarged edition of his critical apparatus*. He also laid down some principles for textual criticism* such as *lectio difficilior**.

Benisch, Abraham (1811–78). A Hebraist who was born in Bohemia and studied medicine in Vienna. Editor of *Jewish Chronicle*, 1854–69 and 1875–78. Translator of Jewish School and Family Bible*, 1861.

Benoit, Pierre (1886–1962). Successor to de Vaux* at the Ecole Biblique and one of the key figures in the production of the Jerusalem Bible*, especially the New Testament.

Bensley, Thomas (d. 1833). Printer of the Murderer's Bible*.

Bentley, Richard (1662–1742). Master of Trinity College, Cambridge, English classical scholar and literary critic, and the first to accept the value of the ancient versions as a way of approaching the Greek. He planned a critical edition* of the NT in both Greek and Latin on the principle of preference for the oldest mss., but the task was too great for him and he never completed it.

Berkeley Version, 1945 (NT), 1959 (complete). The Berkeley Version of the New Testament, a dynamic equivalence* translation by Gerrit* Verkuyl*, 'to bring us God's thoughts and ways' in 'the language in which we think and live rather than that of our ancestors who expressed themselves differently'. Called after Berkeley, California, where he lived, and published by James J. Gillick, Berkeley. Twenty scholars subsequently worked on

a translation of the OT, with Verkuyl as Editor-in-Chief, 1945–59, resulting in a similar translation, to give The Holy Bible: The Berkeley Version in Modern English, published in the USA and in London. Revised to become the Modern Language Bible, 1969*. Accurate and similar to the RSV* but more conservative, with copious footnotes to clarify the text, some of which approximate to moralizing observations.

Beza, Theodore (1519–1605). Celebrated French classical and biblical scholar who succeeded Calvin as minister of the church in Geneva* and published nine editions of the Greek New Testament between 1565 and 1604, four of which were independent and the remainder reprints, with annotations, his own Latin version, Jerome's Vulgate* and textual information drawn from his own collection of Greek mss. It differed little from Stephanus's* fourth edition, 1551, but Beza's work is noteworthy because it popularized the Textus Receptus* and the editions of 1588–89 and 1598 were used by the translators of the AV*. Owner of Codex Bezae*, which he presented to Cambridge University in 1581, and Codex Claromontanus*, though he used neither in preparing his Greek NT because they departed too far from the generally received text of the time. The first scholar to collate the Syriac New Testament, 1569.

Bible. *Biblos*, a Greek word meaning originally the inner bark of the papyrus* plant, came to refer first to the paper made from the bark and then to the scroll* and the codex* and eventually to the whole collection of Old and New Testament books. *Biblion* (pl. *biblia*) was the diminutive, meaning a scroll. In the LXX* both singular and plural were used to denote any kind of written document, but Christianity from the beginning retained the plural to denote the Hebrew scriptures plus the books which went to make up the NT, thus creating a closed and fixed list of books (or canon*) with authority for faith, and usually referred to as 'Scriptures'. John Chrysostom* appears to have been the first to use the word *biblia* of the Old and New Testaments together in this way.

What is less clear is which books the early church included and excluded, and if we are to judge by the way in which different centres of Christianity disagreed on the subject and by the time it took the early church to come to a settled conclusion, there is good reason to believe that they took a much more liberal view of what was 'in or out' than we often imagine. Like the Jews before them (and like many of us!) they tended to respect old books, books associated with familiar and reputable authors, and books which they frequently heard read in synagogue or church.

Once the canon was determined there was an inevitable tendency to interpret one part in relation to another part, thus turning what began as a collection of books into a single, composite volume with a special kind of divine authority. In some cases, it led to a search for consistency and unity of message one might reasonably expect to find in a book but which one would not necessarily expect to find in a collection; on occasions, to anxiety because it was not there, and sometimes even to attempts to create it artificially. This trend was re-inforced once the codex replaced the scroll, giving the appearance and in some cases the reality of a unified statement, and in the Middle Ages by the use of *biblia* as a feminine singular rather than a neuter plural which persisted in European languages, giving us 'Bible' and its equivalents. Theological consequences then followed in the Reformation and post-Reformation period with the new enthusiasm for bib-

lical teaching. For as long as the Bible was thought of as one book readers not only expected consistency but also found it possible to envisage it as 'word of God'; if on the other hand it were a collection, then divergence was more acceptable and 'word of God' language more difficult.

Recent discussion has centred on the fact that not only did the church establish a canon but it also established it in a certain way. This means that not only do we have to pay attention to the content but also to the shape or form, so that, for example, Psalms 1 and 150 are not to be read as individual psalms but in relation to the rest for which they provide the beginning and the end. In other words, arrangement and position modify, even if they do not entirely dictate, meaning.

Translations* (or versions) in Latin*, Syriac* and Coptic* appeared as early as c. 180 CE. Gothic* and Slavonic* translations existed as a single version from the start, but in the case of most others it is difficult to determine whether there was a single ancient version from which the others came or whether a variety of versions converged into a single text.

Bible in Basic English, 1941 (NT), 1949 (complete). Basic English is a form of the English language, produced by C.K. Ogden*, using only 850 English words. For this version 50 special 'Bible words' were added plus a further 100 needed for English verse, thus making 1000 words in all. The translation was made from the original texts by a Committee under S.H. Hooke* and published by the Cambridge University Press.

Bible in Modern English, 1895 (NT), c. 1903 (complete). A dynamic equivalence* translation into modern English, considered by some to be a paraphrase*, from the original Hebrew, Greek and Aramaic languages, by Ferrar Fenton*, and published in London. Romans appeared first (1882) followed by the epistles (1884). Despite being launched so soon after the RV* and amid much controversy as to whether new translations were needed anyway, the work had considerable popularity, with two new impressions in 1941 and 1944, despite the Second World War.

The text is broken up by the insertion of subject headings and there is some introductory and explanatory material. Unusual features include: the translation of Gen. 1.1 where Fenton rejected 'In the beginning...' on the grounds that the Hebrew word was plural and instead gave us, 'By periods God gave us that which produced the solar system; then that which produced the earth'; some peculiarities of translation and spelling, such as Mikah (Micah) and Zakariah (Zechariah), because Fenton transliterated names according to how they would sound in Hebrew; and an unusual arrangement of books, the OT following the Hebrew canon but the NT putting John and 1 John at the beginning of the NT, because Fenton thought they were earlier than the other books and belonged together, thus allowing Luke and Acts to stand together.

Bible in Order, 1975. An edition of the Jerusalem Bible*, compiled by Joseph Rhymer, with books in chronological order according to the dates at which they were believed to have been written, and published in memory of Alexander Jones*.

Bible Societies. See British and Foreign, American and United.

Biblia hebraica. One of only two currently critical and complete editions of the Hebrew Bible, containing a selective critical apparatus* and occasionally a short evaluation of variant readings*. The other,

less widely used and with only Isaiah completed, is the Hebrew University Bible Project*.

The first two editions of Biblia hebraica (1905 and 1912), based on the second Rabbinic Bibles*, 1525, were superseded by the third edition (1929–37) edited by Rudolf Kittel (widely known as *BHK*), based on Codex Leningrad* (L) as providing the earliest complete codex of the Hebrew Bible. Editions since 1951 and *Biblia hebraica stuttgartensia*, 1977, edited by K. Elliger and W. Rudolph (known as *BHS*), contain details from the DSS* for some books, but an edition incorporating all significant readings from Qumran* is not yet available. *BHS* is somewhat less free with conjectural emendation* and was used extensively by scholars preparing the REB* and the NRSV*. A fifth edition to be known as *BHQ* is in preparation.

Biblical Criticism. Biblical criticism is reading the Bible as rational human beings, trying to appreciate its finer points by paying attention to language, history and background, the local and cultural circumstances in which it was written and the ever-increasing knowledge as a result of historical and archaeological research available to every generation, and then trying to relate its message and meaning to the world we live in. Understood in this way biblical criticism is as old as the Bible itself.

Change came in the eighteenth century which serves as a watershed between the pre-critical and critical periods, after which biblical scholarship concentrated on the academic and refused to accommodate its researches, discoveries, theories or interpretations to church doctrine. The change was not universal, varying from country to country, from church to church, and even from scholar to scholar. Issues at stake tended to be textual* (or lower) criticism and higher* criticism, which covered topics such as the origins of the various books, their date and authorship, their reliability as history, the relationship between OT and NT, and the interpretation of particular passages, notably those relating to morality and miracles.

In the last quarter of a century there has been an increasing tendency to concentrate on the texts as they are in front of us rather than on their origin, history and development, resulting in a variety of readings—liberation, literary, feminist, and so on.

Bilson, Thomas (1546–1616). Born in Winchester, educated at Oxford and later Bishop of Winchester, responsible with Miles Smith* for seeing the AV*, 1611, through the press.

Bishop Becke's Bible, 1551. A mixture of Taverner's* OT and Tyndale's* NT, compiled by John Daye and edited by Bishop Edmund Becke*, with a few simple notes in the earlier editions and a dedication to the young King Edward VI, instructing him in the duties of kingship, and saying that if only people would devote an hour a day to reading the Bible they would lead much better lives.

Bishops' Bible, 1568. A revision of the Great Bible*, initiated by Elizabeth I in 1563 and carried out by Matthew Parker*, Archbishop of Canterbury, and other biblical scholars, with their own marginal notes, intended to counteract the popularity of the Geneva Bible*, thought by some to favour Puritan views too strongly and to lack the official support of the church establishment. A compromise, a dignified and 'safe' version for public reading, in scholarship an improvement on the Great Bible, less radical than the Geneva Bible but willing to learn from it.

Work began in 1561 with a proposal for revising the Great Bible, submitted by Parker to the bishops of his Province. The revisers (mainly bishops) were only to alter the Great Bible where the original texts showed it to be inaccurate and were to check the Hebrew mss. by reference to the early Latin translations. 'Bitter' notes and controversial matters were to be omitted.

There were 19 editions, plus 11 separate editions of the NT, 1586–1606. A large page size, similar to the Great Bible, but with verse division*. Convocation of Canterbury, 1571, ordered that every bishop and archbishop should have a copy in his house, and there was to be one in every cathedral and (if possible) every church, but it was never formally recognized by the queen and it never quite displaced the popular appeal of the Geneva Bible, particularly for private use.

Important in the chain of revision because the 1572 edition, which was a completely revised text, was used as the official basis of the AV*, though it was somewhat uneven because of the number of people involved. The NT bears more of the marks of scholarship than the OT which follows the Great Bible somewhat slavishly, and the NT was noticeably revised and improved in 1572 whereas the OT stayed much as it was.

Blayney, Benjamin (1728–1801). Oxford Professor of Hebrew who published translations of the OT and played an important role as editor in the 1762 edition of the AV*.

Blyth, Francis (1705–72). Born in London of Protestant parents. Vicar Provincial of the English Carmelites, a convert from Protestantism who collaborated with Bishop Challoner* in the work of revising the Douay-Rheims Bible*.

Bodley, John (b. c. 1575). Father of Sir Thomas Bodley, founder of the Bodleian

Library, Oxford, and one of the English exiles in Geneva* at the time of the appearance of the Geneva Bible*. In 1561 he obtained from Queen Elizabeth I the exclusive right to print the Geneva Bible for a period of seven years.

Bodmer Papyri. Five NT papyri ($\mathfrak{P}^{66}$, $\mathfrak{P}^{72}$, $\mathfrak{P}^{74}$ and $\mathfrak{P}^{75}$), dated c. 175–200, discovered in 1952 at Jabal Abu Mana* and possibly part of an earlier monastic library in Egypt. Purchased by M. Martin Bodmer from a dealer in Cairo* and published 1956–62. Currently in the Bodmer Library of World Literature, Cologny*, near Geneva*.

$\mathfrak{P}^{66}$ (Bodmer Papyrus II) is a codex of John, dated c. 200, measuring 6 × 5.5 inches, and containing Jn 1.1–6.11 and 6.35b–14.15.

$\mathfrak{P}^{72}$ is the earliest known copy of Jude and 1 and 2 Peter, dating from the third century, measuring 6 × 5.75 inches, and containing also Psalms 33 and 34 and some extra-biblical material: the Nativity of Mary, the apocryphal correspondence of Paul to the Corinthians, the eleventh Ode of Solomon, Melito's Homily on the Passover, a fragment of a hymn and the Apology of Phileas. Like $\mathfrak{P}^{66}$ its size suggests it may have been made for private usage rather than reading in church.

$\mathfrak{P}^{74}$ (Bodmer Papyrus XVII) has 264 pages measuring 3 × 8 inches but in a poor state of preservation, dates from the seventh century and contains Acts, James, 1 and 2 Peter, 1, 2 and 3 John and Jude.

$\mathfrak{P}^{75}$ (unlike the first three all of which reflect an Alexandrian* text) is a clear and carefully executed uncial similar to Chester Beatty* ($\mathfrak{P}^{45}$), the earliest known copy of Luke and one of the earliest known copies of John, con-taining 102 out of 144 pages, each measuring 10.25 × 5.125 inches, is more akin to Codex Vaticanus* and for that reason of special interest at certain points to translators.

In the same collection is a copy of the Fourth Gospel in Coptic*, the most extensive Bohairic ms. so far to come to light.

Bologna, Italy. The Pentateuch in Hebrew was first printed here, 1482, and it was probably here that the first portion of the Hebrew Bible (the Psalms) appeared in print, 1477.

Bomberg, Daniel (d. c. 1550). A rich and well-educated printer, brought up in Antwerp*, who studied Hebrew and moved to Venice where he set up a printing press on the advice of Felix Pratensis* and became one of the first and foremost Christian printers of Hebrew books. He introduced a new era in Hebrew typography and in 1516–17 printed two Rabbinic Bibles*, one edited by Felix Pratensis (1516–17) and the other by Jacob ben Chayyim (1524–25), for many years one of the three main recensions* of the Hebrew Bible* and a model for all subsequent editions. He also published nearly 200 Hebrew books, many for the first time.

Bonner, Edmund (1500–69). Bishop of London and one of the first to set up Chained Bibles* in St Paul's cathedral, 1538, but later had reason to doubt the wisdom of it when he found 'Protestants' reading the Bible aloud, holding services around it and sometimes disrupting the regular worship.

Book of Books, 1938. A translation of the New Testament sponsored by the United Society for Christian Literature to celebrate the 400th anniversary of the placing of a copy of the English Bible in every parish church and the Centenary of their own publication (as the Religious Tract Society) of the Annotated Paragraph Bible, 1838*.

Book of Revelation, 1957. A paraphrase by J.B. Phillips* subsequently incorporated into The New Testament in Modern English, 1958*. Published by Geoffrey Bles, London.

Book Order. In English Bibles no definitive order emerged until the invention of printing in the fifteenth century.

If you exclude the Apocrypha*, Protestant and Catholic versions followed much the same order, but the Old Testament differed at a number of points from the Hebrew Bible* with its division into Torah*, Prophets* and Writings*. In the Hebrew Bible, for example, Ruth and Lamentations, along with Song of Songs, Ecclesiastes and Esther, form part of a single unit (the Five Scrolls), Daniel appears among the Prophets, and some of the Writings come between the Former and the Latter Prophets. The order of books at the beginning of the Old Testament (Genesis to Kings) appears to have been determined partly by chronology and partly by size, the larger books coming at the beginning, which may also explain why some particularly long books like Samuel, Kings and Chronicles were divided in two.

In the early days of the NT book order was not fixed. The gospels and the letters of Paul did not always appear in the same order and many explanations have been put forward for all of them. In the Codex Claromontanus* Acts appears after Revelation, whereas the Cheltenham Canon and Codex Sinaiticus* put it after the letters of Paul and before the Catholic Epistles. From the sixteenth century English Protestants have followed the order of the Great Bible*, 1539.

Bourke, Myles (1917–). Monsignor at the St Joseph's Seminary, Dunwoodie, New York, and chairman of the commission responsible for the NT translation of the Confraternity Version*.

Bowyer, Jr, William (1699–1777). The third generation in a long line of London printers who, besides printing, often contributed learned prefaces and annotations to the work he handled. After his father had printed editions of the Textus Receptus* from 1715–60 Bowyer produced his own critical edition* in 1763, based on Wettstein* but introducing readings supported by better mss. and adding nearly 200 pages of conjectural emendations* on the NT.

Bratcher, Robert Galveston (1920–). American Bible Society translator responsible for the translation of the New Testament in Today's English Version*, 1976, the forerunner of the Good News Bible*.

Breeches Bible, 1560. The popular name given to the Geneva Bible* because Gen. 3.7 records that Adam and Eve sewed fig leaves together and made themselves 'breeches'. (For other unusual titles for Bibles, see Some Early Curiosities, p. 35.)

Bristow, Richard (1538–81). Scholar of Christ Church, Oxford, and member of the English College which William Allen* established, first in Douay* and then in Rheims*, and succeeded him when Allen moved to Rome. Worked with Allen in revising the translation of Gregory Martin* which led to the Douay-Rheims Bible* and was responsible for the NT notes there.

British and Foreign Bible Society. The oldest of the Bible Societies, founded in London in 1804 to translate,

---

Some Early Curiosities

*Printers' errors led to some early editions
earning special titles for themselves*

The Bug Bible, 1551. Thou shalt not be afraid for the bugges [terror] by night. (Ps. 91.5) (For 'bugges' read 'bogies'.)

The Place-Maker's Bible, 1562. Blessed are the place-makers [peace-makers]. (Mt. 5.9)

The Treacle Bible, 1568. Is there no treacle [balm] in Gilead? (Jer. 8.22)

The Printer's Bible, 1702. Printers [Princes] have persecuted me without a cause. (Ps. 119.161)

The Vinegar Bible, 1717*. The parable of the vinegar [vineyard] in the heading to Luke 20.

The Ears to Ear Bible, 1810. He that hath ears to ear [hear], let him hear. (Mt. 11.15)

The Unrighteous Bible. Know ye not that the unrighteous shall inherit [not inherit] the kingdom of God. (1 Cor. 6.9)

The Murderers' Bibles*. An edition of 1795 has 'Let the children first be killed [filled]' in Mk 7.27 and another of 1801 has 'These are murderers [murmurers]' in Jude 16.

---

print, promote and distribute the Bible at home and abroad. An interdenominational organization whose Board consisted of 36 lay people, including 15 Anglicans, 15 from other churches and 6 from overseas. Responsible for translating the Bible into many languages. Their decision not to include the Apocrypha* continued the controversy, dating from the Council of Trent* and the publication of the AV*, but changed in the mid- 1960s, as a result of which there is today considerable cooperation between Roman Catholics and Protestants in Bible translation. Member of The United Bible Societies*.

Brooke, Alan England (1863–1939). Biblical scholar, Provost of King's College and Professor of Divinity, Cambridge. Joint editor (with Norman McLean*) of the Cambridge Septuagint*.

Browne, E.H. (1811–91). Bishop of Ely and Chairman of the OT panel of translators for the RV*.

Bryennios, Philotheos (1833–1914). A native of Constantinople* and Professor of Church History, who in 1873, in the library of the Hospice of the Jerusalem Monastery at Constantinople, discovered a group of ancient documents, one of which was copied in 1056 and contained a list of 27 OT canonical books, with names in both Greek and Aramaic. Its original date is uncertain but it is possible that it contains the books of the OT as they were known from the second to the fourth century. The fact that they are in an unusual book order* may suggest that though by this time agreement was being reached on the books to be included there was still a good deal of flexibility and the idea of a fixed canon* had not yet solidified.

Byblos, Lebanon. Now called Jubail. Site of an ancient Hebrew inscription discovered in 1926 and thought to be the earliest actual Hebrew writing yet discovered. Some scholars date it to c. 1200 BCE. The text contained over 100 characters which suggests that each character represented a syllable rather than a letter.

Byzantine Text. One of the most attested text-types in the minuscule* mss., associated with Byzantium*, sometimes called *koiné* Greek*, and the basis for many early translations of the NT

into English, including Erasmus* whose text later became the Textus Receptus*. A fourth-century revision of several editions of the later Greek NT mss., which suffered from frequent revisions from the fourth to the eighth centuries and from corruptions* with years of copying.

An elegant text which reads well and the one that dominated the whole church throughout the Byzantine empire. Characteristics include a tendency towards longer texts and double readings, correction of style, the addition of explanatory elements and modernization of the vocabulary. The discovery of papyrus* mss. ($\mathfrak{P}^{45}$, $\mathfrak{P}^{46}$ and $\mathfrak{P}^{66}$), which have readings only through the Byzantine text, has proved its value but that does not justify its being given an early date.

Byzantium. Ancient name for Constantinople*.

C

Caedmon (c. 675). A labourer attached to the monastery at Whitby*. Legend relates how, ungifted in poetry and song, he stole away from a party one night and went out to the stable for fear he would be asked to sing. He fell asleep and had a dream. A man came and told him to sing. Caedmon asked what he should sing and was told to sing of how things were created. So he did. When he awoke he remembered all he had sung and wrote it down. His gift was recognized and he was invited to join the brotherhood as a monk. As he heard the Bible stories he turned them into verse. His songs became a kind of People's Bible and many people found they could memorize them and sing them for themselves. One of the earliest paraphrases* of the Bible in English.

Caesarea. Site of the completion of Origen's Hexaplar*. Gave its name to the Caesarean text*.

Caesarean Text. A Greek text type which got its name because Streeter* noticed that Origen* had used it in his work at Caesarea after 231 CE. Exemplified in Family 1*, Family 13*, Family Theta* and the Washington Codex*. Contains a small number of unusual readings and close affinities with Alexandrian* and Western* texts.

Cairo, Egypt. Home of the Cairo Geniza* and of the Karaite Synagogue and the Codex Cairo*, whence came its name. Site for the discovery of an Old Syriac* ms. and the place where Charles L. Freer* discovered the Washington Codex* and where Martin Bodmer purchased the Bodmer Papyri*. The only complete copy of the Coptic* translation of the Gospel of Thomas*, found at Nag Hammadi*, is in the Coptic Museum at Old Cairo. See also **Old Cairo**.

Cairo Geniza. In 1890, in the course of renovating a geniza* in Cairo, some 200,000 ms. fragments were discovered dating from as early as the sixth century CE. Many more, found earlier, had been removed to Leningrad in 1870. These newly found ones, divided between Cambridge University Library, the British Library, the Bodleian Library, Oxford* and the John Rylands Library in Manchester*, were studied initially by P.E. Kahle* and provide evidence of masoretic transmission several centuries earlier than anything previously available.

Cambridge, England. Home to the archives of the British and Foreign Bible Society*, and to many ancient mss., including Codex Bezae* and some mss. from the Cairo Geniza* in the University Library, and a copy of the first edition of the Great Bible* in St John's College.

Cambridge Paragraph Bible, 1873.
The first really critical edition[*] of the AV[*], in three volumes, by F.H.A. Scrivener[*], with the text in paragraphs and the verse numbers in the margin, taking into account the whole history of the text and what the printers had done to it over 200 years.

Cambridge Septuagint, 1906–40. *The Old Testament in Greek according to the Text of Codex Vaticanus*, edited by A.E. Brooke[*], N. McLean[*] and H. St J. Thackeray and following the tradition of Swete[*]. Four volumes containing Genesis to Nehemiah, plus Esther, Judith and Tobit, according to Codex Vaticanus[*] with some assistance from Codex Alexandrinus[*] and Codex Sinaiticus[*] and a critical apparatus[*]. Used by scholars for precise research.

Campbell, Alexander (1788–1866). Born in Ireland, emigrated to the USA in 1809 and became founder of the Disciples of Christ. As a scholar in Bethany, Virginia, he came across an 1818 translation of the NT which combined the skills of Philip Doddridge[*], George Campbell[*] and James MacKnight[*], which he then used alongside Griesbach[*] to produce his own translation, 1826, which was frequently revised and reprinted though thought to be weak in its English diction.

Campbell, George (1719–96). Theologian, educated in Edinburgh and Aberdeen. Author of one of three popular eighteenth-century translations, in this case covering the gospels, the other two being Philip Doddridge's[*] translation of the NT, 1739–56, and James MacKnight's[*] A Translation of all the Apostolical Epistles, 1795[*]. In 1818 a combined translation appeared in London, susbequently revised and published by Alexander Campbell[*],1826.

Canon.
Definition and Canonization.
A Greek word meaning 'a straight rod' (lit.) and then 'a measure', used in the ancient world in a variety of ways when referring to guides, models, regulations and grammar, but first used in relation to the Bible[*] by Eusebius[*] and then from the fourth century CE, by both Jews and Christians, to define the books recognized as 'biblical'. A Jewish source defines the canon as

> [Books] accepted by Jews as authoritative for religious practice and/or doctrine, and whose authority is binding upon the Jewish people for all generations. (S.Z. Leiman)

By changing 'Jew' to 'Christian' Christians would have no difficulty with the definition, but there are significant differences in understanding between the Jewish and the Christian communities, in that the concept itself arises primarily within the NT scene, Hebrew has no equivalent word for 'canon', and phrases such as 'defile the hands' in rabbinic discussions, though similar, are not quite the same.

The means by which sacred texts become authoritative is much more the result of a measure (or indeed several measures) being applied over a long period (probably 1000 years for the OT and 400 years for the NT) rather than any particular test, agreement or approval at one point. Scholars recognize a five-fold process of composition, circulation, revision, collection and recognition (or canonization), and the final stage was reached more easily in the case of some books than of others.

Opinions differ as to the precise process. The prevailing view is that even at the end it was gradual and more a recognition of the status which certain books had received than an actual choice of books to be included (with inclusion or exclusion hotly contested), that the

Synod of Jamnia* was not necessarily the final authority it was once thought to be, and that there is evidence of different collections of books circulating and being accorded different authority in different places.

Signs of the final definitive list, both for OT and NT, emerged in the first and second centuries from which it is possible to form some judgments about the criteria being applied.

For the Jews, the overriding factors were authority and antiquity, which, in the case of the Torah*, were fairly well settled by this stage. Recognition of the Prophets* depended very much on their association with the prophets (or the name of a prophet), and the test for the Writings* was largely one of their capacity for inspiration, though 'canonicity' and 'inspiration' were not regarded as synonymous. Other factors, which also applied to some extent to the NT, were the extent to which texts were cited and used, their consistency (both within themselves and in relation to other texts) and their relevance to the times combined with their capacity for a wider and more universal interpretation.

In the case of the NT the crucial test was orthodoxy, faithful witness to the apostolic faith, and being untainted by the heresies of the first and second centuries. After that, four other factors played a part though they were not of equal status and the weight of authority varied according to churches and their leaders:

> *The authority of Jesus.* Books which were clearly related to his life and teaching were more likely to be acceptable.
> *Apostolicity.* Not necessarily apostolic authorship but ideally some connection with an apostle.
> *Church usage.* Books which had established a special place in the life of the churches and were used frequently in

worship, though here there were regional differences. For example, Revelation was more acceptable in the West, Hebrews in the East, and some churches used non-canonical books.

Inspiration, though it is often debatable whether books were placed in the canon because they were thought to be inspired or thought to be inspired because they were in the canon.

In the case of Christianity, three other factors influenced the process of canonization and to some extent hastened it: the pressure from persecution and martyrdom, the need to distinguish Christianity from Judaism as the Jews defined their canon and the churches increasingly became a mixture of Jews and Gentiles, and as a defence against heresy. A fourth factor, in the case of the gospels, was the need to establish some in order to discount others.

The Hebrew Bible

The Hebrew Bible* appears to have come together in three stages: the Torah* c. fourth century BCE, the Prophets* c. 200 BCE, and the Writings* c. 100 CE. How they actually came together is unclear but a general view suggests that serious interest in texts and collections dates from Josiah and the Deuteronomists in the sixth century BCE (certainly as far as the Pentateuch is concerned) and was well acknowledged by the time of Ezra. Jews in Palestine and elsewhere appear to have had no difficulty 'adopting' the Torah and a somewhat varied collection of other Writings but these were not clearly defined for several centuries. Tradition ascribes the decision to the Synod of Jamnia* at the end of the first century CE but no such list or record has been preserved, and it is likely that final decisions came much later.

Josephus*, for example, writing about

the same time as Jamnia, mentions 22 books, including 4 that contain hymns and offer guidelines for daily living, but does not specify what they are.

2 Esdras, similarly and about the same time, refers to a sacred collection among the Jews dating from the return from Babylon, consisting of 24 books which are regarded as 'special' or 'sacred' (but again without specifying what they are), plus a further 70 'for the wise among your people', thus giving rise to the idea of books 'on the edge of the canon' which became 'apocrypha'* or 'hidden'.

The book of *Jubilees* has several references to a 20-book collection, which may hark back to Josephus, but again without specifying which they are so we cannot even be sure that they are referring to the same collection, much less the same books.

Traditional Jewish literature for the first 600 years into the Christian era gives little indication as to how such a collection of books became 'sacred scripture', though there are references to books which 'soil the hands', seemingly referring to books which have a specially sacred, but perhaps not necessarily canonical, character.

The Christian Bible.
Here the process of recognition was in two parts, giving a Canon of the OT and a Canon of the NT.

The early church accepted the Alexandrian canon (the LXX*) well before the shorter rabbinic (Hebrew Bible*) canon was established, which may account for the fact that the OT differs from the Hebrew Bible, mainly in Book Order*, and differs within itself as between Roman Catholic, Reformed and Orthodox traditions. Subsequently, the Catholic tradition accepted the Apocrypha*, though making a distinction between proto- and deutero-canonical

books, the Reformed stayed with the Hebrew Bible, and the Orthodox maintained various collections rather than a single one.

In the case of the NT, there appears to have been no felt need for defining a list of books until the middle of the fourth century, the first indication being the Council of Laodicea* c. 363. The Muratorian Fragment* could not have been promulgated by the Church of Rome c. 200 and is now generally thought to have been more than a century later, though by the end of the second century the four gospels seem to have achieved a position of authority comparable to that of the OT and could almost be called scripture.

As with Judaism, the NT achieved recognition in three stages:

the first century, when the life and teaching of Jesus and oral tradition were more highly regarded than writing;

the second century, with the making of 'collections', such as the gospels and the letters of Paul, and with increasing recognition as they were circulated, widely read and quoted;

the fourth century, when, under the pressures of heresy and the threat of persecution by the state, there was a need for clarification of belief, authority, a sense of unity and sacred texts.

Once the canon was clear Christian scholars then turned their attention to the standardization of the text.

The role of Church Councils*, insofar as they were involved at all, and particularly in the West, was generally late on the scene and always more a recognition of what was already a fact than a creative initiative. The various stages of debate and development therefore can best be understood by a study of the writings of such early Christian scholars as second-century Irenaeus*, Papias*,

Polycarp*, Marcion*, Justin Martyr*, Ignatius*, Melito* and Tatian*, third-century Origen* and fourth-century Eusebius*, Cyril of Jerusalem* and Athanasius*, though the fact that they list books, accepting some and rejecting others, does not mean that they are defining a 'canon'; all they are doing is witnessing to a process of growth and development over two to three centuries out of which the canon emerged from the fourth century onwards, and even after that, agreement is neither general nor final.

Carbon 14 Test. See Radio Carbon dating.

Castlebrae, Scotland. The home of two twins, Agnes Smith Lewes* and Margaret Dunlop Gibson*, who found a copy of the Old Syriac* version in Sinaitic Syriac towards the end of the nineteenth century.

Catholic Epistles. James, 1 and 2 Peter, 1, 2 and 3 John and Jude. 'Catholic' in the sense of 'general' and therefore sometimes called General Epistles, though not grouped together under this title until the fourth century, and the Peshitta* omits 2 Peter, 2 and 3 John, Jude and Revelation. As with the Pauline Corpus*, for evidence of their significance for the early church and for the way in which they achieved recognition it is necessary to refer to the early church Fathers, and in particular to Polycarp*, Irenaeus*, Hippolytus, Clement of Alexandria*, Tertullian*, Origen*, Cyprian, Eusebius* and Jerome*, and the Muratorian Canon*.

Caxton, William (c. 1422–91). Founder of English printing who set up his press in 1476 at the site of the Red Pole in the Almonry at Westminster, on the site of the modern Tothill Street*. His output was huge, including Chaucer and *Morte d'Arthur*, and he printed some portions of the biblical text in English in his translation of *The Golden Legend*, but the Constitutions of Oxford* were still in force and prevented him from printing and distributing the English Bible as a whole.

Centenary Translation of the New Testament, 1924. A dynamic equivalence translation* by Helen B. Montgomery*, in the language of everyday life without departing too much from translations already familiar and loved, to mark the centenary of the American Baptist Publication Society. Noteworthy for the introductions to the various books, the titles Montgomery gave to chapters and paragraphs, and the indenting and italicizing of quotations for clarity. Published by the Judson Press, Philadelphia.

Chained Bibles. In sixteenth-century Britain, when many people were unable to read, when threats and persecution had been handed out to those who translated the Bible into English, and when many clergy and laity were still resistant to the idea of Bible readings in church, Edmund Bonner*, Bishop of London, set up six copies of the Bible in English in St Paul's, chained them to the pillars, and put a notice over each urging people to read it quietly and reverently. Other bishops followed his lead, including Nicolas Shaxton*, Bishop of Salisbury, who in 1538 required his clergy to chain an English Bible to the desk in their parish church so that parishioners could either read it for themselves or have it read to them. Some churches chose Coverdale's* translation and others Matthew's*. On 5 September 1538 a national injunction to this effect was published in the name of the king and with the support of Cromwell*. Cromwell probably had the Great Bible* in mind though at this time it was not quite ready. Unfortunately many Protestants insisted on reading aloud, disrupting the services and even using the content to challenge the authority of the clergy, so that by 1541 the Bishop of London was asking for the Chained Bibles to be taken out.

Chaldee. Since Aramaic was put into the mouth of the Chaldeans in Dan. 2.4 it came to be called Chaldee, but as it was realized that this was not so, since the language of the Chaldeans was Akkadian, the word was superseded by Aramaic.

Challoner, Richard (1691–1781). Born in Sussex, son of a wine-cooper and rigid dissenter*. His mother was probably a practising Catholic and he was an Anglican until he was 12. Financed by a fund for poor boys, he went to Douay* to train for the priesthood where he remained until 1730 when he returned to England to work among the poor, though continuing his studies and writings. Consecrated a Roman Catholic bishop, 1741, Vicar Apostolic of the London district, 1758, and a scholar who undertook a complete revision of the Douay-Rheims Bible* and published it in 1749, followed by five successive revisions of the NT, 1749–72, and two of the OT, 1750 and 1763. A convert from Protestantism, his familiarity with the language of the AV* is reflected in his work.

Chapter Division. Early Hebrew, Greek and English mss. had neither chapter nor verse* division as we know them. Chapter division in the Hebrew Bible is first mentioned c. 1330, largely the result of Christian practice brought about partly by the change from scroll* to codex* and probably originating in the Vulgate* where it is accredited to Lanfranc, Archbishop of Canterbury (d. 1089). Chapter division in the English Bible is attributed to Stephen Langton* and as we know it today goes back to the pattern laid down by Felix Pratensis*.

Charles I (1600–49). Presented in 1627 with a Greek ms. of the Bible which was older than any biblical ms. previously available in the West. Dating from the fifth century it became known as Codex Alexandrinus* and led to much greater accuracy in Bible translation.

Cheke, John (1514–57). Professor of Greek at Cambridge and tutor to Edward VI. Began a novel attempt at Bible translation in 1550 using only words of pure English origin. 'Resurrection' became 'uprising', 'crucified'* became 'crossed', and so on. The ms. remained unpublished until 1843 when it was edited and published by James Goodwin.

Chester Beatty Papyri. A collection of papyri, discovered by A. Chester Beatty of Dublin, an American collector of mss., in Egypt, c. 1930, buried in jars in the ruins of an ancient building, possibly a church. Though most of the biblical books were represented, none was complete but they were a century older than other known mss. of the Bible and throw light on the conditions in which these books were originally known and circulated. The greatest discoveries since Codex Sinaiticus* and the Washington Codex*. Edited, with introductions and discussions, by F.G. Kenyon, and currently in the Beatty Museum, Dublin.

Eight are mss. of the OT, three of the NT and one of the Apocrypha*, all in Greek. The earliest is a copy of Numbers and Deuteronomy, c. 120–50 CE. Large portions of Genesis, Isaiah, Ezekiel, Daniel and Esther are from the third century. The NT books, published 1933–51, are of special importance, four papyri in particular.

$\mathfrak{P}^{45}$ contains the gospels and Acts, probably in the order of the Western* text (i.e. Matthew, John, Luke, Mark, Acts), dates from the first half of the third century, and consists of 30 of an original 110 leaves, 8 × 10 inches (wide), with small writing in a single broad column, 39 lines to a page.

$\mathfrak{P}^{46}$ contains Romans, Hebrews, 1 and 2 Corinthians, Ephesians, Galatians, Philippians, Colossians and 1 Thessalonians, is the most significant piece in the puzzle of reconstructing the Pauline Corpus*, demonstrating its existence in the middle of the third century, and consists of 86 near-perfect leaves out of a total of 104, 5.5 × 8.75 inches (wide), from a date not later than 250 CE.

$\mathfrak{P}^{47}$ contains 10 out of an original 32 leaves of Revelation, c. 250–300 CE.

$\mathfrak{P}^{52}$ is the John Fragment*.

Further importance arises from the fact that they are written on papyri* but in codex* rather than scroll* form, thus marking an intermediate stage between the papyrus scroll and the vellum codex.

Their evidence was added to the critical apparatus* of the 16th edition of the Nestle* text, 1936, and so influenced the translation of the RSV* at one or two points.

Chrysostom. See John Chrysostom.

Church Councils. Church Councils played a less significant role in the growth of the NT canon* than is often supposed and where they did it was more one of recognizing a position already arrived at than actually creating anything new, so that their records are more important for the lists they endorse than for the decisions they make. The three most important in the early church are the Council of Laodicea*, 363, the Council of Hippo*, 393, and the Council of Carthage*, 397. Further clarification came for Roman Catholics with the Council of Trent*, 1545–63, and the First Vatican Council*, 1869–70, and for Protestants with the

*Belgica**, 1561, and the Thirty-Nine Articles of the Church of England*, 1562, 1571.

Clark, Kenneth Willis (1898–1979). An American NT scholar, educated at Duke University, who researched documents in the John Rylands Library, Manchester* relating to The Twentieth Century New Testament*, 1902, and published his findings in the Bulletin of the John Rylands Library, September 1955.

Clarke, Samuel (1675–1729). One of a number of scholars who in 1701 produced a paraphrase* with bracketed explanatory material into the text of the AV*.

Clay. Possibly the earliest form of writing materials* and used by the Sumerians in Mesopotamia. No reference to clay as writing material in the Bible, but the Ras Shamra Tablets* provide a good example.

Clement of Alexandria (c. 150–215). Born at Athens of pagan parents and converted to the Christian faith. Philosopher and head of the famous Catechetical School in Alexandria*. Accepted the notion of four gospels as scripture, following Irenaeus*, and was the first to distinguish John (a 'spiritual' gospel) from the other three, known as the Synoptic Gospels*, which he regarded as more down-to-earth. Seems also to have recognized and accepted Acts, 14 of Paul's letters, including Hebrews, 1 and 2 John, 1 Peter and Revelation. In common with Tertullian* and the general opinion of his day he accepted Jude, though this came to be challenged later by Eusebius* and Jerome* because of its use of apocryphal books.

Clement of Rome (64–96). Bishop of Rome, known only for one letter (1 Clement), but around whose name much early literature formed itself, including a sermon (2 Clement) probably by a different author. Seems to have been acquainted with a document in Rome relating to the teaching of Jesus, similar to the gospels (particularly Matthew and Luke) but not to be identified with them, and had a closer acquaintance with some of Paul's letters in that he makes specific reference to Romans and Corinthians as well as Galatians and Philippians, though it is not clear whether he had seen them separately or whether at that time they were part of a Pauline Corpus*. First to provide a definite allusion to Hebrews and it is possible that he also knew James, Peter and Acts. 2 Clement (c. 160) has allusions to Romans, 1 Corinthians, Galatians, Ephesians, Philippians, Hebrews, and possibly James and Peter, but neither 1 Clement nor 2 Clement suggest the existence at this time of a canon* of Scripture.

Clermont, France. Site for the discovery of Codex Claromontanus*.

Cochlaeus, Johannes (1479–1552). A vigorous enemy of Martin Luther and the movement to reform the church. When he was at Cologne*, seeing a book through the press, he heard the printers boasting about the new successes being won by the Reformers in England. Anxious to know more, he invited the printers to his home and when they were all well filled with wine they revealed they were printing 3000 copies of Tyndale's Translation* in English. Cochlaeus immediately informed the authorities at Cologne who put a stop to the work, but Tyndale escaped with the printed sheets to Worms*. Because Cochlaeus had sent a description of the work to England Tyndale put it on one side for the time being and issued a different edition. Of the quarto edition begun at Cologne there is one fragment still in existence, in the British Library.

Codex. (pl. Codices) A replacement for the scroll*, dating from the second century CE, and the forerunner of the book as we know it, formed by taking one or more sheets of papyrus* or vellum* and sewing them together at the spine. The Latin codex originally meant the trunk of a tree but later was used of a block of wood split into a number of tablets or leaves.

The codex had many advantages over the scroll: it was generally easier to handle, particularly when it came to finding specific passages; it enabled several mss. to be grouped together so that it was possible, for example, to have all four gospels or all the letters of Paul in one format; and it was double sided, which not only made it more economical but meant it could hold more.

Extensive use of the codex form by Christians began in the second century. The early Christian community seems to have found the codex more convenient whilst at the same time its introduction emphasized the break with Judaism with its preference for a scroll, so that by the third century most Christian literature was commonly found in codex form, and of 172 fragments of biblical texts 158 are from codices and only 14 from scrolls.

The Hebrew Bible in codex form for non-liturgical use was well established by the eighth century CE, but for liturgical use the scroll remained the norm.

Codex Aleppo. c. 925 CE. A good example (perhaps the earliest) of a complete Hebrew text, containing all 24 books, with the Ben Asher* system of vocalization*, complete with masoretic notes, and preserved by the Jewish community in Aleppo. Used for many years as a standard text in the correction of books because of its connection with Ben Asher. Wrongly thought to have been destroyed by fire in 1948. Three-quarters of it has been preserved, though not the

Torah*. Now in the Hebrew University, Jerusalem.

Codex Alexandrinus. Complete ms. of the Greek Bible (save for some 43 leaves containing passages from Matthew, John and 1 Corinthians which suffered mutilation), and including the Apocrypha*, 1 and 2 Clement, Psalms of Solomon and 3 and 4 Maccabees, written on pages of fine vellum in the first half of the fifth century, probably in Egypt. It has 820 leaves, each containing two columns and bound in four volumes, and measures 12.75 × 10.25 inches. Thought to be the work of two scribes. Usually known as A and located in the British Library.

First uncial* ms. to be used by modern biblical scholars apart from the Complutensian Polyglot*. NT text is Alexandrian* except for the gospels which are Byzantine*, of which it is the oldest witness.

Complete edition of the OT produced by John Ernest Grabbe*, a Prussian scholar who settled in Oxford*, 1701–20. Published with the NT in 1786, the first of three major codices of the NT to be published, the other two being the Codex Sinaiticus* and the Codex Vaticanus*. Soon recognized as one of the main Greek mss. of the Bible.

Cyril Lucar*, Patriarch of Constantinople* and former Patriarch of Alexandria*, presented a copy to Charles I in 1627 and it was kept at St James's Palace until 1649. It represented a much more reliable text than that which the translators of the AV* had worked with. Unfortunately it was too late for them to make use of it and its discovery was soon overshadowed by even earlier mss. such as the Codex Vaticanus* and the Codex Sinaiticus*.

Codex Amiatinus. The most reliable complete extant ms. of the Vulgate*, 1029 leaves of parchment, 19.5 × 13.5 inches, written in a regular and beautiful hand with the first lines of each book in red ink, dating from the eighth century, written by order of Coelfrid* and sent as a gift to Pope Gregory II, 716. Located in the Laurentian Library, Florence.

Codex Argenteus. Sometimes known as the Silver Codex. A deluxe edition of the Gothic* Version of the NT by Ulfilas*, dating from the fifth to the sixth centuries, very literal and following a Byzantine* text with the gospels in the order of the Western* text (Matthew, John, Luke, Mark). It has 336 leaves, 7.625 × 9.825 inches, of which 188 have survived. Located in Uppsala.

Codex Bezae. A fifth or sixth century ms. of the gospels and Acts, with a small fragment of 3 John, usually known as D, principal example of the Western* text and located at Cambridge University, to whom it was presented in 1581 by Theodore Beza*. Sometimes known as Codex Cantabrigiensis*. Published in full in 1793 by the University of Cambridge, followed by a new edition in 1864.

The first and oldest preserved example of a copy of the Bible in two languages (Greek and Latin on facing pages) and one which varied from the usual text so much, with its own additions and omissions, that for a long time it was regarded with suspicion. The gospels are in the order of the Western* text (Matthew, John, Luke, Mark), the text of Acts is 10 per cent longer than in other mss., Lk. 6.5 comes after 6.10, and between verses 4 and 6 there is one of the unknown sayings of Jesus*. See entry, p. 15.

Over 500 leaves, 10 × 8 inches, single column, with the text in sense lines and therefore with lines of unequal length.

Codex Cairo. A Hebrew ms., c. 895 CE, containing Former and Latter Prophets, usually known as C (though not to be confused with Codex Ephraemi*) and located in the Karaite Synagogue, Cairo*.

Codex Cantabrigiensis. An alternative name for Codex Bezae* because of its links with Cambridge University.

Codex Claromontanus. A sixth-century ms. of the Pauline Letters, discovered at Clermont, France, usually known as D₂, a Western* text and located in the Bibliothèque Nationale, Paris*. Greek and Latin, 533 beautiful vellum leaves, 9.75 × 7.75 inches, with text in sense lines and very wide margins.

Important for our understanding of the growth of the canon* because in addition to a Latin list of the books of the OT and NT, as recognized c. 300, it includes lists of some non-canonical early Christian literature. Books also appear in a different order from usual. John follows Matthew, Acts follows Revelation, the Pastoral Epistles come before Colossians, and Philippians is missing altogether. Barnabas follows Jude, Shepherd of Hermas, the Acts of Paul and the Revelation of Peter all come after Revelation and Acts, and the OT contains 1, 2 and 4 Maccabees.

Codex Ephraemi. A fifth-century palimpsest* discovered c. 1700, brought from the east to Italy and from there to Paris*. Attention was first called to the underlying biblical text in the seventeenth century and in 1843–45 Tischendorf* published all of the OT and NT that was decipherable. The original contained the whole Greek Bible. NT text is mixed, mostly Byzantine*.

It consists of 209 leaves, 12.5 × 9.5 inches, containing 64 (scattered) lines of the OT (including Ecclesiasticus, prologue to Ecclesiasticus, and Wisdom of Solomon) and 145 (scattered) lines of the NT, one column to a page. Usually

known as C and located in the Bibliothèque Nationale, Paris*. Erased in the twelfth century and re-used for a Greek translation of sermons by Ephraem, a fourth-century Syrian church Father.

The writing is that of the fifth century, perhaps a little later than the Codex Alexandrinus*, and it may well have ranked with the greatest mss. if it had not been defaced by some mediaeval individual in search of writing paper.

Codex Koridethianus. See Family Theta.

Codex Laudianus, 1715. A good sixth-to seventh-century ms. of Acts, used by Bede*, usually known as E₂ and located in the Bodleian Library, Oxford*. Greek and Latin on facing pages, with very short sense lines. Similar in some ways to Codex Bezae* but in general more Byzantine* than Western*. The earliest known ms. to contain the Ethiopian's confession of faith in Acts 8.37.

Codex Leningrad. An ancient and complete Hebrew ms., c. 1009 CE, copied from a Ben Asher* ms., and with vocalization* close to that of Codex Aleppo*. The earliest complete codex* of the Hebrew Bible* which is closest to the Ben Asher* tradition. The basis of *Biblia hebraica* and *Biblia hebraica stuttgartensia*. Known as Codex L and located in the Public Library, St Petersburg*.

Codex Petersburg. A Hebrew ms., c. 916 CE, containing Isaiah, Jeremiah, Ezekiel and the Twelve minor prophets, in a Ben Asher* text but with earlier Babylonian vowel pointing. Usually known as P and located in the Public Library, St Petersburg*.

Codex Sinaiticus. A fourth-century Greek ms., usually known as א (aleph, the first letter of the Hebrew alphabet) or S.

About 720 leaves (or 1440 pages), 15 × 13.5 inches, with four columns to a page except for the Psalms and the poetic books which have two. Thought to be the work of three scribes whose different strengths and weaknesses have been identified.

The earliest complete NT (144 leaves) and the only complete copy in uncial* script. The original contained the whole of the Greek Bible, including in its OT Tobit, Judith, Wisdom of Solomon, Ecclesiasticus, 1 and 4 Maccabees, Letter of Barnabas and Shepherd of Hermas, but most of the first half of the OT had been destroyed before Tischendorf* got hold of it. Of the OT 43 leaves are in Leipzig*, 3 fragments in St Petersburg* and 199 leaves in the British Library. NT text is Alexandrian* with signs of Western* influence.

Differs from many other mss. in that it brings Mark to an end at 16.8, omits the woman taken in adultery (Jn 7.52–8.11) and puts the doxology in Romans after 16.23.

Discovered by Tischendorf* on a visit to St Catharine's Monastery* on Mount Sinai in May 1844 where he had gone to study ancient documents and, after an intriguing story, presented by the Monastery to the Tsar of Russia, where it was published in 1862, at Russian expense, in a luxury edition of 346 leaves plus scholarly commentary. Subsequently published in facsimile, 1911 (NT) and 1922 (OT) by Kirsopp Lake*. In 1933 the British Government bought 80 pages for £100,000. Now located in the British Library. (See Tischendorf and Codex Sinaiticus, p. 48.)

Codex Vaticanus. A fourth-century ms., usually known as B, 10.5 × 10 inches, two columns to a page in the poetic texts and three in the others. Originally complete but severely mutilated (759 out of 820 leaves), having lost Gen.

1.1–46.28, Psalms 106–138, Hebrews 9–14, the Pastoral Epistles, Philemon and Revelation, but includes Baruch, Epistle of Jeremiah, Wisdom of Solomon, Ecclesiasticus, Judith and Tobit. One of the earliest examples of Greek mss. to break up the text into paragraphs. NT text is Alexandrian*.

In the Vatican Library as early as 1481 but little noticed by scholars until Napoleon brought it to Paris* where its value was recognized by a German scholar, J.L. Hug*. After the fall of Napoleon it was returned to the Vatican, where a somewhat unsatisfactory edition was published in 1857. NT text was not published until after Codex Alexandrinus* and Codex Sinaiticus*.

Found (almost by accident) by Tischendorf* when he visited Rome in 1843 but he was not allowed much time to work on it. When he returned he was able to demonstrate that the 1857 edition was not satisfactory and he published the best edition up to that time in 1867.

Coelfrid (d. 716). Abbot of Wearmouth*. Responsible for the Codex Amiatinus* and for presenting it to Pope Gregory II, 716, though he was unable to do so himself because he died on the way to Rome.

Coggan, Frederick Donald (1909-). Archbishop of Canterbury, appointed Vice-President of the United Bible Societies*, 1956, and President, 1957. Chairman of the Joint Committee for the NEB*, 1968, in succession to Alwyn P.T. Williams*, and for the REB*, 1989.

Colet, John (1467–1519). Dean of St Paul's (1505) and founder of St Paul's School, 1510. Translated the Lord's Prayer into English. A representative of the New Learning, his lectures in Oxford on Romans in 1496 explored new methods

Tischendorf and Codex Sinaiticus

In 1844, on a quest for ancient Bible mss., a young German scholar, Tischendorf, found himself staying at St Catharine's Monastery* at the foot of Mt Sinai.

> There 'I discovered the pearl of all my researches. In visiting the library of the monastery… I perceived in the middle of the great hall a large and wide basket full of old parchments; and the librarian, who was a man of information, told me that two heaps of papers like these, mouldered by time, had been already committed to the flames.

On examination, he found 43 sheets of fine vellum with the oldest Greek writing he had ever seen, dating from c. 350 CE and containing 1 Chronicles, some of Esdras, all of Esther, part of Tobit, most of Jeremiah and about half of Lamentations. It was part of the Septuagint*.

He would have been wise to conceal his excitement. His enthusiasm immediately roused the suspicions of the monks who realized they were obviously sitting on something of great value. They refused to let him see the other 80 pages which they said they had though they did allow him to take away about 43 sheets and on returning to Europe he published them, though concealing the place of discovery.

A second visit, in 1853, was equally unproductive, the monks still refusing to let him see any more, but a glimpse of a fragment containing 11 verses of Genesis was sufficient to suggest to him that originally the mss. had contained all the OT and he did not need three guesses to work out what might have happened to the rest.

On a third visit, in 1859, still nothing of consequence emerged until the last afternoon, 4 February, when he gained access to the rest: 199 pages of the OT and all the NT. This is how he describes it:

Tischendorf and Codex Sinaiticus (continued)

I was taking a walk with the steward of the convent in the neighbour-hood, and as we returned, towards sunset, he begged me to take some refreshment with him in his cell. Scarcely had he entered the room, when resuming our former subject of conversation, he said, 'And I, too, have read a Septuagint'... And so saying he took down from the corner of the room a bulky kind of volume, wrapped in a red cloth, and laid it before me. I unrolled the cover and discovered to my great surprise, not only those fragments which fifteen years before I had taken out of the basket, but also other parts of the Old Testament, the New Testament complete, and in addition, the Epistle of Barnabas and a part of the Pastor of Hermas. Full of joy which this time I had the self-command to conceal from the steward and the rest of the community, I asked, as if in a careless way, for permission to take the manuscript into my sleeping chamber to look over it more at leisure. There by myself I could give way to the transport of joy which I felt. I knew that I held in my hand the most precious biblical treasure in existence.

Tischendorf spent the night copying. Next morning he asked permission to take it away but was refused.

Subsequently, in Cairo, Tischendorf met the Abbot of St Catharine's and pleaded for sight of the ms. The abbot not only agreed but actually dispatched messengers to bring it to Cairo, and with the help of two Germans (who knew Greek) and a couple of others, it was copied, eight pages at a time. In two months the job was finished.

Still one more hurdle. The monks of Sinai were looking for a new abbot for their most senior post. They needed support from the Czar of Russia. Tischendorf suggested a gift might help. They saw the point. And what better than the sacred text! Which explains how it came to be in Russia before the British bought it in 1933.

(Quotes from I.M. Price, *The Ancestry of our English Bible*, pp. 60-61.)

of biblical interpretation, abandoning the methods of the mediaeval scholastics and expounding the text in accordance with the plain meaning of the words viewed in their historical context. Colet exercised a considerable influence on Erasmus*, on Sir Thomas More*, particularly with regard to biblical interpretation, and on Tyndale*.

Colines, Simon de (1480–1546). A Parisian printer, stepfather of Stephanus*, responsible for publishing the first attempt to achieve a critical edition* of the Greek NT, using Erasmus* and the Complutensian Polyglot*, with the addition of some unique readings.

Cologne, Germany. The city in which Coverdale's Bible* was printed and possibly the most likely place for the publication of the first English edition of the whole Bible, probably Coverdale's. Home of Peter Quentel* and where Tyndale started to print his English NT before his enemies threatened him and he fled to Worms* taking with him 64 pages of print, subsequently known as the Cologne Quarto*.

Cologne Quarto. Tyndale's* translation of Matthew and the beginning of Mark, plus a prologue, printed at Cologne* by Peter Quentel*. No more were printed because the authorities stopped the work on information received from Johannes Cochlaeus*. Tyndale managed to prevent them being destroyed and fled to Worms*. The first 64 pages appeared in 1834 bound up in a volume with another work and are now in the British Library.

Cologny, Switzerland. A suburb near Geneva* and home of the Bodmer Library of World Literature which houses the Bodmer Papyri*.

Colophon. A note, often found in ancient mss., giving information about the author or the place of origin, and sometimes used to add a prayer or simply to express a scribe's feelings.

Common Bible, The, 1973. An edition of the RSV* published by Collins and approved for use in the Roman Catholic Church. Its roots go back to 1953 when the Catholic Biblical Association approached the RSV Committee with a view to 'making a few amendments' so as to enable its adoption in the Roman Catholic Church, but unfortunately securing Catholic approval took too long and had to wait for the new spirit created by the Second Vatican Council*, 1963–65, by which time some Roman Catholic scholars like Walter M. Abbott* and Robert M. Grant had been quietly assessing the issues and preparing the ground.

In 1965 Nelson published 'a Roman Catholic edition' of the RSV New Testament, followed in 1966 by the whole Bible, with the OT unchanged, the Apocrypha* interspersed throughout the OT, as in the Vulgate*, and an appendix listing 93 verses involving 67 verbal changes, but it was still a Catholic edition of a Protestant Bible rather than an agreed text.

The Common Bible, 1973, had no Catholic notes and divided the Apocrypha into two sections, separating those which Roman Catholics had always regarded as deuterocanonical from the rest.

After a few more changes, and an agreed common text under the leadership of Martini* and Holmgren*, an expanded edition from Oxford University Press in 1977 secured further support from the Eastern Orthodox, thus producing what is described by some as the first truly ecumenical edition of the Bible in English.

Common Translation Corrected, 1718–24. A revised text of the AV* by Edward Wells*.

Communication Theory. A recent development in translation work giving more attention to the impact made on the readers, recognizing, as with dynamic equivalence*, that meaning depends on readers as much as on translations. Earlier translators paid most attention to the intent and meaning of the work for the original author. Communication theory raises the question of 'correct (translation) for whom', recognizing that different cultures, races, ages, etc., all read and understand differently. Adults differ from children, scholars from general readers, and so on. Words even have different meanings for different people and at different times. 'Freedom (from slavery)' means something different for a slave from what it does for a free man. 'Grace' means something different today from what it did in the Middle Ages.

Compilations. Though some books of the Bible seem to have been written as a single, composite unit, such as Ruth or the letters of Paul, and some indeed with a specific purpose, such as Deuteronomy or the Fourth Gospel, many appear to be compilations of material going back to much earlier times, Psalms and Proverbs perhaps being the most obvious examples from the Old Testament, and the rest falling somewhere in between. Scholars, for example, have long recognized the Pentateuch* as a compilation of material over many centuries, two (if not three or more) sources are thought to make up Isaiah, and many other books suggest similar compilations.

In the case of the gospels the stories of Jesus were obviously circulated and used in worship in slightly different forms, and for different purposes, in the different centres of early Christianity and this helps to explain some of the variations between them. Nor were the compilations altogether neutral. Editors and compilers often had their own view-

point. Local or contemporary circumstances sometimes required a particular emphasis.

Complete Bible: An American Translation, 1927, 1935 (revised), 1938 (Apocrypha), 1939 (complete). A dynamic equivalence* translation, beginning with The New Testament: An American Translation*, 1923, by Goodspeed* to which was added first the OT by J.M. Powis Smith* and three other scholars, including T.J. Meek* who was responsible for the revised edition, and (later) Goodspeed's translation of the Apocrypha*. Powis Smith gave two reasons for making a new translation of the OT: one, a greater knowledge of the Hebrew language than the earlier translators had, and, two, a greater awareness of the uncertainty of the Hebrew text and the developments in textual criticism* which enabled safer guesses to be made as to the original. Translators mainly followed the Masoretic Text* but were free to adopt generally accepted conjectural emendations*.

Each book had a short introduction and words like 'thee', thou' and 'doth' were avoided altogether in the NT, though retained in the OT when referring to God. Widely popular among students and very refreshing to many others. The layout is that of a contemporary book, with poetry printed as poetry and recovering some of the stylistic qualities of poetry in the Hebrew. Published by the University of Chicago Press.

Complutensian Polyglot, 1522. A printing of 600 copies of the complete Bible with the NT in Greek and Latin and the OT in Hebrew, Greek and Latin, all in parallel columns, plus a Greek–Latin lexicon of the NT and a Hebrew–Latin dictionary with a Latin–Hebrew index and an etymological dictionary of biblical proper names, deriving its title from the place of publication, Alcalá* in Spain, then called 'Complutum'. A triumph of pre-Reformation scholarship and the culmination of 50 years of printing the Bible in ever-increasing scholarly form.

The Hebrew text was based directly on ms. tradition without relying on earlier printed editions and was the first edition of the text of the Hebrew Bible* to be published under the direction and authority of Christian influences.

The earliest complete printed edition of the Greek NT. Work started on the ms. as early as 1502 by Cardinal Ximenes*, Archbishop of Toledo, and it might have been the first Greek Bible to be published had it not been beaten by Erasmus*. Though printed in 1514, publication was delayed until the whole work (6 volumes) was completed in 1517 and then further delayed until 1522.

The forerunner of the Antwerp*, Paris* and London* polyglots, all of which depended on it, and on the second Rabbinic Bible*, but they too were all based on mediaeval mss. of recent date and scant critical worth.

Concordant Version, 1926. A version based on the principle that every word in the original should have its own English equivalent, but it is rarely the case that the original word can *always* be translated by the same modern word, particularly when dealing with ancient languages.

Confessio Gallicana,**1559.** A statement by the Reformed Churches relating to decisions concerning the Apocrypha* at the Council of Trent, 1545–63*.

Conflation. The process by which scribes, confronted by two different texts or two slightly different versions of the same text in two different sources, preferred to include both rather than choose between them. Simple cases are some-

times called variant readings* but in its more sophisticated forms conflation may result in two accounts of an event being blended together to form a consistent, though not always *wholly* consistent, narrative. Identifying conflation is part of textual criticism*. The later the ms. the more prevalent it is. See Conflations, p. 53.)

Confraternity Version, 1941. Based on current Roman Catholic Canon Law*, a decision in the 1930s to undertake a fresh translation of the Vulgate* led to a revision of the NT of the Douay-Rheims Bible* amounting almost to a new translation, carried out by the Episcopal Confraternity of Christian Doctrine and published in the USA under the title, *The New Testament of our Lord and Savior Jesus Christ*. Based on the latest Greek and Vulgate* texts, with special reference to those places where the Greek and the Vulgate differ. Diction, grammar and syntax have been modernized but the form 'thou' remains. A start was made on a new translation of the OT based on the best Hebrew texts, beginning with Genesis in 1948, and the rest was published in four volumes, 1952–59.

Following the Second Vatican Council*, which authorized direct translation from the Hebrew, Aramaic and Greek, the Episcopal Confraternity of Christian Doctrine (which held the copyright) authorized an entirely new translation from the original texts which resulted in the New American Bible*, 1970.

Conjectural Emendation. A practice by scholars (some would say a last resort), much less common than it was 50 to 60 years ago, to determine what a corrupt text, a text which seems not 'to work', or one that is markedly out of line with other mss. or versions, might have read before it was corrupted, usually resulting in a new reading. Sometimes it

Conflation

Mk 13.11. Jesus counsels his disciples not 'to be anxious' beforehand when facing their persecutors, but some mss. urge them not 'to practise beforehand' as does the Lukan parallel (21.14). Many mss. give both.

Lk. 24.53. Some early mss. have 'in the temple praising God' (as in NEB*) whereas others have 'blessing God' (as in NRSV*). Some later mss. have 'praising and blessing' (as in AV*).

There is also evidence for the addition of 'fasting' especially relating to prayer, as the habit became more common, e.g., Mk 9.29; Acts 10.30; 1 Cor. 7.5.

Acts 20.28. Some early mss. have 'church of God' whereas others have 'church of the Lord'. Some later mss. have 'church of the Lord and God'.

requires a change of a word, more often a consonant and occasionally only a vowel. By definition, most emendations require an element of guesswork or intuition and are of three kinds:

Contextual. Changes derived from a specific understanding of the overall setting. These are by far the most common form of conjectural emendation, and though many are highly disputed a few are now generally accepted.

Linguistic. Changes derived from an understanding of grammar. These are less frequent and most disputed since there are limits to our understanding of Hebrew grammar and we can never presume that everybody writes grammatically all the time anyway.

Metrical. Changes derived from scholarly theories relating to Hebrew poetry, metre, stress, etc. Most scholars regard these emendations with a high degree of scepticism.

Sometimes what was once proposed as a conjectural emendation will come to light in a newly discovered ms., as, for example, in the DSS*, at which point it ceases to be an emendation and becomes a variant reading*.

Constantine I, the Great (275–337). Roman Emperor who gave official recognition to Christianity, previously a persecuted religion, and ordered 50 copies of the Greek Bible to be written on vellum* for his capital, Constantinople*.

Constantinople, Turkey. In ancient times, Byzantium. Christian monks and scholars kept a library of classical mss. here, including some of the NT in Greek, for hundreds of years prior to its capture by the Turks, 1453. Capital of the ancient Greek-speaking world and source for the Byzantine* text. City of the Jerusalem Monastery where Philotheos Bryennios* discovered some ancient OT documents. Now called Istanbul.

Constitutions of Oxford, 1408. Under the leadership of Thomas Arundel, Archbishop of Canterbury, a synod of clergy at Oxford passed 13 provisions against the Lollards*. One provision forbade anyone to translate, or even to read, a vernacular version of the Bible without approval from the bishop. They remained in force until the establishment of Reformed religion in England.

Contemporary English Version, 1991 (NT), 1995 (complete). A dynamic equivalence* common language translation, following in the tradition of Today's English Version* while recognizing the changes in the English language over the last 20 years. Initiated in the mid-1980s by Barclay M. Newman*, one of the translators of the Good News Bible*, and the American Bible Society*. After studying popular forms of modern English to determine how people were speaking and hearing Newman became interested in how people 'heard' when listening to something being read aloud and felt the need to eliminate the rhythm and cadence of the Hebrew and Greek from the modern English. A test carried out on illustrated Bible passages among children showed the version to be so popular that he decided to translate the entire Bible. The NT appeared on the 175th anniversary of the American Bible Society and the OT 4 years later.

In the tradition of the AV*, based on *Biblia hebraica* stuttgartensia* for the OT and the (UBS) Greek New Testament* for the NT, with an emphasis on a text that is faithful to the original, and capable of being read aloud by an experienced reader without stumbling, of being understood by someone with limited English and appreciated regardless of religious or educational background, and with meticulous attention to line breaks because that is where most readers pause. Committed to gender-inclusive language and the avoidance of traditionally theological language and biblical words like 'atonement', 'redemption', 'righteousness' and 'sanctification'.

Contextual Emendation. See Conjectural Emendation.

Contractions. When copying mss. scribes often used a system of contractions for certain sacred words (*nomina sacra**). such as 'God', 'Lord', 'Israel', 'Saviour' and 'Jerusalem', and this sometimes led to errors in copying*. In Hebrew, contraction often meant using just the first letter followed by the equivalent of an apostrophe, for example, 'Y' for 'Yahweh'. In uncial* Greek, contractions may be the first and last letters, the first two and the last, or the first and the last two, and so on, and were usually identified by a horizontal line over both letters, much as we might use a full stop to convey the idea of an abbreviation, e.g., ΘΣ for 'God', using the first and last letters of ΘΕΟΣ, ΠΜΑ for 'spirit', using the first and last two letters of ΠΝΕΥΜΑ, and ΚΩ for 'Lord', using two letters of ΚΥΡΙΩΣ. (See Contractions, p. 55)

Coptic Versions. Translations for the Coptic Church in the language used by Egyptian Christians from the third century. Essentially the non-cultivated speech of rural folk at a time when the Egyptian aristocracy used Greek, Coptic was not committed to writing until around the third century and then solely for the purposes of Bible translation. Derived from hieroglyphics, it developed a simplified alphabetic script of 31 letters in Greek characters, of which 24 were borrowed from the Greek uncial script.

Of seven dialects, only three were known until the 1880s, the first two being the most significant for biblical studies:

Contractions

2 Chron. 21.2 describes Jehoshaphat as 'king of Israel' instead of king of Judah, which may suggest that what the scribe saw was 'king of J', both Israel and Judah beginning with the same letter in Hebrew.

Judg. 19.18. MT has ביתי (*byhy*) (my house) and the LXX agrees, but if the final י (*y*) is separated and taken as the first letter of 'Yahweh' we have י בית 'house of Yahweh [or "the Lord"])'. Both are equally acceptable translations, one reflected in the NRSV* and the other in the AV*, especially if you allow for *scriptio continua**.

Jon. 1.9. MT has עברי (*'bry*) ('a Hebrew') where the LXX appears to have read י עבד (*'bdy y*) ('a servant of the Lord'), treating the final י (*y*) as a contraction* for 'Yahweh' and then reading (or misreading) the ר (*r*) as a ד (*d*).

Jer. 6.11. MT has חמתי (*ḥmty*) and the LXX translates 'my wrath', but some mss. have 'the wrath of Yahweh' by making a word division* before the final י (*y*) and treating it as a contraction* for 'Yahweh'.

Rom. 12.11. Some scribes appear to have read KΩ, a contraction* for KΥΡΙΩ ('Lord'), as KPΩ (a contraction of 'the opportune time'), as in the RV margin.

Sahidic: in the south (Upper Egypt), in the second to the third centuries CE, the standard literary language over the whole of Egypt from the fourth century and the language of educated people until the eighth to ninth centuries, when it was superseded by Bohairic. The oldest version of the Sahidic is 270 CE and by 370 CE all the books of the Bible had been translated into it.

Bohairic: in the north (Lower Egypt), in the third century CE, which took over from the Sahidic in the fourth century, gained mastery in the ninth and continues to be used as the only dialect in the liturgy of the Coptic Orthodox church. Bohairic mss. are numerous though late, twelfth to fourteenth centuries. Used by John Fell* in his Greek edition of the NT, 1675.

Fayyumic: in the region of Oasis Fayyum.

Coptic versions of the OT were made from the LXX* and the John Rylands Library, Manchester*, has a Bohairic Coptic text of Job and a Sahidic Coptic text of Ecclesiasticus both going back to the fourth to fifth centuries. It is not known when the earliest Coptic translations of the NT were made but probably by the end of the second or the beginning of the third centuries. The most extensive Bohairic ms. to come to light is one of the Fourth Gospel, part of the Bodmer* Collection, dated from the fourth century, containing 239 numbered pages, though the first 22 are badly damaged.

Coptic versions of the Bible appeared only in fragments until the beginning of the twentieth century and this is still largely the case, but in 1910, in the ruins of the monastery of Archangel Michael, archaeologists found a large collection of ancient and complete Sahidic mss. dated somewhere between the first half of the ninth and the latter half of the tenth centuries. Fifty-six were biblical works and included six complete books of the OT (Leviticus, Numbers, Deuteronomy, 1 and 2 Samuel and Isaiah), three complete gospels (Matthew, Mark and John), fourteen letters of Paul, 1 and 2 Peter, and 1, 2 and 3 John. They were subsequently acquired by the Pierpont Morgan Library in New York and published in a magni-ficent facsimile edition. Interest in Coptic versions of the NT was stimulated by the discovery of a library of Coptic writings at Nag Hammadi* in Upper Egypt in 1945.

The standard edition of the Bohairic Coptic is that of George W. Horner, four volumes published in London, 1898–1905, complete with introduction, critical apparatus and full English translation. The Coptic Orthodox Society published a one-volume edition of the Bohairic NT in 1934, using Tattam's text published by SPCK, 1847–52. (See Coptic, below)

Coptos, Egypt. Now known as Qift. Site of the discovery of an ancient papyrus* mss., dated c. 200, by John Vincent Scheil* in 1889.

Coptic

The origins of Christianity in Egypt are obscure. If the words, 'in his own country', in Codex Bezae* (Acts 18.25) are accepted as reliable they suggest that Christianity had reached Alexandria (as it had Rome) by 50 CE. There is certainly evidence of a number of Christian documents (mainly apocryphal gospels* and the like but including the John Fragment*) circulating there in the second century, and the Chester Beatty*, Oxyrhynchus* and Bodmer papyri* are all conservatively dated in the early third century.

Monasticism dates from the third century, possibly beginning with Anthony (251–356) who decided in 271 to give all he had to the poor and go into the desert to live the life of a hermit. Athanasius, his biographer, says it all started one Sunday when he heard Mt. 19.21 read in a little village church in southern Egypt. And when Pachomius, the founder of coenobitic monasticism in Egypt, composed his rules c. 320 he required all aspirants to be able to read 20 psalms or 2 epistles or some other parts of the scriptures, and those who could not read were to learn it by heart, all of which suggests that most of the NT and the psalms already existed in the vernacular at that time.

Coptic* represents the final stage in the development of ancient Egyptian, the language of Egypt long before the Christian era, the word being derived from the Arabic Qobt, a shortened form of the Greek for Egyptian.

Copying. The copying of ancient mss. among Jews was a skilled and disciplined procedure. Corruptions* occured, nevertheless, and if a scribe made a mistake or found anything which he considered to be a mistake, either by a previous scribe or by a reader, there were recognized procedures for correcting it. These included cancellation dots, erasure, additions above the line, a note in the margin, reshaped letters or brackets. Sometimes additions* were made and corrections set alongside an error were always liable to creep into the main text at a later date

The same rigidity did not apply to early Christian scribes, many of whom were not professional scribes but educated people making copies for their church, friends and family, some of whom felt free to exercise their individuality or give rein to their inspiration. Moreover, particularly in the early days, they were expecting the imminent return of Christ and did not see themselves as producing sacred text. From the fourth century onwards, with help from the state, scriptoria were set up where one person dictated the text and several scribes wrote it down. As the text became more established and recognized as 'sacred' copying procedures improved and copied texts became remarkably similar, but errors of sight and sound, additions, omissions*, and variant readings* all nevertheless crept in. Later mss. tended to be copied more by monks working alone in monasteries. (See Copying and Correcting, pp. 58-59.)

Cornish, Gerald Warre (1875–1916). Born and educated at Eton and Cambridge. Ordained priest. Master of Sunningdale School. Lecturer in Greek at Manchester University prior to being killed in action in 1916. Among his belongings was found a muddy copybook containing a translation of 1 and 2 Corinthians and part of Ephesians. The work was published in 1937 under the title, St Paul from the Trenches*, 1937.

Corrections. See Corrections, p. 59. See Copying.

Corruptions. A technical term for mistakes in mss., usually due to copying* and of two kinds: accidental and intentional.

In the OT accidental corruptions may be due to damage to the papyrus* or vellum*, unclear handwriting, word spaces or boundaries to text, similar letters*, similar sounds*, dittography*, doublets*, haplography*, homoioteleuton*, homoioarcton* or the transmission from early Hebrew cursive* script to the later square characters. Intentional corruptions may be due to deliberate (though often random and sometimes thoughtless) textual transmission. Issues, however, are rarely clear-cut and what looks like corruption to one may be regarded as correct (or even an improvement) to another.

In the NT, accidental corruptions arise for similar reasons and account for the vast majority of the variant readings*. NT texts, however, are more prone to intentional changes, which may be additions* from different oral or liturgical traditions, from groups with a special interest (such as those who appeared anxious to stress fasting as well as prayer), by pious scribes, the fruit of doctrinal bias or simply an attempt at harmonization*. Most of them happened before the year 200 and as yet there is no means of getting back to earlier versions.

Some help with countering corruptions can be gained from a study of parallel texts* or (because of their dating) the DSS*, but in neither OT nor NT can one presume to get back to a single original autograph* or urtext*. (See Corruptions, p. 59.)

The Price of Copying

Copying* manuscripts was laborious, painstaking, time-consuming, not particularly rewarding, and expensive. Scribes in a fourth-century scriptorium were normally paid per line. In 301 CE Emperor Diocletian set the rate at 25 denarii per 100 lines for top quality production and 20 for medium quality. On this basis Rendall Harris calculated that the cost of producing one copy of the Bible (say Codex Sinaiticus) would be about 30,000 denarii.

But there was more to the cost of copying than money. There was posture. As late as the Middle Ages scribes would stand or sit on a stool or bench, holding the scroll on their lap and so coordinating knee, mss., right hand and stylus, but even at a desk or table sitting in that posture copying for six hours a day month after month must have taken its physical toll.

No wonder scribes occasionally worked off their feelings through a note or colophon, like the one frequently found in non-biblical mss. which says, 'He who does not know how to write supposes it to be no labour; but though only three fingers write, the whole body labours'.

Other similar notes were.

Writing bows one's back, thrusts the ribs into one's stomach, and fosters a general debility of the body.

As travellers rejoice to see their home country, so also is the end of a book to those who toil [in writing].

The end of the book—thanks be to God!

Even the elements took their toll and in one Armenian ms. of the gospels the scribe complains in a colophon that a heavy snowstorm was raging outside, the ink froze, his hand became numb and he dropped his pen!

As if that were not enough, there were also punishments for poor workmanship. In one monastery in Constantinople, in the ninth century, a scribe whose work suffered because he got too interested in what he was copying was liable to be put on bread and water. Soiled or untidy parchment called for 130 penances and the penalty for taking somebody else's parchment or using too much glue, 50.

Corrections

1 Sam. 18.10 refers to 'an evil spirit from God', which has led some commentators to suggest that 'evil' may have been inserted in the margin by a scribe, unable to change the word 'God' but not wishing to attribute some of Saul's behaviour to him, intending it as an alternative or even a 'corrected' reading, but which then finished up in the main text.

The quotation attributed to Jeremiah in Mt. 27.9 is actually from Zechariah (11.12-13), which may explain why some mss. omit the name and others appear to have changed it. Similarly, the quotation attributed to Isaiah in Mk 1.2 is also in Malachi, which may explain why some later mss. read simply 'in the prophets'.

'After three days' in Mk 8.31 seems to have presented problems to some scribes so that it became 'on the third day'.

The discrepancy between Jn 7.8 where Jesus says he is not going up to the feast and two verses later where he says he is apparently led some scribes to change 'not' to 'not yet'.

Since Heb. 9.4 places the golden altar of incense in the Holy of Holies (forbidden in Exod. 30.1-6), Codex Vaticanus* and the translator of the Ethiopic version* move the words to v. 2 where the furniture is simply being itemized.

Corruptions

Judg. 11.20 offers a good example of a double (or even treble) corruption, the result of homoioteleuton* and metathesis*.

MT has '*and Sihon did not trust Israel to cross his border*' but some versions*, presumably working from an earlier Hebrew text, have 'refused to allow'. So how could an early Hebrew 'refused to allow' ever become the MT 'did not trust'?

First, by homoioteleuton*, 'to allow' may have been overlooked by a scribe because of its similarity to the following word or simply omitted because it seemed not to make sense. Second, by metathesis, the accidental transposition of two letters ' and א (*y* and *'*) into א and ' (*'* and *y*) turns אמי (*'my*) ('he refused') into ימא (*ym'*) ('he trusted'), and since that makes no sense a later scribe added the negative to give 'did not'.

1 Sam. 1.24 offers a good example of a double corruption* as a result of *matres lectionis** and word division*.

MT (followed by the Vulgate*) has בפרים שלושה (*bprym šlošh*) ('with three bulls'), as in the AV*, but if you omit the *matres lectionis** ' and ו (*y, o*) you have בפרם שלשה (*bprm šlšh*). A different word division* then gives you בפר משלשה (*bpr mšlšh*) ('a three-year-old bull'), as in the Syriac*, the LXX* and the NRSV*.

Council of Carthage, 397. Confirmed the biblical canon approved at the Council of Hippo*, 393, and possibly the first official endorsement of the 27 books which now make up the NT.

Council of Hippo, 393. Set out a biblical canon for the OT similar to that of Augustine*. Accepted the 27 books of the NT, but separated Hebrews from the letters of Paul. The records were lost but were subsequently confirmed at the Council of Carthage*, 397. The Council of Carthage, 419, issued the same NT list but included Hebrews with Paul.

Council of Laodicea, c. 363. Determined what psalms could be used in the churches and listed the books of the OT canon, which was the same as that of Athanasius* except that it combined Ruth and Judges and followed it immediately with Esther.

Council of Trent, 1545–63. Determined the limits of the OT canon to include the Hebrew Bible*, as accepted by Protestants, plus Tobit, Judith, Wisdom of Solomon, Ecclesiasticus, and 1 and 2 Maccabees, an addition which led to Protestant reaction in the *Confessio Gallicana** and *Belgica**.

Coverdale, Miles (1488–1569). Born in York*, educated in Cambridge, an Augustinian friar (until 1528) and eventually a bishop. Worked as an assistant to Tyndale* on the continent, 1528–35, helping him with the translation of the Pentateuch* and possibly following him from Hamburg to Antwerp*. Enjoyed the patronage of Ann Boleyn and Thomas Cromwell* on his return in 1535, but with Ann's execution and Cromwell's fall he was in danger again and returned to the continent in 1540 where he stayed until Henry VIII's death in 1547, mostly in Strasbourg* where he translated books from Latin and German into English. Returned to England under Edward VI, became Bishop of Exeter in 1551 and enjoyed two years of Bible translation, during which time he was involved in later editions of the Great Bible*. Deposed under Mary Tudor in 1553 and went into exile for a third time, this time in Geneva*, where he had contact with the Reformers working on the Geneva Bible*. Returned to England in 1559 for the last time and took part in the consecration of Matthew Parker* as Archbishop of Canterbury.

Besides Coverdale's Bible* he revised Matthew's Bible* at the request of Cromwell to produce the Great Bible*, published a revised NT with the Latin Vulgate* in parallel columns in 1538, and his version of the Psalms is used in the Book of Common Prayer, 1662.

Coverdale's Bible, 1535. The first complete printed edition of the Bible in English, probably published in Cologne*, and quickly imported to Britain. A dedication to Henry VIII* was added in the second edition (1537), printed in England. Henry sought the advice of the bishops and when they assured him that it contained no heresy he assisted in its publication and distribution; thus it became the first English Bible to circulate freely without opposition from the ecclesiastical authorities. In some churches it was one of the first Chained Bibles*.

Unlike Tyndale*, Coverdale was more an editor than a translator and, knowing little or no Hebrew and Greek, made considerable use of Tyndale's* translation and acknowledged his debt to the Vulgate*, Luther, Zwingli and Pagninus. His best work is in the poetical and prophetic books and he provided the translation of the Psalms for the Book of Common Prayer, 1662. First Bible to introduce chapter summaries and marginal notes, and, following Luther, to separate the Apocrypha* from the rest of the OT. Phrases from Coverdale which have survived in subsequent English versions include 'lordly dish' (Judg. 5.25) and 'enter thou into the joy of thy Lord' (Mt. 25.21, 23).

There are two forms: an earlier form, 13 × 8 inches, printed in double columns in a German black-letter type, with 68 woodcuts providing 158 illustrations, many ornamental letters and a map of the Holy Land, and a later one with the prelims in the English black letter. Reprinted (with some revisions) by James Nicolson (1537), by Christoph Froschauer (1550) and by Richard Jugge (1553), but its true successor was the Great Bible, 1539*. Two copies in the British Library.

Cranmer, Thomas (1489–1556). Archbishop of Canterbury, 1533–56. Very sympathetic to Bible translation and anxious to secure royal authority for an English version. In 1534, an attempt to secure approval for such a version from the bishops having failed, Convocation asked Cranmer to put the request to the king and when Matthew's Bible* appeared Cranmer worked for a royal licence and secured it. Wrote the Preface for the 1540 and subsequent editions of the Great Bible*. Executed in the period of reaction that followed the accession of Mary* to the throne.

Cranmer's Bible, 1539. Another name for the Great Bible*.

Critical Apparatus. Editions of the Hebrew Bible*, the LXX* and Greek Testaments* are either based on one particular source or are a reconstruction from several sources, but in both cases variant readings* in other sources are noted in the margin and in some cases evaluated. This information forms the critical apparatus and the result is known as a critical edition*.

Critical Edition. Since there is a wealth of mss. and textual data, since nobody can be competent enough in all areas to do all their own evaluations, and since years of scholarship is scattered around in commentaries, journals and monographs, it is necessary to have one basic text, complete with the most significant variations, known as a critical apparatus*, to which all can refer.

Bearing in mind everything to be considered there are basically two ways of compiling such an edition. One way is to take one ms. as being generally the most acceptable (e.g. Codex Vaticanus*), make that the basic text, and then fill in the gaps from other established mss. and draw attention to variant readings*, etc., in the margin or at the foot of the page. The other way is to collate all the available sources (mss., versions, quotations, etc.) and then choose what the editor considers to be the 'best' reading in each case, thus producing an eclectic text.

Two critical editions of the Hebrew Bible are Biblica hebraica* and the Hebrew University Bible Project*. In the NT, Swete*, 1887–91, is a good example of the single text, Rahlfs*, 1935 and later editions, the eclectic. Other critical editions of the New Testament include Souter*, 1910, von Soden*, 1913, and Nestle*, 1898, revised 1979, which led to the (UBS) Greek New Testament*.

Cromwell, Thomas (1485–1540). Chief minister of Henry VIII*. Supported Coverdale* in his Bible translation by financing him and thereby financing the very first Bible to be printed in English, 1535. Cooperated with Cranmer* in the production of Matthew's Bible* and received from the king in 1539 the exclusive right for five years to grant a licence for the printing of the Bible in English. Directed the preparation of the Great Bible* and saw it through to its completion, motivated in part by what he saw as the weakness of the two English Bibles already in existence: Coverdale's, because it had been compiled from various sources and was not a translation from the Hebrew and Greek, and Matthew's because it was a compilation of translations of varying value whose marginal notes at points reflected controversy. Cromwell secured the services of Coverdale to prepare a revised Bible free from these objections. Became Earl of Essex in 1540 and was beheaded soon afterwards on Tower Hill. Unsuccessful in his attempts to save Tyndale*.

Cruden, Alexander (1699–1770). Born and educated in Aberdeen* and prevented by ill health from entering the Presbyterian ministry. Instead he went into teaching at the age of 21 and, after several tutorships, moved to London in 1732 where he opened a book shop in the Royal Exchange. In 1737 he began working on his *Complete Concordance to the Old and New Testaments*, described as 'a dictionary and alphabetical index to the Bible', based on the AV*, and containing over 225,000 references, first published in 1844 and today renowned throughout the English-speaking world. There was a major revision by William Youngman in 1920 followed by another by C.H. Irwin, A.D. Adams and S.A. Waters. Published from 1839 by the Religious Tract Society, subsequently the United Society for Christian Literature, and Lutterworth Press.

Cuneiform. The oldest form of writing, probably invented in Mesopotamia c. 3400 BCE. A pictographic system written with a stylus on clay, originally in vertical columns starting at the top right-hand corner and working left. Adopted and modified in Akkadian c. 3000–2500. Vertical writing continued until c. 1100 BCE when it was superseded by the invention of the alphabet, which in the case of the Phoenician script amounted to 22 letters, written from right to left, c. 1150 BCE.

Cureton, William (1808–64). Born at Westbury, Shropshire, and educated at Christ Church, Oxford. Ordained a priest. Sub-librarian at the Bodleian Library, Oxford*, and then Assistant Keeper of Ancient Manuscripts at the British Museum, where he prepared a classified statement of Arabic mss. When a batch of Syriac mss. which had come to light in a monastery in Egypt arrived in the British Museum he learned the language and in the course of classifying them recognized a previously unknown version of the gospels in Old Syriac*.

Curious Hieroglyphic Bible, 1784. A second printing of the first English hieroglyphic Bible, copying earlier volumes in Latin, German and Dutch, representing select Bible passages with emblems and adding a short account on the lives of writers of the gospels. It ran to several editions.

Cursive. A 'running' form of writing Greek, mainly for non-literary purposes such as personal letters, accounts, bills, receipts, deeds and petitions, etc., and very popular in the early days of Christianity. Some of Paul's letters, especially those addressed to individuals, may have been written in this way. It was a modification of the uncial* script by rounding off the letters and joining them up. In the eighth or ninth centuries it led to another form of cursive, the minuscule*.

Cyril of Jerusalem (315–86). Bishop of Jerusalem, from c. 349. In his catechism of 348 he claimed that the OT canon*, consisting of 22 books, was the Jewish Scriptures as found in the LXX* plus

Baruch and the Letter of Jeremiah. Other books, including 2 and 3 Maccabees, Wisdom of Solomon, Psalms and Odes of Solomon, Ecclesiasticus, Esther, Judith, Tobit and Susanna, were to be regarded as permitted reading. In the NT he accepted the four Gospels, Acts, 14 letters of Paul and the Pastoral Epistles.

D

Daily Study Bible, 1954–57. Seventeen volumes of Bible readings and commentary by William Barclay*, published by the St Andrew Press, to give the general reader the benefits of modern scholarship in a form which is precise and meaningful, yet free from technical and theological terms and able to demonstrate its relevance for today. Each volume contains a new translation into modern English so as to provide text and comments side by side. Followed by an OT series by a wider variety of authors.

Damasus I (304–84). Controversial pope who did much to resist heresy and strengthen the position of the see of Rome. Invited Jerome* in 382 to make a fresh translation of the Bible into Latin.

Darby, John Nelson (1800–82). Born in London and educated at Westminster School and Trinity College, Dublin. Called to the Irish Bar but then got himself ordained and became one of the leaders of the Brethren Movement. Worked and travelled extensively in Europe and North America and was involved in hymn writing and in Bible translations into German and French, subsequently adapted into English and known as Darby's Translation*, 1871–85.

Darby's Translation, 1871–85. An English adaptation, by one of the founders of the Plymouth Brethren, who are its main users, of a version which had already appeared in French as the Pau Bible*, and in German as the Elberfeld Bible*, closely shadowing the AV* and paying particular attention to the different ways of referring to God in the OT. The NT contained a full critical apparatus* and was consulted by the revisers of the RV*, but the OT was incomplete when Darby died and was finished from the French and German versions.

Dead Sea Scrolls. Sometimes described as 'the greatest ms. discovery of modern times', mainly because of the light they throw on ancient Bible texts and the evidence they provide for writing*, literary activity in general and a variety of textual traditions.

The original discoveries by an Arab boy in 1947 were 11 scrolls of ancient leather and bronze in earthenware jars, some containing literary compositions, and now located in the Hebrew University in Jerusalem.

Subsequent excavations showed them to be part of a collection of about 800 texts, mostly fragmentary, in Hebrew, Aramaic and Greek, biblical and extra-biblical, found in the Judean Desert, 1947–56, the most important being in Cave 4 at Qumran*, half-a-mile away from the first discovery, and probably copied somewhere between 250 BCE and

150 CE. Most of the biblical scrolls are now thought to belong to the first century CE though some may go back to the second century BCE.

Among the early discoveries was an almost complete copy of Isaiah in Hebrew, subsequently used by the translators of the RSV*. Fragments of all the books of the OT except Esther were discovered subsequently, though most were small. Little is known about their origin or how they came to be there, but because they come from different places and belong to different periods they provide scholars with an interesting textual variety.

Texts, which represent a stage in the Hebrew tradition roughly contemporary with the consonantal text of Rabbi Akibah* but prior to vocalization*, provide some contrasting surprises. Some from Cave 1, for example, show a surprising agreement with the Masoretic Text* of the ninth and tenth centuries, thus testifying to a considerable consistency in transmission. Others from Cave 4 differ from the Masoretic Text but agree significantly with the LXX*, thus reflecting a Hebrew text that differed from the Masoretic Text and so demonstrating the existence of considerable textual pluralism.

By focusing attention on the Hebrew texts at a time when almost as much value was placed on Greek, Latin and Aramaic sources as on the Hebrew, they increase our understanding of Jewish interpretations, of the relationship between the various textual witnesses, and of the historical process of the translation of the Bible into other languages.

By ante-dating previous biblical texts by several hundred years, and so providing a picture of the biblical text which may go back as far as the second century BCE, especially those texts from which the Masoretic Text and the Samaritan Pentateuch* emerged later, they throw

light on the state of the Hebrew text at a time for which there was no previous evidence and assist our understanding of the history of the Hebrew language.

Similarity to the Pre-Samaritan Texts* has helped scholars to distinguish between the text of the Samaritan Pentateuch and the earlier texts which gave it birth. (See The Dead Sea Scrolls, p. 65).

Defective Reading. A Hebrew word where one or more of the *matres lectionis** is missing.

de Lagarde (1827–91). A nineteenth-century scholar who took the views of Bauer* regarding the possibility of an urtext* for the Hebrew Bible and applied them to the Bible as a whole, classifying mss. according to their recensional families* in order to make a judgment on their variant readings* with the intention of arriving at a text corresponding more closely to the original.

de Vaux, Roland (1903–71). French Dominican, Director of the Ecole Biblique, nick-named the 'mountain goat' because of his restless and energetic manner. An archaeologist involved in excavations and discoveries at Qumran*, one of the leaders in the translation of *La Bible de Jérusalem* in 1946, and a key figure in the production of the Jerusalem Bible*, especially the Old Testament.

Deuteronomy Fragment. Eight papyrus fragments of Deuteronomy in Greek, six of which give readable text from Deuteronomy 23–28, a pre-Christian portion of the Greek Old Testament, dating back to the second century BCE and therefore earlier than any other mss. of the Greek Bible. After being abandoned as a literary text some of its blank sides were used for financial accounts, and later still the papyrus sheets were used as packing round a mummy! Unlike most

The Dead Sea Scrolls

Shortly before the end of British rule in Palestine, late 1946 or early 1947, a shepherd boy, who enjoyed searching for caves and was minding his sheep on the shores of the Dead Sea, amused himself by throwing stones at an opening in the cliffs. All at once, one of the stones went into a cave and he heard the sound of broken pottery.

Neither he nor his two companions thought any more of it, but two days later, unbeknown to the others, one of them got up early and squeezed himself into the cave where he found ten jars, each about two feet high, all but two of which were empty. One of the two contained nothing but dirt. The other had three scrolls, two of which were wrapped in linen. They were later identified as a copy of Isaiah, a Manual of Discipline (setting out rules for a community) and a commentary on Habakkuk. Four additional scrolls were found later and removed.

They took them to an antiquities dealer who shared his find with St Mark's Monastery in Jerusalem, but at this point nobody had any idea as to their value, so a deal was made whereby the Bedouin would receive two-thirds of what the antiquities dealer received. But the whole operation at this stage was low-key rather than secretive, and there is a famous story of how when the Bedouin kept an appointment at the monastery to complete the transaction the door was answered by a monk who was unaware of the arrangement and turned away 'the poorly dressed tribesmen', thus nearly depriving the monastery of a chance to acquire such treasure. Fortunately the error was soon rectified and the monastery purchased four scrolls for about £25.

The monastery needed professional help to evaluate what they had purchased and turned, among others, to Professor Sukenik of the Hebrew University of Jerusalem. The British Mandate was almost at an end. Palestine was a dangerous place to be. Travel was difficult. But when Sukenik heard that a dealer in Bethlehem had 'some ancient scrolls' he made a secret visit on the very day that the United Nations created the State of Israel and bought the three remaining scrolls. Two months later he was shown the four scrolls held by the monastery though he did not then know they had come from the same place. He tried to buy them. The monastery refused to sell, so that from the beginning the Dead Sea Scrolls were split into two groups and published under different auspices.

The discovery was announced by the press in 1948. The first archaeological excavation was in 1949, and led to further discoveries and fresh information concerning the Dead Sea Community, the Essenes and ancient texts at a time of considerable significance in Christian history.

surviving copies of the LXX[*], which are Christian in origin, this ms. is unambiguously Jewish and close in time to the original translation of the Torah[*] into Greek. Now located in the John Rylands Library, Manchester[*].

Dissenter. A general term (still in popular use) to refer to nonconformists at the time of the Reformation, mainly Baptists, Congregationalists and Presbyterians, arising from the fact that two from each of these three churches formed the Dissenting Deputies in 1732, an official lobby to deal with the civil disabilities which they suffered as a result of the Test and Corporation Acts, 1662.

Dittography. The copyist's error of writing a letter, word, verse or passage twice instead of once, sometimes as a result of parablepsis[*], and so producing a different word or meaning. The opposite is haplography[*]. (See Dittography, below)

divinatio. The Latin term for conjectural emendation[*].

Documents of the Christian Church, 1934. An independent translation of the books of the NT, expanded and with explanatory phrases in italics, in what their author, G.C. Wade, believed to be their chronological order, plus historical and critical introduction and notes.

Dodd, Charles Harold (1884–1973). Born in Wrexham, son of a school teacher, and educated at University College, Oxford, where he got a Double First

---

Dittography

Isa. 30.30.	Some mss. repeat 'shall make heard'.
Isa. 31.6.	Some mss. repeat 'to him'.
Jer. 51.3.	Some mss. repeat 'draw'.
1 Thess. 2.7.	Some mss. read 'we were gentle' (ἐγενήθημεν ἤπιοι), as in AV and NRSV, whereas others read 'we were infants' (ἐγενήθημεν νήπιοι), as in NRSV margin, a difference readily appreciated if a scribe accidentally repeated the letter 'ν', particularly if there was no word division[*], and even more understandable if the error is found mostly in later mss. or in versions[*] which used them.
Mt. 27.17.	Some mss. insert 'Jesus' before 'Barabbas', as in NRSV, and others omit it as noted in NRSV margin. What is not clear is whether it is dittography[*], the last two letters of the previous word, ὑμῖν, ('for you') being repeated and then read as an abbreviation for 'Jesus', or haplography[*], which may explain its absence from other mss.
Mk 12.27.	Some mss. repeat 'God'.
Acts 19.34.	Codex Vaticanus[*] repeats 'Great is Diana of the Ephesians'.

in Greats. After a short spell teaching in Leeds and Oxford, he was ordained to the Congregational ministry and settled in Warwick before becoming Principal of Mansfield College, Oxford, followed by professorial appointments in Manchester and Cambridge. Vice-Chairman of the Joint Committee and Convenor for the NT panel of the NEB*. Appointed General Director for the whole translation in 1949.

Doddridge, Philip (1702–51). Author of one of three popular eighteenth-century translations of the NT, 1739–56, the other two being George Campbell's* translation of the gospels and James MacKnight's* translation of the epistles. In 1818 a combined translation appeared in London, subsequently revised and published by Alexander Campbell* in 1826.

Douay, France. Home of the English College for Roman Catholics founded by William Allen*.

Douay-Challoner. See Douay-Rheims Bible.

Douay-Rheims Bible, 1582 (NT), 1610 (complete). A translation made from the Latin Vulgate*, begun in 1578 by many prominent Roman Catholics who fled to France to avoid persecution when Elizabeth I* succeeded Mary* Tudor. Gregory Martin* was the main translator, with revisions by William Allen* and Richard Bristow* and notes by Thomas Worthington*. The NT was published first at Rheims and the OT subsequently in two volumes at Douay*, though the OT was actually translated first. Later revised, authorized by the Roman Catholic Church for public and private use, and used by many English Catholics.

A fairly literal translation, sometimes intelligible and sometimes meaningful only to those who already understood the Latin. The Vulgate was chosen because the Council of Trent*, 1545–63, had determined that the ancient and vulgar version should be regarded as authentic. The order of books in the Vulgate is followed, which means that the books of the Apocrypha* are not collected together as in Protestant Bibles.

The NT was re-printed in 1600, 1621 and 1633 and the whole Bible in 1635 but there was no thorough revision until the fifth edition by Bishop Richard Challoner* in 1738, which he saw not so much as an editing of the text as a revision, the language of the earlier version being largely unintelligible to English Catholics, and it is this version which is commonly referred to as the Douay-Rheims Bible, though it might more properly be called the Rheims-Challoner or Douay-Challoner. Contains many annotations, mainly to interpret the text in line with the faith as the editors understood it. Five further editions of the NT followed, 1749–72, and two editions of the OT, 1750–63. In 1810 the Challoner Bible was authorized for use by the English-speaking Roman Catholics of America. Many other revisions followed, some originating in Britain and others in America.

In 1941 a group of 27 Catholic scholars undertook a new translation of the NT from the Latin, a revision of the Challoner-Rheims Version. It takes the older versions of the Vulgate into account and refers to the Greek variations in the notes. Modern paragraphing is used and poetic forms are recognized.

Doublets. A form of conflation* as a result of repeating or combining two or more different accounts of the same event, sometimes done deliberately to preserve different readings.

Driver, Godfrey Rolles (1892–1975). Son of S.R. Driver* and Oxford Professor of Semitic Philology. Succeeded T.H. Robinson* as Convenor for the OT panel of the NEB* in 1950 and Joint Director with C.H. Dodd* for the whole translation from 1965.

Driver, Samuel Rolles (1846–1914). Oxford Professor of Hebrew and a member of the Old Testament panel for the RV*, whose literary contribution to the world of OT scholarship, and particularly his commentaries on Genesis, did much to make German Old Testament scholarship better known and more acceptable to the English-speaking world.

Dublin. Home of Chester Beatty, an American collector of mss. and discoverer of the Chester Beatty Papyri*, and location of the Beatty Museum.

Dynamic Equivalence. A method of translation* which aims at 'sense for sense' rather than verbal equivalence* or 'word for word', first proposed by Eugene Albert Nida*, as an approach to Bible translation to help translators in different cultures, and developed by Cecil Hargreaves who identified two mainstream movements in twentieth-century English Bible translations. One, a general idiomatic, or 'phrase by phrase', approach so as to produce the overall meaning of the text in modern English, such as we find in Moffatt*, Goodspeed*, Phillips*, Knox*, the JB*, the NEB*, the REB*, the New Century Version* and the New Living Translation*; the other, a common-language approach which emerged as a result of the efforts by the American Bible Society* to use linguistic analysis to translate the Bible in international mission contexts, such as we find in Today's English Version*, the Good News Bible* and the Contemporary English Version*. Some similarities to communication theory*.

E

Eadfrith (seventh century). Bishop of Lindisfarne and scribe of the Lindisfarne Gospels*.

Edinburgh, Scotland. Home of Alexander Arbuthnot*, a printer who secured permission to print the first Bibles in Scotland, 1575, subsequently appointed king's printer, and of Andrew Hart*, another Bible printer.

Edward VI (1537–53). Studied at Cambridge under Sir John Cheke*, Professor of Greek, and interested in Bible translation. Affirmed his devotion to the Bible at his coronation. Reacted against the reactionary trends at the close of his father's reign and encouraged a programme of reform. Ordered (in the first year of his reign) one copy of the Bible in English to be installed in every parish church and the Epistle and the Gospel in the Communion Service to be read in English. Made provision for the reading of a chapter from both OT and NT at Matins and Evensong. Editions of Tyndale*, Coverdale* and the Great Bible* poured from the press during his reign and many reformers who had fled to the continent under Henry VIII* returned.

Egbert (d. 766). Bishop of Holy Island who made a translation of the gospels c. 700, a copy of which is in the British Library.

Egerton Papyrus 2. A fragment, sometimes known as 'The Unknown Gospel' because of its similarity to the four gospels (John in particular) and dating from c. 150.

Egyptian Recension. See Recension.

El Bahnasa, Egypt. The modern name for the ancient city of Oxyrhynchus*.

Elberfeld Bible, 1871. The German name for Darby's Translation*.

Elephantine Papyri. A collection of writings in Aramaic, on papyrus*, from Elephantine, a Jewish military colony on an island in the Nile, close by the modern Aswan in Southern Egypt, and discovered in 1903. They consist mainly of legal documents such as marriage settlements, records of lawsuits or deeds relating to property transfer, but they also provide some evidence of correspondence between the Jews in Elephantine and Jerusalem, one letter, for example, relating to their failure to observe the Passover and another appealing to the Persian governor in Jerusalem after the destruction of their temple by the Egyptians. Dating from the fifth century BCE (the time of Ezra and Nehemiah) they are useful not only as a reflection of the life of that community but also for what they teach us about the habit of writing at that time, being among the oldest West-Semitic book scrolls and demonstrating that Hebrew scribes were writing and copying letters and documents on papyrus and books on papyrus scrolls at this time and probably earlier.

Elizabeth I (1533–1603). Took steps to ensure that the Bible in English was available in every church. Usually it was the Great Bible* but during her reign 60 editions of the Geneva Bible* were also issued. Initiated a revision of the Great Bible which led to the Bishop's Bible*.

Ellicott, Charles John (1819–1905). Bishop of Gloucester and Bristol. One of five clergymen who worked with Ernest Hawkins* to produce The Authorised Version of St John's Gospel, revised by Five Clergymen*, 1857, and similar revisions of some of the epistles. Chairman of the NT panel of translators for the RV*.

Elzevir, Louis (1540–1617). A Dutchman who founded a family printing business in Leiden* which ran through three or four generations. Bonaventura and Abraham, son and grandson (though sometimes referred to as the Elzevir Brothers), produced seven editions of the Greek NT, 1624–78, based on Stephanus* and Beza's* edition of 1565. The second edition (1633) contained in its Preface the claim that it was received by all and free from error, and was subsequently known as the Textus Receptus*.

Emphasised Bible, 1872 (NT), 1897–1902 (complete). A very literal translation by J.B. Rotherham*, a competent Greek and Hebrew scholar who added various signs to the text so as to bring out the finer points of the original. The first two editions of the NT were based on Tregelles's* text, the third on Westcott* and Hort*. One of the first versions to render the name of God as Yahweh.

English, E. Schuyler (1899–1981). Born in New York and educated at Princeton University and Wheaton College. Chairman of the committee of nine which was responsible for the New Scofield Reference Bible, 1967*, and author of *Companion to the Scofield Reference Bible*, 1972. Joined the Curtis Publishing Company, 1922, became a faculty member of the Philadelphia School of Bible, 1935–1947, and President, 1936–39. Editor-in-Chief of The Pilgrim Bible, Oxford University Press, 1948.

Epiphanius (315–403). Bishop of Salamis who produced a list of 27 canonical books of the OT, the same as those in current Protestant Bibles and similar to the list produced by Bryennios* though in a more familiar order.

Erasmus, Desiderius (1466–1536). A Dutch humanist scholar who visited England in 1511 and spent most of his time in Cambridge, where he gave himself to a study of Jerome* and the NT and laid the foundations for his own edition of the Greek NT, based on a very few minuscule* mss. none of them earlier than the tenth century. The order of books in his Greek NT was adopted by the Great Bible*, the AV* and other translations after 1539. Printed the first NT in Greek and Latin side by side in Basel* in 1516. Other editions followed in 1519, 1522, 1527 and 1535. One formed the basis for Luther's German NT and for Tyndale's* English NT, first printed in 1525. Despite being carried out with some haste and suffering badly from typographical errors, despite being criticized for the changes it made to the Latin text, and despite the fact that it was based on Greek mss. that were late and of little critical worth, it nevertheless laid the foundations for a standard Greek text which emerged by 1550 and was called the Textus Receptus*.

Estienne, Robert. See Stephanus.

Ethiopic Version. The early history of Ethiopia is shrouded in legend, the story of early Christianity there difficult to determine, and the date of the Ethiopic Version uncertain, probably somewhere between the fourth and the seventh centuries.

The OT has been studied more than the NT but it is not clear whether it was translated from the LXX* or the Syriac* and some scholars think they can find traces of Hebrew influence.

The NT is very mixed, sometimes very literal, sometimes very free and predominantly Byzantine*. In the Pauline letters the agreement with Chester Beatty* ($\mathfrak{P}^{46}$) is striking. There are about 300 Ethiopic mss. containing one or more books of the NT, mostly from the sixteenth to the nineteenth centuries, in Europe and America. Until recently the oldest was a copy of the four gospels in the Bibliothèque Nationale, Paris*, thought to have come from the thirteenth to the fourteenth centuries but several older mss. came to light in the 1960s, mainly of individual books.

The first printed edition of the NT was in Rome, 1548–49, in two quarto volumes, the work of a printer who did not know the language and therefore containing many typographical errors. It is included in the London Polyglot* with a Latin translation and there was an edition published by the British and Foreign Bible Society*, 1826–30.

Eumenes (d. 159 BCE). King of Pergamon in Asia Minor who made Pergamon a centre of learning. Wanting to create a library and unable to get papyrus* because his rival King Ptolemy of Egypt refused to allow it to be exported, Eumenes was the first to use vellum* for writing.

Eusebius (c. 260–340). Bishop of Caesarea* and a Christian historian, whose writings, c. 325, reflect the beginnings of scripture becoming a 'canon'*; possibly the first to use the word in that connection and one of the first to refer to the OT* and, later, the NT*. His *Church History* contains a list of 'accepted books', including the four gospels (listed for the first time in the order in which we now have them), Acts, 14 of Paul's letters, 1 Peter, 1 John and possibly Revelation. Unlike Athanasius*, whose list is very similar but with much firmer edges, Eusebius still has room for flexibility. He sees the books in question falling into one of three categories: those universally acknowledged, those which he believes to be spurious, and 'disputed' books. Of the 'disputed' books Eusebius accepted 1 Peter, questioned Jude, as did Jerome*, and put 2 Peter on his 'disputed' list along with Hebrews, James, and 1, 2 and 3 John. His criteria for recognizing scripture include universal acceptance, correct doctrine and apostolic authorship, though there may well have been some rationalization and books may well have been accepted or rejected first on other grounds.

Exemplar. The ms. from which a scribe is copying, not to be confused with an autograph* or urtext*.

Expanded Translation of the New Testament, 1956–59. A three-volume translation by Kenneth S. Wuest*, to introduce readers without Greek to the shades of meaning in the originals and to bring out the theological and philological nuances.

Eynsham, Oxfordshire. Home of Abbot Aelfric*.

F

Family 1. A group of four minuscule* mss. with a text close to Theodotion*, dating from the twelfth to the fourteenth centuries, subsequently numbered 1, 118, 131 and 209, allied to each other by certain similarities or curiosities identified by Kirsopp Lake* in 1902. The numbers represent the arabic numbers allocated to minuscule mss. and the Family bears the name of the first to be listed. Some connection also with Family 13* and the Caesarean* text current in the third and fourth centuries.

Family 13. Four minuscule* mss., discovered c. 1875 and published in 1877 by two Irish scholars, W.H. Ferrar* and T.K. Abbott*, known as 13, 69, 124 and 346, whose similarities suggested a common ancestry. The numbers represent the arabic numbers allocated to minuscule mss. and the Family bears the name of the first to be listed. Subsequently a few other mss. with similar characteristics (211, 543, 713, 788, 826 and 828) were added to the Family. Apparently a connection with the Old Syriac*.

Three of the originals were written in Southern Italy in the twelfth or thirteenth century and the fourth in England in the fifteenth century.

The most notable characteristic is that they remove the story of the woman taken in adultery from John 8 (where it seems not to belong) and put it after Lk. 21.38.

Family Theta. A late-ninth-century uncial* ms. of the gospels in a monastery at Koridethi* and first noticed by von Soden* in 1906. When it was published in 1913 strong similarities with Family 1*, Family 13*, and some other minuscules were noted as a result of which it was combined with these Families and the whole was given the title Family Theta. The name is derived from the Greek letter *theta*, used to identify the uncial mss. Now located at Tbilisi*. B.H. Streeter* pointed out that this kind of text stood midway between Westcott* and Hort's* Western* and Neutral* texts and was used by Origen* when he was at Caesarea*. Hence the name, Caesarean text*.

Fell, John (1625–86). Dean of Christ Church and Bishop of Oxford. Printed an edition of the Greek NT in 1675, the first to be published at Oxford, in small size (3.75 × 6.5 inches), in which he drew on the Elzevir* 1633 edition and claimed to have used over 100 mss. and demonstrated how they varied. They included those used by Stephanus* and Walton* but also some mss. from the Bodleian and some Coptic* and Gothic* versions. Editor of the 1708 edition of

Paraphrase on the Epistles of St Paul by Abraham Woodhead*, Richard Allestry* and Obadiah Walker*, first published anonymously in 1675.

Fenton, Ferrar (b. 1832). A London businessman who believed he was 'the only man who has ever applied real mental and literary criticism to the Sacred Scriptures' and that he had discovered 'the Hebrew laws of Syllabic verse'. He translated Paul's epistles in 1883, followed by other portions from time to time leading eventually to The Bible in Modern English*, 1903. One of the first to tackle the Bible single-handedly, the forerunner of people like Moffatt*, Weymouth*, Phillips* and Knox*, and significant for keeping alive the idea of continuous translation and moving it forward.

Ferrar, William Hugh (c. 1835–71). A biblical scholar, Junior Dean of Trinity College and Professor of Latin at Dublin University, who worked with T.K. Abbott* and c. 1875 discovered four minuscule* mss., subsequently numbered 13, 69, 124 and 346 and known as Family 13*. Author of *A Comparative Grammar of Sanskrit, Greek and Latin* (1869) and *A Collation of Four Important Manuscripts of the Gospels* (1877).

First Vatican Council, 1869–70. Reaffirmed the decision of the Council of Trent, 1545–63* regarding the extent of the canon of the OT.

Florence, Italy. Site of the Laurentian Library, home of Codex Amiatinus*.

Form Criticism. A method of biblical criticism* which concentrates on the prehistory of written documents or sources, classifying them according to their literary form or *genre* (e.g. stories, sayings, legends, pronouncements, etc.).

Four Gospels, a New Translation, 1933. A translation by Charles C. Torrey* reflecting his view that an Aramaic original underlay the text of the gospels. Contains an essay on 'The Origin of the Gospels'. Revised in 1947.

Four Gospels, The, 1898. A new Roman Catholic translation directly from the Greek, with reference to the Vulgate* and the ancient Syriac*, by F.A. Spencer* and published in New York. The whole New Testament was published posthumously in 1937.

Four Prophets, The, 1963. A paraphrase of Amos, Hosea, Isaiah 1–35 and Micah by J.B. Phillips*. Published by Geoffrey Bles, London.

Freer, Charles Lang (1854-1919). An American collector, with a museum in Washington*, who visited Cairo* in 1906 and purchased a group of biblical mss., later to become known as the Washington Codex*.

Full Reading. A Hebrew word containing *matres lectionis*.

G

Geddes, Alexander (1737–1802). A Scottish biblical scholar and liberal-minded Roman Catholic critic who studied in Scalan and Paris*. Trained for the priesthood but was suspended from his post for attending a Presbyterian service and for hunting. Went on to make a new translation of the English Bible for Roman Catholics, the Holy Bible, translated from the Corrected Texts of the Originals*, 1792–1807.

Genealogical Evidence. A phrase used principally by Westcott* and Hort* to express the idea that 'community of reading implies community of origin', leading to the notion of 'families of manuscripts' and the drawing up of a 'family tree'.

Geneva, Switzerland. City of Coverdale's* third exile in 1553 under Mary Tudor* and where he became an elder of the church and had contact with the Reformers working on the Geneva Bible*, whence came its name.

Home of John Calvin, a Protestant scholar of the Reformation who wrote many commentaries on the Bible, and the city where many Reformers, including William Whittingham* and other exiles, fled to escape the Marian persecutions because of its freedom from political and religious restrictions.

Home of Martin Bodmer, owner of the Bodmer papyri*, and of Theodore Beza*, owner of Codex Bezae* and Codex Claromontanus*, who succeeded Calvin as minister of the church.

Geneva Bible, 1560. The Bible of the Reformers, John Calvin and John Knox. The work of a group of Puritans, with a good knowledge of Hebrew and Greek, who had fled to Geneva* to escape the persecutions of Mary Tudor*. Their names are not known but William Whittingham* was probably the main inspiration and editor, supported by Anthony Gilby, Christopher Goodman, Thomas Sampson, William Cole and the ageing Miles Coverdale*. The version with the greatest influence on the AV* after Tyndale*.

The OT is a thorough revision of the Great Bible*, especially in those books which Tyndale had not translated and which therefore had not previously been translated from the original texts, thus bringing the existing versions of the Prophets* and the Writings* into line with the Hebrew text, and even the Hebrew idiom. The NT is Tyndale's latest edition revised in the light of the Codex Bezae* Latin version. Words with no equivalent in the original text but essential to the sense were printed in italics, as later in the AV*. The Apocrypha*, as in Coverdale*, appeared as an appendix to the OT.

First printed in Geneva, there were 70 editions of the complete Bible and 30 of the NT during the reign of Elizabeth I*, with 150 editions altogether, the last in 1644. Costs appear to have been borne mainly by John Bodley*. In 1576 a revised edition of the NT was produced by Lawrence Thomson* and found its way into subsequent editions of the Bible. The bishops seem to have welcomed it.

A Scottish edition appeared in 1579, the first Bible to be published in Scotland, accompanied by an Act of Parliament requiring every person worth more than a certain amount to have a Bible in the common language, under penalty of £10. Subsequently the version appointed to be read in churches in Scotland.

The first English Bible to have numbered verses, to be printed in roman type as against the black gothic letters, and to be regularly used in the home. Smaller in size and cheaper than previous Bibles, and complete with maps, tables and marginal notes which later achieved some notoriety because they annoyed James I* so much.

Popularly called 'the Breeches Bible'*, the Bible of William Shakespeare, and the household Bible of the English-speaking Protestants, as against the Great Bible* which became the Bible of the church. The version taken to America by the Pilgrim Fathers on the *Mayflower*.

Geniza. A Jewish word meaning 'that which is withdrawn' or 'stored' and can refer both to the documents themselves and to the physical place where they are kept. In some cases mss. were withdrawn because they were thought to be heretical; in other cases scrolls were withdrawn from common use, possibly due to age, and replaced by new ones, but in both cases their sacred nature meant that they could not be destroyed and they were therefore placed in a geniza. One of the more well known where many ancient fragments have been found is in Cairo*.

Georgian Version. One of the earliest versions of the NT and one of the least familiar to Western scholars. Its origins are unknown but its text is basically Caesarean*.

Gesenius, Heinrich Friedrich Wilhelm (1786–1842). German biblical scholar and professor at Halle University who contributed considerably to the knowledge of the Hebrew language. The first person to prepare a critical classification of the differences between the Samaritan Pentateuch* and the Masoretic Text*, in 1815.

Gezer, Canaan. An ancient city on the border of the Philistine Plain, some 20 miles north-west of Jerusalem, on the road to Joppa. The object of extensive archaeological excavation at the beginning of the twentieth century and best known as the site of the Gezer Calendar*. It was populated as early as the fourth millennium BCE, is mentioned in Egyptian records in the fifteenth century and was ceded by Egypt to Israel in the time of Solomon who rebuilt it. Inscriptions go back to an early date, cuneiform tablets going back to the fifteenth and fourteenth centuries, including one fragment of pottery containing three Canaanite characters, scratched in clay before being fired, possibly the earliest example of an alphabetic script.

Gezer Calendar. One of the earliest examples of ancient Hebrew writing dating from the tenth century BCE. A small inscribed limestone tablet (4.25 × 2.75 x 0.625 inches), found in 1908 in Gezer*, which lists the appropriate agricultural activities for successive months. Written in an archaic Southern Semitic dialect, similar to the one found in the Siloam Inscription* (c. 700 BCE). Possibly a schoolboy's tablet for learning to write.

Gibson, Margaret Dunlop (b. 1843). Twin sister of Agnes Smith Lewes*, sometimes described as the Ladies of Castlebrae*, who towards the end of the nineteenth century found a second copy of the Old Syriac* version at St Catharine's Monastery*, Mount Sinai, reflecting the Sinaitic Syriac text.

Gideon International. An organization of Christian business and professional people committed to Bible distribution, founded in the United States at the beginning of the twentieth century, established in the UK in 1949, and currently distributing Bibles at the rate of a million a week in over 150 countries. Best known for placing Bibles in hotel rooms for the use of guests.

Glasgow, Scotland. Birthplace of James Moffatt*.

Glosses. Marginal or interlinear interpretations, usually made in the first instance by scribes in the process of copying* and carefully kept outside the main text, but sometimes becoming additions* to the text at a later date and thus the subject of textual criticism*. Some are straightforward copying errors, some are attempts at improvement or explanation, some are self-defence, some are errors of judgment and some would appear to be errors through lack of judgment. (See Glosses, p. 78.)

Good News Bible, 1976. A British edition of Today's English Version*, 1976, published by Collins.

Goodspeed, Edgar Johnson (1871–1962). A contemporary of James Moffatt* and sometimes regarded as his American counterpart. Studied Greek from the age of 12 and was educated at the Old University of Chicago and Yale. Travelled in Europe for two years, joining an archaeological party on a visit to Greece where he unearthed a mass of valuable (non-biblical) papyri* and was one of the first

to focus attention on the links between the Greek of the papyri and that of the NT. Spent most of his working life on the staff of the Chicago University, 1898–1936. Produced his own translation of the NT in the American idiom, The New Testament: An American Translation*, 1923, subsequently referred to as Goodspeed's Translation*. Did not feel competent to tackle the OT, but translated the Apocrypha* in retirement, 1938, which was then included in The Complete Bible: An American Translation*, 1939.

Goodspeed's Translation. The name popularly given to The New Testament: An American Translation*, 1923 and The Complete Bible: An American Translation*, 1939.

Gospel of Thomas. One of the apocryphal gospels*. A collection of traditional wisdom sayings, parables, prophecies and proverbs, probably read frequently in the early church and sometimes referred to as 'the secret sayings which the living Jesus spoke', many of which have parallels in the canonical gospels. Three Greek fragments, found at Oxyrhynchus*, are located in the British Library, the Bodleian and Harvard University. The only complete version, a Coptic translation from the Greek and found at Nag Hammadi*, is in Old Cairo*.

Gospel of Truth. A Coptic text on the Christian life, recently discovered at Nag Hammadi*, thought by some to be the work of Valentinus, a second-century theologian, and showing an awareness of the four gospels, several of Paul's letters, Hebrews and Revelation. If such an early date could be established it would be one of the earliest pointers to a collection of references to the OT and NT writings with a decidedly Western orientation.

Glosses

Attempts at improvement or explanation

Gen. 14.3.'that is, the Dead Sea'.

Gen. 36.1.'that is, Edom'.

Josh. 15.8.'that is, Jerusalem'. This may also be an addition because it is missing from the parallel passage (Josh. 18.16).

Error

Josh. 18.13. 'that is, Bethel' relates to Luz, not to the slope of Luz, southward.

Explanation of a difficult word

Isa. 51.17 and 22. AV has 'cup' twice in each verse whereas some translations (e.g. NEB) have 'cup' the first time and 'bowl' the second. קֻבַּעַת (*qb't*) ('bowl') is a rare word, occurring only here. Some scholars have therefore suggested that a scribe unfamiliar with the word inserted the more familiar 'cup' in both verses. (Some would offer a similar explanation for the use of 'waters' in Gen. 6.17 and 7.6.)

Zech. 6.3. AV* describes the horses as 'grizzled and bay' but the second word is not a colour and means 'strong', as suggested in the AV margin. One explanation is that 'and bay [strong]' was added as a gloss to explain the Hebrew word translated 'grizzled' which was unknown in 1611 but which we now know means 'piebald' or 'dappled' as in NRSV*.

Possible glosses that worked their way into the main text

Jn 5.3b-4. 'for an angel went down at a certain season into the pool, and troubled the water; whoever then first after the troubling of the water stepped in was made whole from whatever disease he had' is not found in all mss.

Rom. 8.1. 'who walk not according to the flesh but according to the spirit' may also be a marginal gloss*.

Gospels, The, 1952. A paraphrase by J.B. Phillips* subsequently incorporated into The New Testament in Modern English, 1958*. Published by Geoffrey Bles, London.

Gothic Version. The Goths invaded and ravaged Asia Minor in the third century and there were several instances of evangelistic efforts by Christian priests whom they captured. Gothic is a dead language which has come down to us in not more than 280 pages of texts, almost all translations of various books of the NT (well over half is the gospels), plus three pages of Nehemiah, fragments of Genesis 5 and two half-verses of Psalm 52. The Gothic version of the NT, by several centuries the earliest surviving literary monument in a Teutonic language, is a fourth-century translation by Ulfilas* who had to create an alphabet in order to do it. Six mss. are preserved, the most complete being the Codex Argenteus*.

Göttingen Septuagint, 1931. A precise and thorough critical edition* of the LXX* in three volumes, edited by Rahlfs* and others, containing the Pentateuch* and all the Prophets*, plus Esther, Judith, Tobit, Ezra A, 1, 2 and 3 Maccabees, Job, Wisdom of Solomon and Ecclesiasticus, originally on the principles and methods established by de Lagarde*. Subsequently published in an abridged form by Rahlfs.

Grabbe, John Ernest (1666–1711). A Prussian scholar who settled in Oxford and produced a complete edition of the OT of Codex Alexandrinus*, 1701–20.

Grafton, Richard (d. 1572). Publisher of Matthew's Bible* in Antwerp* and one of the printers of the Great Bible*.

Great Bible, 1539. Translated by Coverdale*, based on Tyndale's* translation and the Latin Vulgate*. Owed its origin to Cromwell's* desire for a revision of Matthew's Bible* and his request to Coverdale to undertake it. Owed its title to the size of its pages, 16.5 × 11 inches. In the OT it is essentially Matthew's (Rogers*, Tyndale, Coverdale) edition revised, with many of the controversial notes of Matthew dropped. In the NT it is mainly Tyndale, based on the Vulgate.

Changes the order of the books of the NT. Earlier translations had followed Luther in putting Hebrews, James, Jude and Revelation at the end in a group by themselves. The Great Bible follows the order of Erasmus* in his Greek NT, a practice followed by the AV* and other translations after 1539.

Printing began in Paris* by Grafton and Whitchurch, producers of Matthew's Bible and noted for their devotion and technical skill, but was delayed because the French Inquisitor-General forbade the printers to continue and confiscated their sheets. Representations were made and type, paper and printers were transferred to England, but what had been confiscated was not released, so most of the work had to be done all over again.

An improved edition appeared in 1540, with a preface by Cranmer* and therefore sometimes referred to as Cranmer's Bible, and containing at the foot of the title page the words, 'This is the Byble appoynted to the use of the churches'. Five further editions appeared between July 1540 and December 1541. The fourth and sixth editions contain a reference to Cuthbert, Bishop of Durham. This is Cuthbert Tunstall*, formerly Bishop of London, who had resisted Tyndale.

One of the first Bibles to be set up officially in churches, often chained to a pillar or lectern, and the basis for the 1549 Book of Common Prayer. A copy of the first edition, printed on vellum* in block letters, is in the library of St John's College, Cambridge*.

Greek–English Diglot for the Use of Translators, 1958–64. Several slim volumes intended primarily for translators, covering about 18 books of the NT, under the directorship of W.D. McHardy* and distributed privately by the British and Foreign Bible Society*, each containing the Greek and English text on facing pages. Forerunner of The Translator's New Testament*.

Greek Language. The language of classical Greece and the NT. Similar to English in a way that Hebrew* and Aramaic* are not, many English words having Greek origins. By NT times the classical age of Greek literature (sixth to fourth centuries BCE) had come to an end and the language had changed as a result of contact with other languages and cultures. NT Greek therefore is known as *Koiné* (or common) Greek*, and there are different *Koiné* styles in the NT. Revelation and Mark are very *Koiné* (or rough). Matthew and Luke, often following Mark, are almost engaged in a tidying-up process, whilst Hebrews is very literary. Paul's letters fall somewhere in the middle.

Greek New Testament. The Greek NT began life not as a book but as a collection of mss. In 1989 there were 5488 such mss., including 96 papyri*, 299 uncials*, 2812 minuscules*, and 2281 in various ancient lectionaries. Only 59 are complete. 1500 contain only the gospels. Only 287 include Revelation. Most of the papyri are only fragments, the smallest being the John Fragment* and the most substantial being the Bodmer* and the Chester Beatty*. Of the ones on parchment or vellum* the oldest are the Codex Vaticanus* and the Codex Sinaiticus*.

The first Greek texts of the NT to be printed were the Magnificat and the Benedictus, published together with the Psalter, in 1481, in Milan★. The first printed edition of the Greek text of the NT was in the Complutensian Polyglot*, completed in 1514 though not actually published until 1522, by which time Erasmus* had published his. The earliest complete printed editions of the Greek NT were not editions of early Greek mss. but of later ones and represent a revision which was undertaken in the fourth century and became known as the Byzantine* text.

Greek New Testament is also the title of a critical edition* of the Greek NT, an eclectic text intended as a tool for translators, the work of an editorial international committee under Bruce Metzger*, Allan P. Wikgren, Arthur Voobus, Kurt Aland and Matthew Black, with 25 consultants, and published by the United Bible Societies★, 1966, followed by a second edition, 1968, with Roman Catholic cooperation through Cardinal Martini. A third edition, 1982, a major revision with full Roman Catholic participation, followed the new edition of the Nestle-Aland* text (the twenty-sixth) resulting in the same text with different punctuation and critical apparatus*. There was a fourth edition, 1992.

Gregory, Caspar René (1851–1932). Native of Philadelphia, trained at Princeton and Professor at Leipzig University, 1899, where he prepared an edition of the Greek New Testament*, 1884. Building on Wettstein's* work of classifying mss. by letters and numbers he devised several other categories, listed papyrus* mss. separately from parchment or vellum* by allocating to them a letter 'p' followed by a number, and, as the number of uncial* mss. exceeded the number of letters in the Latin, Greek and Hebrew alphabets combined, started to use Arabic numerals preceded by a zero.

Gregory of Nazianzus (329–89). A theologian, son of the Bishop of Nazianzus and one of the Cappadocian Fathers who produced a list of 22 books to be regarded as the canon* of the OT, omitting Esther and dividing Judges and Ruth into separate books.

Grenfell, Bernard Pyne (1869–1926). Oxford Professor of Papyrology and British archaeologist who researched in Egypt, 1893–1906. Worked with A.S. Hunt* in Oxyrhynchus* in 1897 in search of ancient documents and was among the first to discover NT papyri* there.

Griesbach, Johann Jakob (1745–1812). An eighteenth-century German biblical scholar, pupil of J.J. Semler* and professor at Jena, who laid the foundations for all subsequent work on the Greek text of the NT. By 1805 he had set out 15 canons of textual criticism*, including *lectio brevior**, and taken Semler's classification of mss. and added the increased material collected by Wettstein*, assigning each to its appropriate group. Like Bengel* and Semler he believed that the smaller groups of earlier witnesses were superior in weight to the mass mss. in the Byzantine* group. He classified mss. into three groups: Alexandrian*, Western* and Byzantine (corresponding to Hort's* Neutral*, Western and Syrian* groups) and on this basis drew up a list of readings which he thought superior to the Textus Receptus*. Published a Greek edition of the NT, 1774–77, and another, 1796–1806.

Gutenberg Bible, 1456. Another name for the Mazarin Bible*.

Guyse, John (1680–1761). Independent minister. One of a number of scholars who produced a paraphrase*, 1739–52, with bracketed explanatory material into the text of the AV* in the eighteenth century. His three-volume *Exposition of the New Testament in the Form of a Paraphrase* appeared in a sixth edition in 1818.

H

Hagiographa. See Writings.

Hammond, Henry (1605–60). Anglican divine, educated at Eton, Archdeacon of Chichester and President of Magdalen College, Oxford, who prepared *A Paraphrase and Annotations on the New Testament*, 1653, a pioneer work of English biblical criticism*, often reprinted, the last reprint being in four volumes, 1865, and who also assisted Walton* in the production of the London Polyglot*.

Hampden-Cook, Ernest (1860–1932). A Congregational minister, educated at Mill Hill School, Lancashire College and St John's, Cambridge, where he distinguished himself in mathematics and Hebrew. One of the translators of The Twentieth Century New Testament*, 1902, who took Weymouth's New Testament* when Weymouth* died prior to publication, added some notes, including a few opinions of his own, and saw it safely through the press.

Hampole, Yorkshire. A small village in South Yorkshire where Richard Rolle*, a hermit, translated the Psalms into the northern dialect in the fourteenth century.

Hampton Court Conference, 1604. Summoned by James I* and made up of leading churchmen and theologians, including 17 Anglicans and 4 Presbyterians. Passed a resolution, proposed by John Reynolds*, to make a new translation of the Bible from the original Greek and Hebrew mss., *without* marginal notes, to be used in divine worship. The result was the KJV 1611*, better known in Britain as the Authorized Version*, though never actually 'authorized'.

Haplography. The omission of a letter, word, line or even a paragraph, usually because of its similarity to what came immediately before, and so producing a different word or meaning and becoming the subject of textual criticism*. Sometimes the result of parablepsis* and not always easily distinguishable from dittography*. (See Haplography, p. 83.)

Harmonization. The result of scribal changes*, usually deliberate, so as to avoid apparent contradictions within the one ms. Sometimes it may be nothing more than ensuring that a person's name always appears in the same form; in other cases it may mean bringing parallel texts* into line with one another, and the more scribes became familiar with the various mss. and texts the greater the tendency. (See Harmonization, p.83.)

Harmony of the Gospels, 1756. A popular eighteenth-century translation by James MacKnight*.

Haplography

Josh. 21.36-37 is not found in some mss., possibly because the scribe's eye jumped from 'four cities' at the end of verse 35 to the same phrase at the end of verse 37.

Judg. 20.13 should probably refer to 'Benjaminites' or 'sons of Benjamin' but 'Benjamin' stands alone in some mss, possibly because בני (*bny*) ('sons of') is identical with the beginning of בנימן (*bnymn*) ('Benjamin'), so enabling a scribe to overlook it and inadvertently to change the meaning.

1 Sam. 14.41 in LXX*, Vulgate* and the Old Latin*, reads,

And Saul said unto Yahweh, God of **Israel**, *'Why hast thou not answered thy servant this day? If this iniquity is in me or in my son Jonathan, oh Yahweh, God of Israel, give Urim; but if this iniquity is in thy people* **Israel**, give Tummim.'

MT omits the words in italics, so did the scribe's eye jump from one 'Israel' to the other, omitting everything in between?

1 Kgs 8.16 reads

'I have not chosen…building a house *where my name might abide*, but I have chosen David to rule my people Israel'. The parallel account in 2 Chron. 6.5-6 has a fuller statement with two pairs:

I have not chosen…for building a house **where my name might abide**, *nor did I choose anyone to be the leader of my people Israel, but I chose Jerusalem* **where my name might abide**, and I chose David to rule my people Israel.

Chronicles is usually thought to be preferable because of its pairs (negative and positive) and because the omission of the words in italics can be explained as haplography.

Mt. 12.47 is missing from some mss., possibly because of its similarity of ending to 12.46.

Lk. 10.32 is missing from Codex Sinaiticus*, possibly because it ends with the same verb ('to pass by on the other side') as 10.31.

Lk. 14.27 is missing from more than a dozen mss., possibly because the last few words are identical with the end of 14.26.

Jn 17.15 reads, 'I do not pray that thou shouldest take them from the *world but that thou shouldest keep them from the* evil one'. Codex Vaticanus* omits the words in italics to give, 'I do not pray that thou shouldest take them from the evil one', an understandable omission* if you imagine two lines of Greek text,

I do not pray that thou shouldest take *them from the*
world but that thou shouldest keep *them from the*
evil one,

the scribe's eye easily slipping from the end of one line to the end of the next.

1 Cor. 9.2 is missing from Codex Alexandrinus*, possibly because it ends with the same words as 9.1.

Harmonization

Isa. 1.15. Is the one ms. which adds 'your fingers with iniquity' an attempt to harmonize with Isa. 59.3?

Mt. 19.17. Earlier mss. have 'why do you ask me about what is good?' Later mss. have 'why do you call me good?' Is this an attempt to harmonize with Mk 10.18 and Lk. 18.19?

Lk. 11.2-4. The shorter form of the Lord's Prayer was assimilated in many mss. of Luke to harmonize with the longer form in Mt. 6.9-13, seen also as the most likely source for the addition of the phrase, 'but rescue us from the evil one', found in some mss.

Jn 19.20. 'It was written in Hebrew, and Greek, and Latin' appears in many mss., possibly harmonizing with Lk. 23.38.

Acts 9.5-6 is adjusted in many mss. to harmonize with 26.14-15.

Rom. 13.9. Paul cites four commandments but some mss. add 'you shall not bear false witness'.

Col. 1.14. Some later mss. add 'through his blood', as in Eph. 1.7.

Rev. 1.5 has 'washed' in some mss. and 'freed' in others, but since the more reliable mss. have 'freed' a scribe may well have substituted 'washed' because of a similar phrase in 7.14.

OT quotations in the New Testament are often enlarged or made to conform to the more familiar LXX wording.

Mt. 15.8 appears in a fuller version in later mss., probably inspired by scribes familiar with Isa. 29.13.

Hart, Andrew (d. 1621). Edinburgh* printer, responsible for an edition of the Geneva Bible*, 1610, including Lawrence Thomson's* revision of the NT, which continued in use for 50 years with some evidence that it was still being used in Aberdeenshire as late as 1674.

Hartman, Louis Francis (1901–70). Professor at the Catholic University of America and chairman of the commission responsible for the OT translation of the Confraternity Version*, 1941.

Harvard, USA. Home to a fragment of the Oxyrhynchus Papyrus*, in Harvard University Library.

Harwood, Edward (1729–94). A Nonconformist minister, biblical and classical scholar, and author of A Liberal Translation of the New Testament*, 1768.

Haupt, Paul (1828–1926). Baltimore editor of *The Sacred Books of the Old and New Testaments*, more popularly known as the Polychrome Bible*, 1893.

Hawkins, Ernest (1802–68). Educated at Balliol College, Oxford. Canon of Westminster and Sub-Librarian of the Bodleian Library, Oxford. Secretary for the Society for the Propagation of the Gospel who in 1856 brought together five scholars (Henry Alford*, John Barrow*, C.J. Ellicott*, W.H.G. Humphrey* and George Moberly*) to undertake a revision of the Authorized Version of the Fourth Gospel. The result was The Authorised Version of St John's Gospel, revised by Five Clergymen*, 1857. Subsequently they went on to revise Romans, Corinthians, Galatians, Ephesians and Philippians.

He-Bible, The, 1611. A by-name given to the first edition of the AV* because it translated '*he* went' (subsequently changed to '*she* went') in Ruth 3.15. In the first three years of its existence the AV was running two editions, the 'He' Bible and the 'She' Bible, according to the rendering of this text in Ruth.

Hebrew Bible. Mss. of the Hebrew Bible are to be found from the ninth century CE, with a few (mainly fragments) going back to the beginning of the Common Era and a plethora coming from the Middle Ages. None could be described as the Hebrew Bible, though all may contribute. The study of these variations is part of textual criticism*.

The Masoretic Text* is the standard version, but here too there are differences, since the different printed editions reflect different Hebrew mss. and sometimes the views of different editors. Errors also crept in even after the invention of printing, and these are sometimes corrected in later editions. There are also variations between editions when it comes to book order*, chapter division*, verse division* and layout, or because one editor chooses a poetry format where another chooses prose. Most of the differences are slight and not impor-

tant but it is important to recognize that they exist.

The transmission of the text of the Hebrew Bible, from its beginnings to where it is today, was in three stages.

> from its origins (date unknown) until the destruction of the Second Temple (70 BCE), during which time there was considerable variation between the various texts, though usually amounting to little more than a letter, word or phrase;
>
> from the Second Temple to the eighth century CE, when there was very little change;
>
> from the eighth century until the end of the Middle Ages, with the arrival of the Masoretic Text* around the ninth century, by which time there were many Hebrew mss., but the work of the Masoretes*, incorporating many variants in early mss., had led to the emergence of a significant few and the Hebrew text became standardized almost (but not quite) completely.

While substantially the same as the English OT (in the Reformed tradition), the Hebrew Bible has a different book order, with 24 books compared to 39 in the OT, taking Samuel, Kings, Chronicles and Ezra–Nehemiah as single books and the 12 'minor prophets' grouped together in the Book of the Twelve.

From the Renaissance to the end of the nineteenth century three recensions* of the Hebrew text were available. Differences were due to the limited possibilities which Renaissance editors had for collating mss., the degree of attention they paid to punctuation, accents and masoretic notes, and the public for which the recension was intended. They were the Soncino edition*, 1494, the Complutensian Polyglot*, 1514–17, and the second Rabbinic* Bible of Jacob ben Chayyim, 1524–25.

Later editions of the Hebrew Bible,

offering a mixed text dependent on one or more of these three to varying degrees, included Kennicott (Oxford, 1776–80) and de Rossi (Parma, 1784–88) in the eighteenth century, who attempted to collate all the variant readings* in the mss. which had been preserved; *Biblia hebraica* (Halle/Berlin 1818, drawing mainly on Kennicott and de Rossi), Ginsburg (London, 1926), *Biblia hebraica* (third edition, Stuttgart, 1929–37), Cassuto (a corrected Ginsburg, Jerusalem, 1952) and Snaith (London, 1958), who in the nineteenth and twentieth centuries attempted to establish a reliable comprehensive text, Biblia hebraica* becoming the one most used in the twentieth century.

In modern academic usage the term 'Hebrew Bible' is widely preferred to 'Old Testament' on account of the latter's specifically Christian connotations.

In the ancient world the Hebrew Bible was translated into Greek (LXX*), Syriac (Peshitta*), Jewish Aramaic (Targumim*), and Latin (Vulgate*).

Hebrew Language. One of the Semitic languages*, similar to Babylonian, Assyrian, Chaldean and Phoenician, and the language of the OT. Originally a cursive script, known as archaic or palaeo-Hebrew, the written form subsequently developed the square Aramaic alphabet characters with which we are now more familiar. An alphabetic script consisting of 22 letters, written from right to left and only in consonantal form until the arrival of the Masoretes*.

Hebrew Scriptures Translated, 1865. A revision of the OT by Samuel Sharpe*.

Hebrew University Bible Project. One of only two currently critical editions* of the Hebrew Bible*, the other, more widely used, being *Biblia hebraica*. Based on the tenth-century Codex Aleppo* which, though incomplete, accurately represents the best vocalization* system in the Ben Asher* tradition and is therefore thought by some to be of a better quality than Codex Leningrad*. It also includes variant readings* from the DSS*. Differs from *Biblia hebraica* in several respects: there are no conjectural emendations*, variant readings* are not evaluated, and the critical apparatus* is in four parts (ancient translations, Hebrew texts from the Second Temple period, and two selections of mediaeval codices, one with consonantal differences and the other with differences in vocalization and accents).

Hebrew Writing. Early Hebrew writing was similar in appearance to Phoenician. The 'square' characters in the Hebrew Bibles of today emerged c. 400 BCE and thereafter became standard form for mss. of the scriptures. Here are some examples:

מ י ט ח ג א

Hendry, George Stuart (1904–). Born in Aberdeenshire, minister of the Church of Scotland, and Professor of Systematic Theology at Princeton Theological Seminary from 1949. The Representative of the Presbytery of Stirling and Dunblane who in 1946 proposed to the General Assembly of the Church of Scotland that a new translation of the Bible be made 'in the language of the present day' which led to the NEB*, and subsequently Secretary of the Joint Committee responsible for it.

Henry VIII (1491–1547). Gave encouragement to the publication of Coverdale's* NT which was dedicated to him in 1535 and licensed by him in 1537. Made an unsuccessful appeal to Charles V of the Holy Roman Empire for a stay of execution of William Tyndale*. In 1543 Parliament discussed Tyndale's translation, made it a crime for an unlicensed person to read or expound the Bible publicly to others, and even forbade the private reading of the Bible by people belonging to the lower classes of society. In 1546 Henry went further and declared that nobody was to receive, have, take or keep Tyndale or Coverdale's NT. Large numbers of copies were collected and burned at St Paul's Cross*.

Hereford, Nicholas of. See Nicholas of Hereford.

Hermas of Rome (second century). A Jewish Christian, author of *Shepherd*, which contains many allusions to OT phrases. References to NT books are less clear though he does seem to have been aware of Ephesians.

Hesychius (c. 300 CE). A bishop and biblical textual critic credited with having produced an Alexandrian recension* of the LXX*, corrected according to the Hebrew, with a view to finding the oldest readings, eliminating accretions and removing grammatical errors in transmission. It is not possible, however, to identify a clear Hesychian text nor is it clear whether it was made from the Hebrew text or was simply a stylistic revision.

Hieroglyphic Bibles. An unusual Bible format, mainly for children, containing brief verses of scripture and substituting small pictures for some of the words.

Hieronymous. See Jerome.

Higher Criticism. A term rarely used in contemporary scholarship to describe a method of biblical criticism* which concentrates on the study of ancient documents to determine such details as date, authorship, structure, and relationship with other books and mss.

Hilary of Poitiers (315–67). One of the early church Fathers and Bishop of Poitiers c. 353, whose list of books in the OT followed that of Origen* to which he added Tobit and Judith to give a 24-book canon. Like Cyprian and Ambrose he combined Lamentations and the Epistle of Jeremiah with Jeremiah.

Historical Books. See Prophets.

Holmgren, Laton E. (b. 1915–). Officer of the ABS* for three decades and Chairman of the UBS* Council, 1963–66, and of the Executive Committee, 1963–72. A diplomat and one of the architects of the changed relationships with the Bible Societies* following the arrival of the UBS. Chief Protestant negotiator with the Roman Catholic Church (the opposite number to W.M. Abbott*) in discussions relating to cooperation in Bible translation and particularly in compiling the 'Guiding Principles for Interconfessional Cooperation in Translating the Bible' which he helped to shape in three principal meetings, 1967–68.

Holy Bible from Ancient Eastern Manuscripts, 1957. More popularly known as Lamsa's Translation*.

Holy Bible, Translated from the Corrected Texts of the Originals, 1792–1807. The work of a liberal-minded Roman Catholic, Alexander Geddes*, beginning with Genesis–Joshua (1792), followed by Joshua–2 Chronicles and *Prayer of Manasseh* (1797) and the Psalter (1807), posthumously.

Holy Scriptures according to the Masoretic Text, 1917. A verbal equivalence* translation of the Hebrew Bible*, similar in idiom to the AV*, and published by the Jewish Publication Society of America, Philadelphia. Followed by

A New Translation of The Holy Scriptures according to the Masoretic Text, 1963.

Homoioarcton. The omission of a section of text, sometimes the result of parablepsis*, where two words, lines or sentences with an identical beginning are so close to each other that the copyist's eye accidentally slips from one to the other, omitting what comes in-between, thus becoming the subject of textual criticism*. Similar to homoioteleuton*.

Homoioteleuton. The omission of a section of text, sometimes the result of parablepsis*, where two words, lines or sentences with an identical ending are so close to each other that the copyist's eye accidentally slips from one to the other, omitting what comes in-between, thus becoming the subject of textual criticism*. Similar to homoioarcton*.

Hooke, Samuel Henry (1874–1968). Professor of OT at the University of London and best known for his work on Myth and Ritual. Director of the Bible in Basic English* translation.

Hort, Fenton John Anthony (1828–92). Born in Dublin and moved with his family to Cheltenham when he was nine. Entered Rugby, 1841, and Trinity College, Cambridge, 1846, where he was much influenced by F.D. Maurice. Ordained, 1846, and became a country parson. A medical condition prevented him from doing any parish work for two years, 1863–65, and this gave him the time to study the NT in Greek. A return to the parish led him to realize how absorbed he had become in Greek and he became a lecturer in theology at Emmanuel College, Cambridge, 1872, and Professor of Divinity, 1878.

One of the translators of the RV*, who was engaged at the same time with B.F. Westcott* in their epoch-making edition of the Greek NT, *The New Testament in the Original Greek*, a new text taking into account all the variant readings* in the available mss. The work appeared five days before the RV of the NT. Volume 1 contained the Greek text and volume 2 an introduction and appendix setting out the critical principles in detail, including the distinction between intrinsic probability* and transcriptional probability*.

Worked with B.F. Westcott on the classification of mss., based on genealogical evidence*, continuing the principles already laid down by Griesbach*, whereby all textual authorities were divided into four groups (or families): Neutral*, Alexandrian*, Western* and Syrian*. Westcott and Hort then formulated rules to evaluate the four groups. They regarded the Neutral as the main authority and recognized the Alexandrian as very similar. They regarded Western (with its tendency to exercise a freedom of addition, and sometimes omission) as inferior and rejected the Syrian because of its lateness. No reading from the Alexandrian or the Western was to be regarded as reliable without some support from the Neutral.

Hug, Johann Leonard (1765–1846). A Roman Catholic professor at the University of Freiburg who worked on a theory that at the beginning of the third century the NT text degenerated rapidly to produce the Western*, text but his attempts to connect three recensions* of the LXX* with three types of NT text failed.

Humphrey, William Gilson (1814–86). Vicar of St Martin-in-the-Fields, educated at Cambridge, and one of five clergymen who worked with Ernest Hawkins* to produce The Authorized Version of St John's Gospel, revised by Five Clergymen*, 1857, and similar revisions of some of the epistles.

Hunkin, Joseph Wellington (d. 1950). Bishop of Truro and first Chairman of the Joint Committee responsible for the NEB* in 1947.

Hunt, Arthur Surridge (1871–1934). British archaeologist and Oxford Professor of Papyrology who went with B.P. Grenfell* to Oxyrhynchus* in 1897 in search of ancient documents and was among the first to discover NT papyri* there.

Ignatius of Antioch (c. 50–c. 107 CE). Bishop of Antioch, whose seven letters, pleading for Christian unity and written on his way to martyrdom, are important evidence for early Christian writings. He also makes references and allusions to most of Paul's letters and some scholars think that in a letter to the church at Ephesus in the second century he supplies evidence for the existence of a Pauline Corpus*, possibly including 1 Thessalonians, 1 Corinthians, Romans, Colossians and Ephesians, but nowhere does he refer to 2 Thessalonians, Philemon or the Pastorals and he appears not to have known 2 Peter. Some suggest he may also have been aware of two or three gospels (Matthew, John and perhaps Luke) but he did not regard them as scripture and at this date no written document is likely to have been credited with ultimate authority.

Immersion Versions. In a revision of the New Testament published in 1864, with further revisions in 1865 and 1891, the American Bible Union made a determined effort to establish the word 'immerse' as the correct translation of the Greek word normally translated 'baptize', following an earlier attempt by Nathaniel Scarlett*. In 1883 they merged with the American Baptist Publication Society and produced a further revision in 1913 using 'baptize (immerse)' as alternatives, but the idea was not accept-

able and sales were small, though the translation was excellent.

Ink. The use of ink for writing goes back to the Egyptians, c. 3000 BCE. The word comes from the Greek for 'black', the earliest forms being carbon based, made from soot, gum and water, and black in colour. Improvements and changes took place over the centuries.

International Bible Society. Founded in New York, 1809, with a commitment to serve the church by distributing Bibles and facilitating Bible translation around the world. Their first grant, in 1810, was $1000 to William Carey, a Baptist missionary in India, to translate the Bible into Bengali. Subsequently Bibles were distributed to soldiers, hospitals, prisoners, hotels and Sunday Schools, with particular attention to immigrants at New York's Ellis Island at the beginning of the twentieth century and to Eastern European countries at the end. Publisher of the New International Version*.

International Children's Bible, 1983 (NT), 1986 (complete). The work of 20 scholars, some of whom had served as translators on the NASB*, the NIV*, the NKJV* and the RSV*, all from conservative, evangelical and Protestant denominations, inspired by the simplicity and readability of an earlier translation for people with hearing difficulties which had emerged from the World Translation Center. It avoided long sentences, used modern weights and measures, maintained a consistent and familiar use of place names, a vocabulary limited to the Living World Vocabulary, a reference guide used in the preparation of World Book Encyclopedia. Sometimes criticized for its anti-Jewish phrases and sentiments, particularly in the sub-headings. Forerunner to a similar translation, the New Century Version, 1991*, for adults.

Interpolations. The insertion of text into the original by a copyist, sometimes intentionally, sometimes not, and the subject of textual criticism*.

Intrinsic Probability. Textual criticism* often requires editors of ancient texts to choose between two or more variant readings* on the basis of which looks more probable. Hort* coined the phrase 'intrinsic probability' for situations when he was appealing to what an author was likely to have written, as against 'transcriptional probability'* when he was appealing to what the copyists were likely to have made of it.

Irenaeus (c. 150–202 CE). One of the early church Fathers, possibly a native of Asia Minor, who became Bishop of Lyons and one of the first to refer specifically to the Old Testament* and the New Testament*. Stressed the importance of the OT for Christians, was the first to refer to four gospels and crystallized the belief in them with the idea that there should be no more and no less. Seems to have recognized and accepted Acts, most of Paul's letters, though not Philemon, and 1 John, and was the first to make extensive use of the Pastoral Epistles.

Istanbul, Turkey. The modern name for Constantinople*.

Itacisms. Errors arising in mss. as a result of dictation where two or more words sound alike but have different spellings and meanings, or where scribes, repeating the text to themselves, simply mis-spell. In the case of the OT there was always a danger of further confusion because of the similar ways in which different Hebrew letters could be pronounced. In the NT itacisms sometimes arose as a result of certain Greek vowels and diphthongs losing their distinctive sound which occasionally explains why one particular ms. appears to be out of step with all the rest. (See Itacisms, p. 92.)

Itacisms

Obvious English examples are 'there'/'their', 'sight'/'site'/'cite', 'hair'/'hare', 'night'/'knight', etc. לֹא *and* לֹו *(l'/lo) is a good example in Hebrew, meaning a straight negative when spelt one way and 'to him (it)' when spelt another.*

1 Sam. 2.16. 'No, hand it over now…' makes good sense, following the LXX and the *Qere**, but MT has the somewhat nonsensical 'to him'.

1 Kgs 11.22. 'But *do not* let me go' in some mss., as in REB and NRSV, seems odd for a man who has been pleading to go, whereas 'let me go *to it*', as in 27 mss., including the LXX, and reflected in AV and RSV seems to make better sense. The Hebrew word is '*lo*', but spelt one way it is the negative and spelt another way it is 'its'. The sound is the same in both cases.

Isa. 9.3. Similarly, in a passage regularly read at Christmas, AV surprisingly has, 'Thou hast multiplied the nation, and *not* increased the joy', whereas at least 20 mss. including the LXX have, 'and increased *its* joy'.

Similarity in pronunciation of Hebrew letters also causes confusion. In English 'c' sounds like 'k', the soft 'g' like 'j', 'b' and 'p' are very close, and so on. In Hebrew א (aleph) (transliterated by ' and scarcely pronounced), ה (he) (a soft 'h'), ח (ḥeth) ('ch' as in 'loch') and ע (ayin) (transliterated by ' and very close to ḥeth) all sound very similar.

Gen. 31.49. MT has מצפה (*mṣph*) ('hear'). Samaritan Pentateuch has מצבה (*mṣbh*) ('the pillar').

1 Sam. 17.7. Kethib* has חץ (*ḥṣ*) ('arrow'). *Qere** has עץ (*ṣ*) ('shaft').

1 Kgs 1.18. MT has ועתה (*w'th*) ('and now'). The LXX obviously read ואתה (*w'th*) ('and you').

Itacisms (continued)

Itacisms presented a new problem in the early Christian centuries when certain vowels and diphthongs lost their distinctive sound. For example, the short 'o' and the long 'o' (two separate letters in Greek, o and ω) merged, ε and αι were pronounced with a short 'e' sound, and η, ι, υ, ει, οι and υι all tended to be pronounced like the English 'ee'. Dictated mss. therefore provided plenty of opportunity for variant readings, mostly raising questions and allowing for a variety of interpretation but occasionally helping to explain how one particular ms. came to be out of line with all the others and obviously in error.

Mt. 11.16. Is it 'others' (ἑτέροις), as in NRSV*, or 'fellows' (ἑταίροις), as in AV*?

Jn 5.39. Jesus refers to 'they who bear witness' (αἱ μαρτυροῦσαι) but Codex Bezae has 'they are sinning concerning me' (ἁμαρτανοῦσαι).

Rom. 5.1. Is it 'we have' (ἔχομεν), as in AV and NRSV, or 'let us have' (ἐχῶμεν), as in NRSV margin?

1 Cor. 15.54. Is it 'victory' (νῖκος) or 'conflict' (νεῖκος)?

Heb. 4.11. Is it 'disobedience' (ἀπειθείας) or 'truth' (ἀλήθειας), as in Codex Claromontanus*?

Rev 4.3. Is it 'rainbow' (ἶρις) or 'priests' (ἱερεῖς)?

More confusing in Greek is the similarity between 'our' (ἡμῶν, with a long 'e' and 'o') and 'your' (ὑμῶν), with similar confusion with 'we', 'you' (plural) and 'us'.

Gal. 4.28. Is it 'you', as in AV and NRSV, or 'we', as in NRSV margin?

2 Thess. 2.14. Is it 'did he call *you*' (or *us*)?.

1 Jn 1.4. Is it '*our* joy', as in NRSV, or '*your* joy', as in AV and NRSV margin?

J

Jabal Abu Mana, Egypt. Site for the discovery of one of the Bodmer Papyri*, not far from Nag Hammadi* the site of similar discoveries.

James I (1566–1625). James VI of Scotland. Summoned churchmen and theologians to the Hampton Court Conference*, 1604, which passed a resolution to make a new translation of the Bible, resulting in the AV*.

Jamnia, Synod of. With the fall of Jerusalem in 70 CE, after which Judaea no longer existed as a nation, the Jews found it necessary to define their canon*. Much discussion took place among rabbis, though mainly only about one or two books, subsequently included in the Writings*, because by this time there seems to have been no doubt about the Torah* and the Prophets*. Discussion seems to have ceased after the Synod of Jamnia, c. 112 CE, which suggests that Jamnia was responsible for the final decisions, though this is seriously questioned by many scholars who believe that the most Jamnia did was to recognize a situation which had already been arrived at.

Jarrow, Tyne and Wear. Home of Bede* and one of two possible sites for the copying of the Codex Amiatinus*, the other claimant being Wearmouth*.

Jeremiah Fragment. One of the earliest dated Hebrew mss. in existence, dated c. 964 CE, and now located in the John Rylands Library, Manchester*.

Jerome (c.342–420). A monk and a scholar, the son of Christian parents, educated in grammar and rhetoric in Rome and the best exegetical schools of the Greek orient, who learned Hebrew from the rabbis and developed a feeling for literary style as a result of studying the Latin classics. Invited by Pope Damasus I* in 383 to make a new translation of the gospels from the Greek into Latin, though there is evidence that other scholars were involved and it is doubtful whether Jerome did the epistles, Acts and Revelation.

Moved by what he called *hebraica veritas*, Jerome saw that what was needed was not simply a revision of the Old Latin* in relation to the Greek but (in the case of the OT) a new translation from the Hebrew*. He began work in 391 and, with the help of Jewish scholars, finished in 405, working first in Rome and then in Jerusalem. Again, it is important to distinguish between what Jerome translated from the Hebrew and what he merely revised. Not surprisingly, unlike Augustine*, he paid no attention to the Apocrypha*. The Vulgate* was the result.

Like the later Reformers he accepted the Hebrew canon* and then identified two other categories: books which were edifying and therefore suitable to be read in churches but not canonical (in which he put Esther, Wisdom of Solomon, Ecclesiasticus, Judith, Tobit, the *Didache* and the Shepherd of Hermas), and apocryphal books, to be avoided altogether.

He wrote commentaries on most of the biblical books, revised the Old Latin texts on the basis of the Greek texts and the old Latin Psalter on the basis of the LXX* which appeared in 384 and was known as the Roman Psalter to distinguish it from the Old Latin Psalter. He met severe criticism and did not live long enough to receive appreciation, but his version became the main Bible of all Western Christendom and was without rival for 1000 years.

Jerusalem Bible, 1966. A response to a Roman Catholic desire for a Bible translated from the original languages rather than the Latin. 'Catholic' in the sense that it was produced *by* Catholics, not *for* Catholics. In contemporary idiom (no 'thees and thous') whilst at the same time preserving the poetic and the sacral, and aimed from the start at general acceptance by all Bible readers, but particularly by Protestants, psalm numbers following the Hebrew rather than the LXX* or Vulgate*, as in Protestant Bibles, and proper names having the more familiar Protestant forms. The apocryphal books are placed in their LXX or Vulgate positions, except for Maccabees which are placed with the historical books. The scholarship is that of the 1940s though some account is taken of the DSS*.

A new dynamic equivalence* translation, based on Hebrew, Aramaic and Greek originals, reflecting sound scholarship, inspired by *La Bible de Jérusalem*, a version made by Roman Catholic scholars, principally de Vaux* and Benoit* building on the work of Lagrange*, at the ecumenical Ecole Biblique in Jerusalem*, and regularly consulted where questions of variants or interpretation arose. The work of Alexander Jones* (editor) and 27 collaborators, and published by Darton, Longman and Todd on an initiative by Frank Sheed* and Michael Longman*.

Includes a translation from the introduction and notes to *La Bible de Jérusalem*, stating that its purpose is to elucidate the text rather than reaffirm traditional interpretations, and those which reflected Catholic doctrinal positions were removed from the Reader's Edition, 1968, the one with which most English-speaking readers are familiar.

Special features are the use of 'Yahweh' rather than 'God', pluralizing the word 'grace' (the only English language translation to do so), superb typography, with clear type, printed right across the page, poetry in metrical form, helpful tables and maps, though no modern equivalents for weights and measures. The first edition may also be thought to have been accident prone: the Belgian printer apparently dropped the type on the way to the machine and put it together hastily without a further proof read, as a result of which Gen. 1.1 has 'siprit' for 'spirit', Ps. 78.66 (AV 'he smote the enemy in the hinder parts') reads 'The Lord woke up to strike his enemies on the rump', and one popular newspaper couldn't resist drawing attention to 'Pay for the peace of Jerusalem' (Ps. 122.6).

The first print run was 50,000 copies and by the time the New Jerusalem Bible* appeared sales were well over three million.

Jerusalem, Israel. Location of Ecole Biblique which provided much of the inspiration for *La Bible de Jérusalem*, which led in turn to the Jerusalem Bible*. Home to some of the original discoveries of the DSS*, in the Hebrew

University, and to many other ancient mss.

Jewish Publication Society Bible, 1917. A translation of the Hebrew Bible by USA Jewish scholars, led by Marcus Jastrow and sponsored by the Jewish Publication Society of America. A Jewish version of the RV*, 1885, and the standard Bible of the American Jewish community until the New Jewish Version*.

Jewish School and Family Bible, 1861. An early Jewish translation of the Hebrew Bible by Abraham Benisch*.

Johannine Corpus. The Fourth Gospel, 1, 2 and 3 John, and Revelation. Authorship is attributed to John, the apostle, though Revelation is the only one which actually identifies him (1.4). Doubts were raised in the early church about the inclusion of the letters on the grounds of disputed authorship and Origen* and Eusebius* had them on their 'disputed' list, but Irenaeus* accepted 1 John and all three are listed in the Muratorian Canon*. Revelation was popular in the West in the second century but the Eastern Church was questioning its inclusion in the canon* until the fourth century when Athanasius* endorsed it and the Council of Carthage*, 397, confirmed it.

John Chrysostom (347–407). Bishop of Constantinople*, 397–407, and the first to use the word *biblia* or 'Bible'* of the Old and New Testaments together.

John Fragment. The oldest witness to the Fourth Gospel, the oldest example of a NT text and probably the earliest Christian extant writing. A small piece of papyrus codex, 3.5 × 2.5 inches, containing verses from John's Gospel (18.31-33, 37, 38) and dated from the first half of the second century, possibly as early as 125. Usually known as $\mathfrak{P}^{52}$. Part of the

Chester Beatty Papyri* collection now located in the John Rylands Library, Manchester*, which acquired it along with other papyri in 1920 but did not fully recognize it and appreciate its significance until 1934.

Jones, Alexander (d. 1974). Senior Lecturer in Divinity in Christ's College, Liverpool. Translator and General Editor of the Jerusalem Bible* which he began in 1957. Most of the scholarship came from the Ecole Biblique but Jones translated and edited their notes with the help of 27 colleagues. It is said that he devised 'a special kind of semi-circular stall' in which he sat surrounded by Hebrew, Greek and French texts plus English drafts from a team of experts, comparing one against the other, a process of revision and counter-revision that lasted eight years.

Josephus (37–100 CE). Jewish historian and the most important resource for Palestine in New Testament times, expounded in *The Jewish War* and *Jewish Antiquities*. He believed Jewish culture to be superior to Greek and in defending it in his work, *Against Apion*, provided early evidence for the development of the canon* by referring to a '22-book canon', sometimes said to consist of the Pentateuch* and 13 books of prophets (probably Joshua to Kings and the Psalms), though the evidence is unclear.

Joye, George (1490–1553). Native of Bedfordshire, educated at Cambridge and Fellow of Peterhouse. Early associate of William Tyndale* who produced a translation of Martin Bucer's Latin version of the Psalms (1530 and 1534), Isaiah (1531), Jeremiah (1534), Proverbs and Ecclesiastes (1535). Except Proverbs and Ecclesiastes, most of his work was printed abroad, probably in Antwerp*, and such were his relations with Tyndale that it is not always clear just how much was his. Lacking scholarship and a nicety of taste he has been described as 'an interesting minor figure in the story of the English Bible'. When there was increasing demand for Tyndale's Translation* some pirate printings took place, often with words altered. Joye was responsible for some of these and Tyndale admonishes him in the prologue to his revised NT, 1534.

Judaean and Authorized Version of the New Testament, 1969. Intended to be a version without any anti-Semitism. Passages therefore which may give rise to hostile feelings between Christians and Jews were changed, the more familiar AV* text appearing in the footnotes.

Justin Martyr (c. 100–165 CE). A second-century Greek apologist who came from Palestine to Rome and suffered martyrdom, defended the OT as pointing to Jesus, made specific reference to the first three Gospels (or 'memoirs of the apostles' as they were then called) and their being read in worship alongside the prophets, and the first to make direct reference to Revelation, but provides nothing more than allusions to Paul.

K

Kahle, Paul Ernest (1875–1964). Joint editor of Kittel, *Biblia hebraica**, third edition, 1929–37. A twentieth-century scholar who studied some of the mss. found in the Cairo Geniza* and questioned the possibility of the urtext* on the grounds that no recension* was the result of a single act but rather the end result of much editing and revision. Attributed agreements between the LXX* and the Samaritan Pentateuch* to the fact that they came from the same 'common' tradition.

Kenrick, Francis Patrick (1797–1863). Roman Catholic Archbishop of Baltimore, Maryland. Born in Dublin and educated in Rome, where he trained for the priesthood and developed a love of Greek and Hebrew, Kenrick established a seminary to train priests and made a revision of the Douay-Rheims Bible* which he published in six volumes, 1849–60.

***Kethib* and *Qere*.** In some cases (anything from about 1000 to 1500), the Hebrew text instructs the reader to ignore what is written (*kethib*) and to read (*qere*) what it says in the margin. In most cases the consonants remain intact but the vowels change to give a different meaning. *Kethib/Qere* is used for a variety of reasons, including the need to avoid profanity, to correct error, or to offer a euphemism.

Kibworth, Leicestershire. Birthplace of Ronald Knox*.

Kilpatrick, George Gordon Dinwiddie (1887–1975). Oxford Professor of Exegesis and successor to T.H. Robinson* as Convenor of the Apocrypha panel for the NEB*.

King James Version. See Authorized Version.

Kittel, Rudolf (1853–1929). Editor of *Biblia hebraica**.

Knox, Ronald (1888–1957). Born in Kibworth, Leicestershire, son of an Anglican clergyman later to become Bishop of Manchester. Educated at Eton, where he began his literary career, and Balliol College, Oxford. Tutor and Fellow of Trinity, leading to ordination. Became a Roman Catholic, 1917, a Roman priest, 1919, and Professor of Old Testament at St Edmund's, Ware, Hertfordshire, 1922–26, when he moved to Oxford to become Chaplain to Catholic Undergraduates, a position he held for 13 years. Translator of Knox's Bible* and author of *On Englishing the Bible*, a set of lectures and articles on Bible translation setting out the principles on which he worked.

Kethib/Qere*

The classic example of the Kethib/Qere is the divine name, but there are others.*

To avoid utterance of the divine name, Yahweh, the consonants of the name (YHWH) were retained in the text as *Kethib*, but the vowels to produce the *Qere* were those of 'adonai' ('a', 'o', 'a'), normally translated and always pronounced in Hebrew as 'adonai' (never 'Yahweh') to give the English 'Jehovah' ('YaHoWaH'), a transliteration of the *Kethib* and the *Qere*.

1 Sam. 5.6, 9, 12. 'Haemorrhoids' (*Kethib*) in the AV* has become 'tumours' (*Qere*) in the NRSV*. Cf. 1 Sam. 6.4, 5.

Deut. 28.30. 'He shall enjoy her' (*Kethib*) has become 'he shall lie with her'(*Qere*). The *Qere* is a less obscene word in the Hebrew. Cf. Isa. 13.16, Jer. 3.2, Zech. 14.2.

2 Kgs 20.4. 'The city' (*Kethib*) has become 'the court' (*Qere*), as reflected in the AV margin and some other translations.

Knox's Bible, 1945 (NT), 1949 (OT), 1954 (complete). A Roman Catholic dynamic equivalence* translation into 'timeless English' by Ronald Knox* and published by Burns and Oates, London, with extensive and accessible footnotes to clarify difficult passages and provide references to particular Greek mss.

Describes itself as 'a translation from the Latin Vulgate* in the light of the Hebrew and Greek originals'. This is the Clementine Vulgate, authorized by Pope Clement VIII, 1592, and the standard text for the Roman Catholic Church since that time. Knox felt unable to exercise the freedom of the revisers of the Confraternity Version* and go behind the Clementine Vulgate to the purer Jerome* even where it was obvious to him that the Clementine was corrupt.

Modern paragraphing, verse numbers in the margin, using much modern vocabulary but not poetic forms and retaining the use of 'thou' and thee'. Though inevitably suffering from the fact that it is still a translation of a translation, its strength lies in the fact that Knox was committed to dynamic equivalence and as a translator has an uncanny knack of getting the right word or phrase in any given context. NT has copious footnotes, discussing points of text or rendering, especially where the Latin deviates from the Greek.

Authorized for use in the churches by the hierarchies of England and Wales, and Scotland, and until the arrival of the Jerusalem Bible* the best-known twentieth-century Roman Catholic version.

***Koiné* Greek.** The Greek of the NT. A popular, or common, form of the Greek language*, as distinct from classical Greek, spoken in the Hellenistic period from the time of Alexander the Great until the sixth century. Popularly known as NT Greek. Sometimes used to mean the Byzantine* text.

Koridethi. The site of a monastery near the Caspian Sea where in 1906 von Soden* drew attention to a ms. which formed the basis for Family Theta*.

L

Lachish Letters. Twenty-five pieces of pottery, discovered in 1935 and 1938, letters written by a Judaean military commander to the Jewish forces defending Lachish, 589 BCE, when Nebuchadnezzar (of Babylon) was attacking Judah prior to his attack on Jerusalem*. They belong to the period of Jeremiah and Zedekiah.

Lachmann, Karl Konrad Friedrich Wilhelm (1793–1851). Professor of Classical Philology in Berlin who opened a new era in textual criticism*, being the first to reject altogether the text as it is (Textus Receptus*) and to attempt to apply scientific principles to the study of the rest to reconstruct the text according to the ancient authorities, thus establishing the method of genealogical evidence* which has determined textual criticism* up to the present day.

He undertook a reconstruction of the fourth-century Greek text of the NT (completed by Tregelles*) and printed a small edition, 1831, and a larger edition, 1842–50, in which he also introduced the practice of classifying the Old Latin* mss. by a lower case italic letter.

At times, he tended to be unduly mechanical and rigid in his methods and though he undoubtedly made a contribution to the study of the Bible, his work suffered because his preoccupation with a fourth-century text led him to assume too readily that the earlier mss. were more likely to be accurate and to ignore the mass of late mss., as a result of which his list of authorities was too small.

'Ladies of Castlebrae, The'. Popular description of Agnes Smith Lewes* and Margaret Dunlop Gibson*, twin sisters who found a copy of the Old Syriac* version in the Sinaitic script, taken from the title of a lecture telling their story, and delivered by A. Whigham Price to the Presbyterian Historical Society in Durham, 1964.

Lagrange, Marie Joseph (1855–1938). A French Dominican who, after studying Assyrian, Egyptian, Arabic and Talmudic Hebrew in Vienna, was sent to Jerusalem* at the age of 34 to do a feasibility study on a proposal to found a biblical school in the Holy Land. He presented a positive report and the School, the Ecole Biblique, opened under his leadership in 1890, reputedly with only a table, a blackboard and a map. He also founded *Revue Biblique*, 1892, and wrote several books, including *History of the New Testament Canon*, 1933, and *Textual Criticism of the New Testament*, 1935, thereby laying the foundations for the Jerusalem Bible (French version), work on which started in 1946, some eight years after his death, though his writings and influence were not lost on men like de Vaux* and Benoit*.

Lake, Kirsopp (1872–1946). A biblical scholar who discovered certain similarities among four minuscule* mss. (nos. 1, 118, 131 and 209) and so established Family 1*. In collaboration with Helen Lake he also published a facsimile edition of Codex Sinaiticus*, 1911–22.

Lamsa's Translation, 1940–57. A verbal equivalence* English translation of an Aramaic text for the entire Bible, by George Mamisjisha Lamsa, a native of Kurdistan, whose mother tongue was akin to the old Syriac (Aramaic) language and who had a high regard for the originality and accuracy of the Peshitta*, from which he had first translated the Aramaic text itself. Published as The New Testament According to the Eastern Text*, 1940, followed by the complete Bible, The Holy Bible from Ancient Eastern Manuscripts, 1957, and published by A.J. Holman Co., Philadelphia.

Langton, Stephen (c. 1150–1228). Archbishop of Canterbury and leader of the barons in the struggle that gave birth to Magna Carta. Responsible for the division of the English Bible into chapters by installing them in the Vulgate*. Verse division* was not applied to the NT until 1551.

Languages. Apart from ten chapters in Aramaic (all in Ezra and Daniel) plus one verse in Jeremiah, the biblical languages are Hebrew (OT) and Greek (NT).

Latin Versions. The language of the Roman Church was Greek until the third century but Old Latin* versions of the Bible go back to the second century, first in Northern Africa and then in Italy, the Vulgate* being the most significant. Their origins are uncertain, though (with the exception of the Pentateuch*) they are most likely to have been in the Christian rather than the Jewish communities in that there is no evidence of the use of Latin in synagogue worship and insufficient evidence to assume that they originated in the Jewish communities. Besides providing the basic terms of Western theology and the formulas of the Latin liturgy the Latin Bible is important as a guide to the earliest Greek texts and even some of the Hebrew readings*, as well as assisting in an understanding of Latin as a language and of European language and literature.

Lattey, Cuthbert Charles (1887–1954). A Roman Catholic scholar, general editor of the Westminster Version*, 1935.

Law, The. See Pentateuch and Torah.

Lawrence, Giles (1539–84). Oxford professor of Greek whose scholarly criticisms of the Bishops' Bible*, particularly the NT, led to its revision, 1572.

lectio brevior. Where two possible readings occur in different mss., apart from an obvious case of haplography*, the shorter text is usually thought to be preferable on the grounds that scribes were more likely to add than to omit.

lectio defectiva. The Latin term (sometimes referred to as *scriptio defectiva*) for defective reading*.

lectio difficilior. Where two possible readings occur in different mss. the more difficult (or unlikely) reading is usually thought to be preferable, on the grounds that scribes were more likely to attempt to simplify or clarify a reading than to make it more difficult, but the principle is by no means infallible. Sometimes two readings are equally difficult, sometimes scholars disagree as to which is the more 'difficult', and sometimes an error in copying may produce a *lectio difficilior* without it necessarily being right, so there is a great deal of subjectivity when it comes to making decisions. (See *lectio difficilior*, below.)

lectio plene. The Latin term (sometimes referred to as *scriptio plene*) for full reading*.

Leeser, Isaac (1806–68). US rabbi, writer and lecturer. Born in Westphalia, educated at Munster and worked mostly in America where he moved in 1824. Published the first Hebrew primer for children (1838), founded a Jewish newspaper, the first Hebrew High School (1848) and the Jewish Publication Society of America, and was the first Jewish translator of the Hebrew Bible* in the USA, a translation which took him 17 years to complete, was published in 1845, and became the standard American Jewish Translation, accepted in all American synagogues until the Jewish Publication Society edition of 1917. A revised edition was published in London in 1865.

Leicester, England. Home of Nicholas* of Hereford, Canon of the Abbey of St Mary of the Meadows, thought to be partly responsible for the translation of Wycliffe's Bible*.

Leiden, Netherlands. Home of the Elzevir* printing firm and the Textus Receptus*.

Leipzig, Germany. City of publication for the first edition of Kittel's *Biblia hebraica** and home to 43 leaves of the OT of Codex Sinaiticus*.

Letters of St Paul, 1901. A translation of the epistles by Arthur S. Way*, omitting Hebrews in the first edition but including it in a second revised edition in 1906.

Letters to Young Churches, 1947. A paraphrase of the NT epistles by J.B. Phillips* subsequently incorporated into The New Testament in Modern English, 1958*. Published by Geoffrey Bles, London.

Leviticus Scroll. Fragments of a targum containing Lev. 16.12-15, 18-21, dating from the second century BCE, and found at Qumran* among the DSS*.

Lewis, Agnes Smith (1843–1926). Twin sister of Margaret Dunlop Gibson*, sometimes described as the Ladies of Castlebrae*, who towards the end of the nineteenth century found a second copy of the Old Syriac* version at St Catharine's Monastery*, Mount Sinai, reflecting the Sinaitic Syriac text.

Lewis, Clive Staples (1898–1963). Born in Belfast, son of a solicitor, Fellow of Magdalen College, Oxford, 1925–54, and Professor of Mediaeval and Renaissance English at Cambridge, 1954–63.

---

lectio difficilior

In Lk. 14.5 Codex Sinaiticus* has, 'Which one of you, if his ass or his ox fall in a well, will hestitate to pull it out, even on the Sabbath day?' Codex Vaticanus*, Codex Alexandrinus* and a few other mss. have, 'his son or his ox', a more difficult reading. Two mss. combine the two ('his son or his ass or his ox'), clearly not original. But was the more difficult reading the original or was there a tightening up with the passing of time?

Popular writer and broadcaster and member of the Literary Panel for the NEB*. Recognized the importance of J.B. Phillip's* translation, Letters to Young Churches, encouraged its publication and wrote an introduction in which he defended the importance of modern translations of the Bible.

Libby, Willard Frank (1908–80). An American chemist who worked on research into the atom bomb, 1941–45, and became Professor of Chemistry at Chicago where he worked for the Atomic Energy Commission and was awarded the 1960 Nobel Prize in chemistry for his part in the invention of the Radio Carbon Dating* method of determining the age of an object.

Liberal Translation of the New Testament, 1768. A none-too-successful attempt by Edward Harwood* 'to translate the sacred writings with the same freedom, spirit and elegance, with which other English translations from the Greek Classics have lately been executed', otherwise described as a free rendering or paraphrase* of the AV*, prior to the appearance of the RV*, possibly suffering from the fact that reading was not a high priority for many people and those for whom it was were either not yet into the niceties of translations or were opposed to the very idea. Once described as 'a literary curio'.

Lietzmann, Hans (1875–1942). A church historian who studied philosophy and theology and was a lecturer at Bonn and a professor at Jena. Discovered three families of text in the Pauline letters: the *Koinē** (most recent), the Western* (of great antiquity) and the Egyptian (often the most primitive).

Lindisfarne Gospels. An interlinear Latin copy of the gospels, written by Bishop Eadfrith* towards the end of the

seventh century, from a text which Adrian, a friend of Archbishop Theodore, had brought to England in 669, and now in the British Library. A monk, Ealdred, made an interlinear translation in the Northumbrian dialect, c. 950.

Originally kept at Lindisfarne, Northumbria, together with the remains of St Cuthbert in whose honour the ms. had been produced, but in 875 the Danes invaded and drove the monks to carry away both the body and the book. The monks wandered for several years in northern England and eventually decided to go to Ireland, but legend has it that the saint was angry at being taken from his own land and the ship ran into a terrible storm in which the precious volume was washed overboard and lost. Realizing that they had incurred the wrath of the saint the monks returned to England with much penitence and one of them subsequently found the ms. washed up on the shore almost uninjured by its immersion. Doubters may take some comfort from the fact that any precious book like this would only be allowed to travel in a very strong container, and several pages of the book do in fact show some signs of having suffered from water!

Three of the gospels are identical with the Rushworth Gospels*, a copy of which is in the Bodleian Library, Oxford*.

Lingard's Gospels, 1836. The first Catholic translation from the Greek, by an English historian, published as 'by a Catholic'.

Linguistic Emendation. See Conjectural Emendation.

Literal Translation of the Bible, 1862. More popularly known as Young's Translation*.

Living Bible, 1971. An American paraphrase* of the ASV* (or AV*), 1901, by Kenneth N. Taylor* which began in parts, 1962–70, and was published complete by the Tyndale House Press, USA, including an edition in 1988 with the books in alphabetical order, beginning with Acts and ending with Zephaniah. A British edition appeared from Kingsway Publications, 1974, and there are several editions in other languages. Though the dangers of paraphrases are recognized the translator adopts a thoroughly evangelical position, aiming 'to simplify the deep and often complex thoughts of the word of God'.

Lollards. A body of travelling preachers sent out by John Wycliffe* each of whom carried a Bible in English from which he read to the people. They were unpopular with the church establishment and Archbishop Courtenay, with the backing of the king, took out sanctions against them, turning them into an underground movement. In 1408 a Synod passed the Constitutions of Oxford* against them. Many were burned as heretics.

London, England. Location of the British Library (formerly British Museum), Lambeth Palace Library, Dr Williams's Library, King's College Library, St Paul's and Westminster, most of which have resources and documents relating to the English Bible. These include 199 leaves of the OT of Codex Sinaiticus*, a fragment of the Oxyrhynchus* Papyrus, the Lindisfarne Gospels*, King Alfred's Psalter, one copy of the West Saxon Gospels*, the Cologne Quarto*, Coverdale's Bible*, Matthew's Bible*, King George III's copy of the Mazarin* (Gutenberg) Bible, two copies of Tyndale's Translation* and the Vespasian Psalter*. The site of Caxton's* first printing press, in Tothill Street*, the home of the Ben Judah-Loeb family of translators and printers, including Alexander Alexander*, of the king's printer, Robert Barker*, and site for the printing

of the AV*. Tyndale's Bibles were burned at St Paul's Cross* on the authority of the Bishop of London.

London Polyglot, 1657–69. Eight volumes, edited by Brian Walton*, sometimes known as Walton's Polyglot, containing Hebrew (OT), Greek, Latin, Syriac, Ethiopic, Arabic and Persian (NT), with Latin translations in all cases, plus the Samaritan Pentateuch* and various targumim* or paraphrases*. The Greek text is that of Stephanus*, 1550.

The first systematic collection of variant readings* and quite the most important of all Polyglot Bibles*, mainly because in the notes Walton added readings from Codex Alexandrinus* and 15 other mss., besides the 15 used by Stephanus, and including Codex Bezae* for the fifth-century gospels and Acts and Codex Clarimontanus* for the sixth-century Pauline epistles.

Longman, Michael (1916–78). A director of Longmans Green who persuaded his fellow-directors to follow up a proposal from Frank Sheed* of Sheed and Ward to negotiate with the French publishers, Editions du Cerf, for the rights to arrange for an English translation of *La Bible de Jérusalem* with a view to publishing the Jerusalem Bible* in England.

Lower Criticism. See Textual Criticism.

Lowth, Robert (1710–87). Bishop of London who discovered the principle of parallelism in Hebrew poetry, whereby the second line of a verse repeats the first in different but synonymous terms, and in so doing opened up a new vista for the interpretation and translation of the OT. In 1778 he published *Isaiah: a new Translation, with a Preliminary Dissertation, and Notes.*

Lucar, Cyril (1572–1638). Patriarch, first of Alexandria* and then of Constantinople*, who presented the Codex Alexandrinus* to Charles I*, 1627.

Lucianic Text. Possibly the first major recension of the LXX*, with an eye on the cultured reader, attributed to Lucian of Antioch, theologian, biblical scholar and founder of an exegetical school in Antioch who died a martyr's death c. 311 CE.

A collection of fragmentary, Greek, minuscule* mss., discovered in the nineteenth century and reflecting some important Hebrew readings and striking agreements with certain Hebrew texts in the DSS*.

Identified mainly in the prophetic books, Judges, Samuel and Kings, and recognizable in certain extant mss. and in the copious biblical quotations of John Chrysostom* and Theodoret, but found only in one uncial* and a few cursive* mss., in the Gothic* and Old Slavonic* versions, and in the first printed version of the LXX*, the Complutensian Polyglot*.

Since the second-century Old Latin* and the first-century Josephus* texts seem to reflect a Lucianic text before Lucian, it is not certain what Lucian himself carried out but the characteristics of the Lucianic text are clear: additions* to adapt it to the rabbinic Hebrew text, some stylistic improvements, explanatory notes, such as proper names, pronouns, etc., and the replacement of Hellenistic forms by Attic equivalents.

It leaned more to the Western* text than the Alexandrian*, became the predominant text throughout the Greek-speaking world from the fourth century and (with minor changes) the Textus Receptus* of the Greek Orthodox Church and so the Greek version behind the AV*.

Luther's German New Testament, 1552. Based on one of the editions of Erasmus's* NT.

Lutterworth, Leicestershire. Home of John Wycliffe*.

LXX. Traditional way of describing the Septuagint*.

M

Mace, Daniel (d. c. 1753). A Presbyterian minister whose free rendering of the New Testament resulted in The New Testament in Greek and English...corrected from the Authority of the most Authentic Manuscripts*, 1729.

MacKnight, James (1721–1800). Biblical critic. Educated in Glasgow and Leiden. Author of A Harmony of the Gospels*, 1756, and A Translation of all the Apostolical Epistles*, 1795, the latter being one of three popular eighteenth-century translations, the other two being Philip Doddridge's* translation of the NT, 1739–56, and George Campbell's* translation of the gospels. In 1818 a combined translation appeared in London, subsequently revised and published by Alexander Campbell* in 1826.

Mainz, Germany. City where John Gutenberg invented printing with movable type, c. 1454, and the site for the printing of the Mazarin Bible*, the first major work to come from the printing press, 1456.

Manchester, England. Home to a Bohairic Coptic* text of Job and a Sahidic Coptic text of Ecclesiasticus, some mss. from the Cairo Geniza*, the Deuteronomy Fragment*, the Jeremiah Fragment*, the John Fragment*, the Titus Fragment*, a palimpsest of 1 and 2 Peter, a Syriac*

NT containing all 27 books and the original documents for the Twentieth Century New Testament*, 1902, in the John Rylands Library.

Manuscript. A hand-written document by which the text was conveyed long before the invention of printing*.

Marcion (c. 100–165 CE). A wealthy ship-owner and church founder in Asia Minor who caused dissension in the church of the second century by becoming a bishop but then created his own community and was eventually dismissed as a heretic. In 140, in Rome, he rejected the OT* and reduced the NT* to an abbreviated Luke and his own edited version of ten letters of Paul, arranged as Galatians, 1 and 2 Corinthians, Romans, 1 and 2 Thessalonians, Ephesians, Colossians, Philippians and Philemon, though in so doing he provides some early evidence of a Pauline Corpus* and may have been instrumental in encouraging the more orthodox to re-examine their own presuppositions and the church to define its canon*.

Mari Tablets. 20,000 tablets, excavated since 1936 at Mari, on the right bank of the Euphrates, and dating from the eighteenth century BCE, round about the time when the city was destroyed by the soldiers of Hammurabi, king of Babylon, while it was undergoing a period of great prosperity.

Mari features in the history of Mesopotamia and, since the population was mostly Semitic, customs and language reflect the culture of Semitic life at that time and so have much to offer towards an understanding of the OT. According to Genesis, Mesopotamia is the country of Abraham and Terah and the texts make reference to the Habiru who are thought by some to have a connection with the Hebrews.

The tablets include letters written by north-western Semites in a Babylonian script full of West-Semitic words and grammatical usages. Thousands of proper names shed light on many OT names, particularly some in the earlier books of the Bible, and in some cases the legacy of Mari has helped in an understanding of some previously obscure Hebrew phrases, such as 'cut a covenant' (Gen. 31.44).

Martin, Gregory (d. 1582). Born in Sussex, tutor in the Howard family, Scholar of St John's College, Oxford, and Professor at the English College at Rheims*, founded by William Allen*, from 1570. Ordained to the priesthood and taught Hebrew. Roman Catholic translator of the Vulgate* into English for the benefit of English-speaking Roman Catholics, which led to the Douay-Rheims Bible*. Beginning in 1578, he translated two chapters daily, working from the Latin but keeping one eye on the Greek and even using some of the English versions which he had previously condemned. He translated the OT first and then the NT, but his NT appeared first, in 1582, when he was at Rheims and is properly known as the Rheims New Testament. The OT appeared 1609–10 when the College had returned to Douay and hence the name Douay Old Testament, or Douay-Rheims Bible and was followed by the Apocrypha*. As each section was completed it was revised by William Allen and Richard Bristow*.

Martini, Carlo Maria (1927–). Cardinal Archbishop of Milan, who argued that the distancing of the Church from the scriptures in order to establish its authority was a relatively recent phenomenon following the Council of Trent*, 1545–63, and that the affirmations of the Second Vatican Council* were a return to an earlier way of thinking. In so doing he prepared the way for closer cooperation with the Protestants and worked with Holmgren* and others to achieve a common text leading to the Common Bible*, 1973.

Mary I (1516–1558). Came to the throne in 1553 and reversed the reforming policies of her brother. Men like John Rogers* and Thomas Cranmer* were executed and many Bibles were burned, but the Great Bible* remained unassailed and could still be found in most churches.

Masorah. The origins of the word are uncertain and even its spelling is disputed, some preferring 'massorah', 'massoretes', etc. One view is that it comes from *'sr* ('to tie'), the other that it comes from *msr*, a post-bibical word meaning 'to transmit'. Transmission is what it commonly means. Its purpose is to preserve the text in its entirety and to interpret it. Hence it consists of a collection of scribal data or code of instructions, dating from somewhere between 500 and 1000 CE, to accompany the Masoretic Text*, traditionally going back to the time of Ezra and continuing the work of the Sopherim*, for preserving, copying* and reading (aloud) the biblical text, including *kethib/qere**. In some cases notes deal with doubts, possibly misunderstandings affecting a letter or word (such as *matres lectionis**), accents or grammatical forms.

There are two masorah traditions, one from Babylon and the other from Palestine, both of which developed after the second Jewish revolt against the Romans (132–35 CE).

Masoretes, The. Jewish scholars charged with achieving a consistent and reliable Hebrew text of the OT. They began work c. 600 CE and did most of their work in the eighth to the tenth centuries, leading to the Masoretic Text*, now the standard Hebrew text for the OT.

Usually applied to the work of Ben Asher* (the most famous family of Masoretes) and a group of Tiberian scholars who defined the consonantal base, developed from earlier traditions from the seventh to the eleventh centuries and reflecting a tradition going back 1000 years to the days of the Second Temple, sometimes described as Proto-Masoretic*. A different masorah, more rigid and consistent, came from Ben Naphthali, another family of Masoretes, contemporaries of Ben Asher.

Ancient Hebrew writing* had only consonants and no vowels and though there was considerable consistency in the written text it was not unknown for one verbal tradition to work on one set of vowels and another verbal tradition on a different set. The Masoretes provided vocalization*, defined the text, added accents and created the apparatus of the Masorah*.

Because it was done by inserting 'points' (dots and other small marks) to represent the vowels, one part of the process is known as 'pointing' and the result described as 'a pointed text'. In the interests of accuracy dots (*puncta extraordinaria**) were put over letters where the rabbis doubted their correctness. In the interests of consistency they counted the words and letters of every book, determining (for example) the middle letter

and word of each book so as to be alerted when anything went wrong in the copying, but verse division*, verse numbers and chapter division* owe more to Latin tradition than to the Jewish.

Masoretic Text. A group of ancient Hebrew mss. that achieved a final form in the Middle Ages when the Masoretes* defined them and added a critical apparatus*. The most commonly used form of the Hebrew Bible from the second century CE, first in its Proto-Masoretic* form and then in its vocalized form as a result of the work of the Masoretes*. The central text for the Hebrew Bible, for the OT, and for biblical scholarship, with which all other ancient Hebrew texts are compared, but not the only textual tradition that was around immediately before the birth of Christianity and therefore not to be regarded as the one and only reliable version.

matres lectionis. Some Hebrew consonants occasionally do duty also as vowels and over the years the custom developed of adding them to certain words for clarification. Judging by early Moabite and Phoenician texts (we do not have any Hebrew texts from the same period) they were probably not used in the days of the First Temple, but they were around by the time of the DSS*. Even after their arrival their use was not universal or consistent, leading to a distinction between a defective reading* where one or more of the *matres lectionis* was missing and a full reading* with one or more included. Most *matres lectionis* do not affect the meaning of the text but their insertion does reflect the understanding of the person adding them.

Matthaei, C.F. (1744–1811). Professor at Wittenberg and Moscow. Worked on a list of mss., drawn up by J.J. Wettstein*, and added a further 57 to produce an edition of the Greek text with the Latin Vulgate* in 12 parts, 1782–88, with a second edition (without the Vulgate) in three volumes, 1803–1807. Possibly the first to draw on Slavic mss., of which he had ten. Paved the way for the later work of J.M.A. Scholz* and Caspar René Gregory*.

Matthew's Bible, 1537. Thomas Matthew was a pseudonym for John Rogers*, friend of Tyndale*, burnt at the stake under Mary*, and responsible for taking the text of Tyndale and Coverdale* and editing it.

The text is substantially Tyndale's NT and as much of the OT as Tyndale had translated (probably Genesis to Chronicles), edited by Rogers. 1112 pages, 11.25 × 6.5 inches, two columns, each with 60 lines. Title page carries the words, 'Set forth with the kinges most gracyous lycence', partly due to the efforts of Thomas Cranmer* and Thomas Cromwell*.

Many notes and references. Divided into chapters and paragraphs, but not into verses. Printed entirely in black letters. The first version to carry the apocryphal Prayer of Manasseh in English and one of the first Chained Bibles* in some churches. Failed to satisfy the scholars because it was not made from the originals and offended some of the traditionalists by its notes and comments.

Published in Antwerp* by Richard Grafton*. The British Library has 2 copies of the original edition of 1500 copies, most of which were destroyed.

Mazarin Bible, 1456. The first major work to come from the printing press after the invention of printing* by moveable type by Gutenberg, 1454, a Latin Bible so-called because one copy belonged to the library of the French statesman, Cardinal Jules Mazarin. Often

called the Gutenberg Bible, which some people consider more appropriate. Printed in two columns. About 40 copies are extant. King George III's copy is in the King's Library at the British Library and some years ago the USA Congress paid £60,000 for a copy for the National Library at Washington*.

McHardy, W.D. (1911–). Educated at Aberdeen, Edinburgh and Oxford, where he became Professor of Hebrew. Specialist in Aramaic* and Syriac* and Curator of the Mingana Collection of Oriental Manuscripts, 1947. Director of A Greek–English Diglot for the Use of Translators*, 1958–64, and leader of a team of 35 scholars who produced The Translator's New Testament*, 1973. Chairman of the Apocrypha* panel for the NEB*, Deputy Director for the whole translation from 1968 and Joint Director from 1971. Director of the Revised English Bible*, 1973–90.

McLean, Norman (1865–1947). Orientalist, educated in Edinburgh and Cambridge, a specialist in Semitic languages* and a lecturer in Aramaic*. Joint editor (with A.E. Brooke*) of the Cambridge Septuagint*.

Meek, Theophile James (b. c. 1881). Biblical scholar in the University of Toronto. Translated the first eight books of the OT, Song of Songs and Lamentations for The Old Testament: An American Translation*, 1927, and subsequently revised the whole work for The Complete Bible: An American Translation*, 1931, often known as Goodspeed's translation*.

Melito of Sardis (d. c. 190). A bishop who was interested in the differences between Jews and Christians when it came to decisions about sacred texts. When he visited Palestine in 170, for example, he discovered that the Jerusalem

Church was using the OT without Esther, so this became the recognized canon* for Asia Minor, and Melito's list of 22 books, all with Greek titles, is the oldest surviving list of books of the OT.

Mesropius (d 439). First Armenian* Bible translator and joint translator with Patriarch Sahug* of the Bible and the liturgy. Credited also with the invention of the Armenian script, an alphabet of 36 letters which emerged in 406.

Message: The New Testament in Contemporary Language, The, 1993. A dynamic equivalence* approach by Eugene H. Peterson, a Presbyterian minister, resulting more in a popular paraphrase. Since the NT was written in informal Greek, the street language of the day, the idiom of the playground and the marketplace, Peterson attempts to retain the informal character of the Greek in the modern English translation. No notes or study aids but sometimes marred by Peterson's interpretative comments. Published by NavPress, Colorado Springs.

Metathesis. The transposition (usually accidentally) of two adjacent letters, resulting either in an impossible word or in another word with a different meaning.

Metrical Emendation. See Conjectural Emendation.

Metzger, Bruce Manning (1914–). New Testament scholar, professor at Princeton Theological Seminary and author of many books on the text and canon* of OT, NT and Apocrypha*. Secretary to the Committee of the National Council of the Churches of Christ in the USA, chairman of an international editorial committee for the (UBS) Greek New Testament*, and involved in the

RSV*, the RV of the Apocrypha*, and the NRSV*.

Midrash. A Jewish commentary on the scriptures, from *drsh*, the Hebrew word meaning 'to search out'.

Milan, Italy. Site for the printing of the first texts of the Greek New Testament* (the Magnificat and Benedictus, alongside the Psalter) in 1481 and home of the Ambrosian Library.

Mill, John (1645–1707). A NT scholar and Fellow of Queens College, Oxford, and the first to appreciate the significance of the ancient versions and quotations in the early church Fathers for critical study of the NT text. He produced a NT in which he attached to the text of Stephanus* the variant readings* of 78 other mss., all the versions* he could get hold of, and (for the first time) scriptural quotations used by early Christian writers. He listed 30,000 variant readings and corrected the Textus Receptus* in 31 places. He added a valuable introduction covering the canon* of the NT and the transmission of the NT text, describing 32 printed editions of the Greek NT and nearly 100 mss., and discussing citations of any importance from all the Fathers. The fruit of 30 years work which he completed a fortnight before his death and which remained as the basis for scholarly work on the NT for many years. On the basis of his work a revised NT Greek text was later produced by Edward Wells* and Daniel Mace*.

Minuscule. A way of writing Greek, developed from the cursive* style in common use in the ninth century CE, using small letters joined together as against the earlier and more familiar capital letters each written separately and known as uncials*. The script was known as 'cursive' and the ms. as 'a minuscule'.

The cursive quickly superseded the older uncial script because it was easier and quicker to write, took up less space and made it possible to have smaller books more suitable for personal use. There are over 4000 such mss. of the NT, mostly from the ninth to the seventeenth centuries, outnumbering uncials by about ten to one, many containing only the gospels, and every one tabulated and given an arabic number for the purposes of identification and recognition. Most have the Byzantine* or *Koiné* Greek* text but what determines their value is not their age but the archetype from which they come. Mss. with similar readings comprise a family and several 'families' of minuscules have been identified, including Family 1*, Family 13* and Family Theta*.

Mishnah. A Jewish set of rules elaborating the Torah* dating from the second century CE, from the Hebrew word meaning 'to repeat' or 'to learn'.

Moabite Stone. A monument, dated c. 890 BCE, on which Mesha, king of Moab, recorded his war with the kings of Israel and Judah, and paralleling the records of 2 Kings 3. Discovered by a German in 1868, then in the possession of Arabs who broke it up so that some large portions have been lost. Its lengthy inscription is one of the earliest examples of Semitic writing in a language that differs only slightly from Hebrew.

Moberly, George (1803–85). Educated at Balliol College, Oxford. One of five clergymen who worked with Ernest Hawkins* to produce The Authorized Version of St John's Gospel, revised by Five Clergymen*, 1857, and similar revisions of some of the epistles. Later Bishop of Salisbury.

Modern Language Bible, 1969. A revision of the Berkeley Version*, published by Zondervan, Grand Rapids.

Modern Reader's Bible, 1896. A dynamic equivalence* translation, the work of R.G. Moulton, a Chicago professor with a commitment to the literary form of the Bible and a desire to avoid many of the controversial issues being raised by biblical scholars and theologians, especially higher criticism*. He began with a series of small booklets, based on the RV* but making full use of the choice provided by the variations in the margin so as to produce the best literary structure. The 21 parts were later put together by Macmillan and published in 1907.

Moffatt, James (1870–1944). Born in Glasgow, son of a Chartered Accountant in the Free Church of Scotland, and educated at Glasgow Academy and Glasgow University, gaining an honours degree in Classics, 1890. An outstanding scholar and the youngest person to receive an honorary DD from Aberdeen when he was 32 for his first published work, *The Historical New Testament*, a piece of original research which arranged the books of the NT in the order of their supposed dates and literary growth. Ordained in 1896, appointed Professor of Greek and New Testament Studies at Mansfield College, Oxford, 1911, of Church History at the United Free College, Glasgow, 1915, and at Union Theological Seminary, New York, 1927. Author of Moffatt's Translation* and one of the best known of all modern English translators in the first half of the twentieth century who helped considerably to popularize an idiomatic approach to Bible translation. Executive Secretary of the Committee which produced the RSV* from 1937 until his death.

Moffatt's Translation, 1913 (NT), 1924 (OT), 1928 (complete). An independent dynamic equivalence* translation by James Moffatt* with the title, *A New Translation of the Bible*, published by Hodder & Stoughton, London. One of the earliest of the modern versions, single-handed, and certainly one of the most popular. The NT had over 70 reprints in 25 years when an illustrated Jubilee edition was published.

His NT text was von Soden's* and he consulted no other versions. He moved freely in the world of Hellenistic Greek without ever taking his eye off the reader and tried to produce a text which would appeal as much to those who understood the original as to those who did not. Usually thought to be more successful with the NT than the OT, probably because he was less sure of his Hebrew than his Greek.

In a day when people were familiar only with the formal language of the AV* Moffatt's translation sounded strange and often struck uneasy chords for some readers, but his over-riding objective was to grasp the feel of the original phrase and then render it into equally original English so as to produce the same impact on the reader as had the original. Sometimes his critics felt the end product was more Scottish than English, in that the list of musical instruments in Dan. 3.10 includes a bagpipe, 2 Sam. 6.14 has David dressed in a linen kilt, Mic. 2.2 has 'yeomen', Lam. 1.6 has 'harts' and Song 4.6 becomes 'I will hie me to your scented slopes'.

He retained the order of books in the AV, printed OT quotations in italics, came up with some original phrases and did much to popularize modern Bible translations, but he did take liberties, like altering traditionally accepted punctuation and changing the arrangement of words and even sections, so that Jn 3.22-30 appears between 2.12 and 2.13 and 1 Tim. 5.23 is missing altogether.

His revised edition (1934), more like a modern book, amounted almost to a fresh translation and is much more accurate.

Montgomery, Helen Maria Barrett (1861–1934). A Baptist leader from Rochester, NY, born in Kingsville, Ohio, and a graduate of Wellesley College. First female President of the American Baptist convention, and translator of The Centenary Translation of the New Testament*, 1924.

More, Thomas (1478–1535). Lord Chancellor of England. A Roman Catholic finally imprisoned in the Tower of London and beheaded because he refused to give up his RC faith. Made a fierce attack on Tyndale's Translation*, 1528, in *A Dialogue Concerning Heresies*, alongside a denunciation of the worship of relics and images, praying to saints and going on pilgrimages. Tyndale replied in *An Answer unto Sir Thomas More's Dialogue*, 1531, to which More responded with *The Confutation of Tyndale*. More argued that Tyndale's NT was not the NT at all but a counterfeit. It was full of errors and to find them was like searching for water in the sea. 'It is easier to make a web of new cloth than it is to sew up every hole in a net', he said. But his charges were not always well founded, he was more sympathetic to Tyndale than he sometimes appears, and closer examination shows that his main objections were to Tyndale's use of non-ecclesiastical words, such as 'congregation' for 'church' and 'senior' for priest'.

Muratori, Ludovici Antonio (1672–1750). Italian historian and antiquary, a priest who worked in the Ambrosian Library, Milan*, preparing and publishing original documents. Discoverer of the Muratorian Fragment* or Canon.

Muratorian Fragment or Canon. A seventh or eighth century fragment of an earlier and larger document, probably written in the vicinity of Rome and translated into Latin from the Greek. Discovered in 1740 by L.A. Muratori*, containing a list of 22 of the present 27 canonical books of the NT, including nearly all those attributed to Paul. Important as an indicator of the existence of a Pauline Corpus* and a guide as to which books were thought to be authoritative at the time, though its value in this regard depends on its dating. Traditionally thought to be the product of the Western church at the end of the second century, arguments not altogether convincing have been put forward for a later date and for an Eastern rather than Western origin.

Murderer's Bible, 1795. An edition of the AV*, printed by Thomas Bensley* in Oxford, in which Mk 7.27 accidentally read, 'Let the children first be killed' instead of 'filled'. Another edition of 1801 renders Jude 16 as 'These are murderers', when it should read 'murmurers'.

N

Nag Hammadi, Egypt. Site of the Nag Hammadi Library, along the Nile in Upper Egypt, 40 miles north-west of Luxor, where 13 papyrus* codices and other writings were found in 1945, 2 of them in poor condition, all fragmentary as regards text, and the most significant being a complete copy of the *Gospel of Thomas**. Written in Coptic* and dating from the fourth century. None of the texts is biblical though they do shed light on early Christianity and the apocryphal gospels*.

Nary's New Testament, 1719. The first Catholic text independent of Douay-Rheims*, translated from the Vulgate* by Cornelius Nary of Dublin.

Nash Papyrus. The only pre-masoretic text known before the discovery of the DSS* in 1947. An old fragment, discovered in Egypt in 1902, dated first or second century BCE, containing the Ten Commandments (a mixture of Exodus 20 and Deuteronomy 5), and the *shema* (Deut. 6.4-5) in Hebrew, written with ink in square characters, in a single column. More liturgical than biblical.

Nestle-Aland Text. A critical edition* of the Greek NT, 1898, produced by Eberhard Nestle until 1927 (the thirteenth edition) when the work was taken over by his son, Erwin. Papyri* evidence

assumed increased importance from then but in all its 80 years the text itself was not changed until the twenty-sixth edition, 1979. Kurt Aland was associated with the work from 1950, and since 1979 it has been known as the Nestle-Aland text. Based on the texts edited by Tischendorf*, 1869–72, by Westcott* and Hort*, 1881, and by Bernhard Weiss*, 1894–1900. Where two of the three sources agree that is what Nestle prints, thus reflecting nineteenth-century scholarship. In the latest editions its apparatus is a marvel of condensation, with a high degree of accuracy and a lot of textual information, much of it discovered in the twentieth century.

Though not universally accepted, this version is essentially the text for the academic study of the NT, allegedly the most widely used and probably the best critical Greek NT available. It is the text of the (UBS) Greek New Testament*, though retaining different punctuation and critical apparatus*, and most English translations work from it, though varying in the extent to which they choose a reading from the critical apparatus. Its influence is apparent in the NRSV*, and the recent revisions of Today's English Version* and The Living Bible*.

Neutral Text. The name given by F.J. Hort* in 1882 to the so-called Alexandrian* text because he thought it to be the purest form of text then in existence, dating from the second century, found in those mss. nearest to the NT times, such as Vaticanus*, Sinaiticus*, eight to ten later imperfect uncials*, a handful of minuscules*, some Coptic* versions and Origen's* texts, and free from error and corruption. Later scholars took a different view and placed more emphasis on the Western* text.

New American Bible, 1970. A new and revised dynamic equivalence* translation of the Confraternity Version, 1941*, with the full title of *The New American Bible, Translated from the Original Languages with Critical Use of All the Ancient Sources by Members of the Catholic Biblical Association of America: With Textual Notes on Old Testament Readings.* Following a papal encyclical of 1943, which authorized translation from the original languages and approved 'co-operation with separated brethren', leading to a new era in Roman Catholic biblical translation, and encouraged by the spirit of the Second Vatican Council*, it was a major breakthrough for the Roman Catholic Church—the first English Bible translated by American Catholic scholars, with several Protestant editors and translators brought in for the later stages. Translated directly from original texts acceptable to professional biblical scholars, both Catholic and Protestant.

Initiated when the Episcopal Confraternity of Christian Doctrine (which held the copyright for the Confraternity Version) approached the Catholic Biblical Association with a request to translate the entire Bible into vernacular English from the best available texts in the original languages, and with the help of the ablest available scholars. Forty-six editors and translators were appointed (including four non-Catholics) and others helped with notes and illustrations. Translators were given considerable freedom and worked less as a team than in some other modern 'official' translations.

Strives to maintain the flavour, style and word order of the original, and is restrained in departures from the Masoretic Text*, conjectural emendation* and gender-inclusive language. Books of the Apocrypha* are printed in their traditional places throughout the OT. Proper names are spelt as in the AV*, a departure from tradition as far as Roman Catholics are concerned. Normally Hebrew versification is followed and attention drawn to differences from the more familiar English usage. Subject headings are brief and lucid, poetry is printed as poetry, introductions to books, notes and cross-references are generally helpful and only occasionally tend to safeguard Roman Catholic doctrines; for example, the 'young woman' (Isa 7.14) is a virgin and 'brothers' in relation to Jesus is said to refer to any kind of relative and not necessarily children of the same parents.

Generally believed to be a good translation in the Challoner* tradition and in the idiom of the twentieth century. Steps were taken in 1986 to produce a revision, beginning with the NT, but pursuing verbal equivalence* rather than dynamic equivalence*.

New American Standard Bible, 1963 (NT), 1971 (complete). A revision and modernization of the ASV*, 1901, but still a conservative and very literal translation, retaining verbal equivalence* to the point of reproducing the ancient word and phrase order. Demonstrates its links with the AV* by way of the ASV*.

Produced by a group of 50 American scholars under the auspices of the Lockman Foundation of California, which also sponsored the Amplified Bible*, in an attempt to be faithful to (and maintain the stylistic characteristics of) the ancient texts, and to be grammatically correct whilst at the same producing a text which can be understood by the masses and is suitable for liturgical use and private reading. Its rigidity makes it a very useful tool for study but the same rigidity and its use of modern language in a traditional way often make it wooden, stilted and unsuitable for public reading. Published by La Habra, California.

Based on the twenty-third edition of the Nestle* text (1957) and able to take into account the various papyrus* mss. which had been discovered, including the Bodmer Papyri*, but sometimes refuses to abandon traditional readings in the light of obvious textual evidence pointing in a different direction, as in, for example, its retention of the longer ending of Mark (16.9-20) and the woman taken in adultery (Jn 7.53–8.11).

New American Standard Bible Update, 1995. A further revision of the NASB* under the auspices of the Lockman Foundation of California. 'Thee' and 'thou' were removed, verbal equivalence* and the ancient word and phrase order were retained, though with concessions to achieve a more fluid translation, the later and more scholarly editions of the Hebrew, Greek and Aramaic texts were consulted, and there were improvements in the grammatical notes and the cross references.

New Century Version, 1991. The work of a team of biblical scholars (all male, except one) from the North American evangelical Protestant world, representing conservative seminaries and colleges such as Fuller, Dallas and Wheaton, motivated by the success of the International Children's Bible*. They aimed to produce a translation which was accurate, free of denominational bias and clear to the widest English-speaking readership, with inclusive language, modernized weights and measures, and clarification of ancient customs, though, as with the International Children's Bible, their acceptance of a limited vocabulary imposed some limits on the quality of the final translation. Published by Word Publishing, Dallas.

New Chain Reference Bible, 1964. A new improved edition of the more familiar Thompson Chain Reference Bible, first published in 1908, the work of Frank and Laura Thompson, over 30 years. AV* text plus a complete numerical system of chain references with every verse classified and catalogued to enable a reader to follow a word, phrase or theme throughout the Bible, plus analyses of books, outline studies of characters, unique charts, a new series of pictorial maps, archaeological discoveries and many other features. Dates are according to Archbishop Ussher, charts and tables reflect idiosyncratic tastes, and allegory and typology feature strongly in OT interpretations.

New English Bible, 1961 (NT), 1970 (complete). A fresh dynamic equivalence* translation, made from the Greek and Hebrew, with the authority of all the major British churches except the Roman Catholic, and so different from all previous translations which had been made either by individuals or by free-lance groups, except for the AV* and the RV* and even they had relied very heavily on earlier individual versions.

On a proposition by G.S. Hendry* the General Assembly of the Church of Scotland, in May 1946, agreed that a new translation (not a revision) of the Bible be made, free from denominational or doctrinal bias. The decision was confirmed by a conference of representatives from the Church of Scotland, the Church of England, and the Baptist, Congregationalist and Methodist churches; and in January 1947 a Joint Committee was set up with representatives from the churches and from the Oxford and Cambridge University Presses. After a year further invitations were extended to the Church in Wales, the Churches in Ireland, the Presbyterian Church of England, the Society of Friends, the British and Foreign Bible Society and the National Bible Society* of Scotland. Subsequently the Roman Catholic Churches of England and Scotland sent observers.

Chairman of the Committee was J.W. Hunkin*, Bishop of Truro, succeeded in 1950 by Alwyn P. Williams*, Bishop of Durham and (later) Winchester, and in 1968 by F. Donald Coggan*, Archbishop of Canterbury. The Directors were C.H. Dodd*, G.R. Driver* and W.D. McHardy*.

Three panels of translators, chosen for their competence in biblical scholarship rather than for their churchmanship, were appointed (OT, NT and Apocrypha*). A fourth panel consisted of advisers on literary and stylistic questions and at different times included both T.S. Eliot and C.S. Lewis*. A book, or part of a book, was entrusted to a translator whose work was then examined by a linguistic expert, discussed by members of the panel, and revised, after which it was passed to the literary panel and their comments passed back to the translation panel for approval. Once that process was complete the text was finally approved by the Joint Committee. Three introductions (to OT, NT and Apocrypha) help the reader to understand the issues involved in translating each section.

It was to be genuinely English in idiom, free from archaisms and transient modernisms—'timeless English'—with sufficient dignity to be read aloud, and to aim at conveying a sense of reality rather than preserving 'hallowed associations'. Characteristics of the finished product include modern speech, textual accuracy without pedantry, vividness of expression and flashes of meaning, and a text printed in paragraph form with sectional headings. Footnotes explain the literal meaning of the Hebrew and of proper names, suggest alternative translations, and elucidate textual corrections, changes in order and the like.

Instead of working on an agreed Greek text, with variations when needed, as had been the usual custom with English translations, the NT translators in this case opted for an eclectic Greek text, including some papyrus* readings and some not previously used by English translators at all. One result of this is that some verses are reordered. Gen. 26.18, for example, now comes between 15 and 16, Jer. 15.13-14 is relegated to a footnote and Mt. 9.34 is dropped altogether. Other significant changes are the omission of titles for the psalms on the grounds that they are not original, the separate treatment plus an explanatory note accorded to Jn 7.53–8.11, changes to the shorter and longer endings of Mark as between the more usual, the NEB earlier versions and the study edition (1976), and the acceptance of the *lectio difficilior* in Mk 1.41, though settling for 'warm indignation' rather than the more outspoken 'anger'. Full advantage was taken of the DSS* and other recent developments in biblical scholarship. The underlying Greek text was then produced by R.V.G. Tasker* and published in 1964 after the translation had appeared.

Though it tended to finish up largely as a text for scholars, it was originally directed at three groups of people: churchgoers who had become too familiar with the text to 'hear it fresh', young people who wanted a more contemporary translation, and people who rarely attended church and were put off by the language of the AV*.

New International Reader's Version, 1995. Not a new translation. Based on the NIV*, retaining verbal equivalence*, with simpler words and shorter sentences for children under eight and adults with limited literacy. Published by Zondervan, Grand Rapids.

New International Version, 1973 (NT), 1978 (complete). Has been described as 'the modern translation for the conservative evangelical community'. Born of a dissatisfaction by American conservatives with the RSV* and many other modern translations, it originated with a decision of the Christian Reformed Church in 1956 to appoint a Committee to study the possibility of a new translation, followed by a similar decision of the National Association of Evangelicals in 1957. 'International' reflects the fact that the translators are drawn from many parts of the English-speaking world. Most of them would describe themselves as 'evangelical' though this does not mean that the translation is sectarian.

In 1967 the New York (now International) Bible Society* took responsibility for the project and appointed 15 scholars to handle it with Edwin H. Palmer* as Executive Secretary. The broad directive was to be faithful to the original Hebrew, Aramaic and Greek, and to produce a text that was in the language of the people, for pulpit and pew, clear and natural, idiomatic but not idiosyncratic, contemporary but not dated. The result, which provides a verbal equivalence* translation (with considerable freedom), is very much the work of teams and committees. At its heart was a Committee on Bible Translation (the 15), mostly biblical scholars and teachers. Each book was assigned its own team of translators whose draft went to an editorial team which supplied a revised translation. That in turn was checked and revised by another editorial team before going to the Committee on Bible Translation who

referred it to their own stylistic consultants before accepting it.

The OT is based on the Masoretic Text*, the Samaritan Pentateuch*, the ancient versions* and the DSS*. Conjectural emendation* is rare. The NT is based on the (UBS) Greek New Testament* bearing general consensus among scholars and able to take into account various papyrus* mss., including the Bodmer Papyri*.

Printed without columns, with brief section headings, tables of weights and measures and 14 maps, meticulous attention to punctuation, poetry set out as poetry, psalms without headings, and published in the USA by Zondervan, Grand Rapids. A British edition, with some changes of idiom and spelling, appeared in 1979 published by Hodder & Stoughton.

Its strengths include good scholarship and readability, modern style but not too far from the AV*, attractively bound and published, a variety of editions and prices, and well marketed. Its weaknesses are that it is very literal, yet not really a verbal equivalence* translation, and essentially conservative with little or no attempt to break new ground or reach new understanding. There is some confusion with modern equivalents for weights, measures and distances in that sometimes we have the original in the text and the modern in the margin and other times the opposite. Using synonyms for the same Hebrew and Greek words to achieve variety sometimes destroys the force of the repetition in the original. Desire for readability sometimes overrules the literalism; for example, 'This is what the Lord says' is not the same as 'Thus says the Lord'. Conservative reputation depends more on the notes than the text and also on challenging some of the charges which had caused trouble for the RSV*; for example, 'Young woman' rather than 'virgin' (Isa. 7.14).

New Jerusalem Bible, 1985. A thorough revision of the Jerusalem Bible*, edited by Henry Wansbrough*, with some books freshly translated and others revised to give a more readable and dignified presentation, in the light of more recent scholarship and the insights of the *La Bible de Jérusalem*, 1972. Designed for worship and study, but its well-written introductions to each book and its explanatory notes make it more suitable for study than for liturgical use. With inclusive language and verbal equivalence* to avoid paraphrase*, it represents a marked change in translation philosophy. As with the NEB*, the translators went for an eclectic text, particularly in their translation of Acts, and there is some evidence of papyrus* influence. Its strength lies in the fact that translation direct from the ancient texts represents the finest Roman Catholic biblical scholarship and takes full advantage of the scholarly work done on the Bible in the last 200 years by others. It also contains the entire range of books regarded by Catholics as canonical, and in canonical order, and retains the rhythm and structure of the ancient languages more than the JB*. Its weaknesses are that sometimes its fidelity to modern English assumes greater importance than an accurate rendering of the ancient texts, and its explanatory notes sometimes support Catholic interpretations that have been under question since the Reformation, though Isa. 7.14 retains 'young woman'. Published by Darton, Longman & Todd, London.

New Jewish Version, 1962–81. A fresh translation of the OT, prepared by leading Jewish scholars with Henry M. Orlinsky* as Editor-in-Chief, and published in stages, beginning with The New Translation of The Holy Scriptures according to the Masoretic Text*, 1963, and resulting in a thorough revision and

translation, leading to the one-volume edition which appeared as Tanakh*, 1985. Some of the prophetic books first appeared in a coffee-table version. Previous Jewish versions had tended to rely on Christian translations as the standard for style and diction.

The work began with a committee of seven: three biblical scholars, one representative from each of the Conservative, Reformed and Orthodox Jewish traditions, and the editor of the Jewish Publication Society Bible*, 1917. An additional committee to expedite the work was appointed to translate the Writings*, 1966. The method of translation was that one member would prepare a draft and send it to the others for comment. The Committee then met for a full day twice a month to discuss and decide, normally by consensus.

Uses contemporary language and avoids wooden, literal phrases and sentences. Rejects verbal equivalence* and replaces coordinate Hebrew sentences connected by 'and' with appropriate independent and subordinate clauses. Maintains a conservative attitude toward changes of the traditional text, but takes account in footnotes of variant readings* and the translators are fully aware of the latest linguistic researches and archaeological discoveries. Follows verse* and chapter* divisions of the Masoretic Text*. Footnotes explain why the translators arrived at the decisions they did. Particularly helpful for scholarly study, not least because of its insight into ancient Jewish customs, idioms and metaphors.

New King James Version, 1982–83. An American Bible, little more than a language update, aimed at readers who were no longer comfortable with the language of the seventeenth century but who really did not want to give up the KJV*, resulting in a curious combination of the old and the new. Ignoring developments in textual criticism*, it relates to the text of the AV* and its reverence for the text is more for the English text than for the ancient texts. Sometimes known as the Revised Authorised Version*. Published by Thomas Nelson Publishers, Nashville.

New Living Translation, 1996. A new dynamic equivalence* translation from the ancient languages, in the tradition of The Living Bible* but with more emphasis on translation than paraphrase*, undertaken by 90 scholars, conservative, evangelical and Protestant, a few British and Australian but mostly North American.

Control was in the hands of the Bible Translation Committee which appointed three scholars to each book of the Bible who jointly produced a first draft which was first revised and then reviewed by the Bible Translation Committee before final approval.

The remit was to revise and update The Living Bible* by reference to the ancient texts and to fashion a new translation that would stand on its own. For the OT they used the Masoretic Text* as in *Biblia hebraica* stuttgartensia* (1977) and for the NT the (UBS) Greek New Testament* and Nestle-Aland*.

Makes significant changes from The Living Bible and aims at a higher reading level than either the New Century Version* or the Contemporary English Version*. Modernizes time, weights and measures but (somewhat confusingly) translates currency according to weight in precious metals. Metaphors are 'explained' or 'elaborated'.

Published by Tyndale House Press, USA, who claim that it is 'easy to understand' and 'relevant to today' and whose commitment may be judged by the fact that the initial print run was 950,000 and the promotion budget, with promotion on the WWW, was 2.5 million dollars.

New Revised Standard Version, 1990. A thorough revision of the RSV*, by a committee of translators, ecumenical and international (though mainly American), who were able to benefit from the gains of scholarship over the previous 50 years, as well as to take account of inclusive language and other changes in the English language between the 1950s and the 1990s, without sacrificing fidelity to the ancient texts and reverence for the linguistic qualities of the AV*. The guiding principle was 'as literal as possible, as free as necessary'. Published by Oxford and Cambridge University Presses, Collins and Mowbrays. (See Changes from RSV to NRSV, below)

New Scofield Reference Bible, 1967. A new edition of the Scofield Reference Bible, 1909 (revised, 1917), the work of a committee of nine with E. Schuyler English* as chairman. The text is AV*, with changes to avoid obsolete, archaic or indelicate words or expressions, or

---

Changes from the RSV to the NRSV

'I will take no bull from your house' becomes 'I will not take a bull from your house' (Ps. 50.9).

'I was stoned' becomes 'I received a stoning' (2 Cor. 11.25).

words which have changed their meaning (mostly identified by a vertical bar on either side), plus a concordance and indexes to subject chain references and annotations. Like the earlier versions it retains Scofield's views on plenary inspiration, inerrancy and dispensationalism.

New Testament. The earliest written documents of the NT are the letters of Paul, c. 50–62, almost all the rest being written by the middle of the second century. Mss. then appear to have come together to form groups or collections, possibly with a collection of the writings of Paul by the end of the first century and a collection of the four gospels no more than 50 years later. By the end of the second century they were translated into Latin* and Syriac*, and textual criticism* shows how they circulated from the fifth century in various text types: Western*, Egyptian, Caesarean* and Syrian*.

The title 'New Testament' first appears in the writings of Irenaeus*, Tertullian* and Origen* towards the end of the second century, sometimes as 'new covenant' to distinguish the 'old covenant' inaugurated with Israel from the 'new covenant' inaugurated in Jesus, but was not regularly employed until the fourth century. The word 'testament' then appears as a Latin translation of the Greek for 'covenant'.

New Testament: A New Translation in Plain English, 1952. More popularly called The Plain English New Testament*.

New Testament: A Translation in the Language of the People, 1937. A popular dynamic equivalence* translation by Charles B. Williams, a biblical scholar at Union University, Jackson, Tennessee, and first published in America by Bruce Humphries, Boston, with a revised edition in 1949 by the Moody Bible Insti-

tute, Chicago. An attempt to translate the NT into the practical everyday words of 'the cobbler and the cab-driver', paying attention more to the thoughts than to the actual words, and in a flowing paragraph style with verse numbers barely visible. His other concern, however, to keep as close as possible to the original Greek, sometimes led to undue emphasis on the exact shade of meaning of the Greek tenses (particularly the differences between the present and aorist tenses in imperative and infinitive moods) and made his work rather heavy, hardly the language of the people, and (in the view of some scholars) at times actually misleading.

New Testament according to the Eastern Text, 1940. More popularly known as Lamsa's Translation*.

New Testament: An American Translation, 1923. A dynamic equivalence* translation by Goodspeed*, based on a Westcott* and Hort* text, which became part of The Complete Bible: An American Translation, 1939*. An attempt to translate the NT into 'the simple, straightforward English of everyday expression' by a translator who thought that the language of the AV* put people off reading a whole book at a sitting which he believed was how they should be read. Sometimes described as the American counterpart to Moffatt*.

New Testament and Psalms: An Inclusive Version, 1995. A revision of the NRSV*, retaining verbal equivalence* with considerable freedom, and making the language more gender-inclusive. Sometimes called the 'PC Bible' because of its emphasis on political correctness. So gender-inclusive language leads to the idea of God as 'Father–Mother', concern for the victims of race and physical disability gives us 'enslaved people' (for 'slaves'), 'blind people' (for 'the blind') and 'people with leprosy' (for 'lepers'), and God's 'right hand' becomes his 'nearness' or 'power' to avoid the social or political notions of right and left. For these reasons it has sometimes been criticized for failing to present a faithful translation reflecting the conditions of the day on the grounds that the ancient texts portrayed the world of the Bible as it was and not as some people today would like to present it. Published by Oxford University Press, New York.

New Testament in Greek and English...corrected from the Authority of the most Authentic Manuscripts, 1729. A free rendering of the NT by Daniel Mace*, based on the work of John Mill*. Corrections of the Greek text reflect good scholarship despite some Greek typographical eccentricities, but the English was too close to the colloquial style of the day to be of lasting value.

New Testament in Modern English, 1958. One-volume edition of the NT translations by J.B. Phillips*, revised in 1971 on the basis of the (UBS) Greek New Testament* with every Greek word re-evaluated and obsolete colloquialisms from the earlier editions removed or replaced. Published by Geoffrey Bles, London.

New Testament in Modern Speech, 1903. Popularly known as Weymouth's New Testament*.

New Testament Letters, prefaced and paraphrased, 1943. A translation produced in Australia by Bishop J.W.C. Wand*, written in the kind of language a bishop might use in writing a monthly letter for his diocesan magazine. Subsequently revised and published in England, 1946.

New Testament, translated from the Greek of J.J. Griesbach, 1840. A revision of the AV* in the light of Griesbach's* Greek text, by Samuel Sharpe*.

New Translation of The Holy Scriptures according to the Masoretic Text, 1963. See New Jewish Version.

New World Translations of the Scriptures, 1950–60. A translation, published by the Watchtower Bible and Tract Society, reflecting the particular biblical interpretation of the Jehovah's Witnesses, based on good Greek and Hebrew texts, which eschews paraphrase*, sets out to be 'as literal as possible' and which by 1971 had sold over 10 million copes in five languages. It faithfully renders the divine name as 'Jehovah' (rather than 'God' or 'Lord') but the English style leaves something to be desired and both translation and notes suffer at times from a concern to maintain the teachings of the Jehovah's Witnesses, particularly in the NT.

New York Bible Society. See International Bible Society.

Newcome, William (1729–1800). Archbishop of Armagh who pleaded that a revision of the AV* be authorized and produced *An Historical View of the English Bible Translations*, 1792, a harmony of the gospels in Greek, 1776, and in English,1800, a revision of the Minor Prophets,1785, and of Ezekiel,1788. His NT, based on Griesbach's* critical edition* of the Greek text, was printed in 1796 and published in 1800 under the title, *An Attempt towards revising our English Translation of the Greek Scriptures, or the New Covenant of Jesus Christ: and towards illustrating the sense by philological and explanatory notes*, with the English text in paragraphs, verse numbers in the margin and quotation marks for direct speech. Sometimes known incorrectly as the Unitarian Version*.

Cultural Differences

One of the problems of translation is illustrated by a visit to Africa in 1948 by Eugene Nida*.

One African language, Shilluk, had a very definite way of talking about forgiveness. When a case was settled and the accused declared innocent, the judge would spit on the ground. That meant that the case would never come into court again. One way to translate God's forgiveness into that language therefore was to say that God spits on the ground.

Newman, Barclay Moon, Jr (1931–). One of the translators of the Good News Bible* and originator of the Contemporary English Version*.

nomina sacra. A system of contractions* used by Christian scribes for certain sacred words.

Nicholas of Hereford (d. 1420). Canon of the Abbey of St Mary of the Meadows, Leicester. A Lollard and Fellow of Queens College, Oxford, who assisted and befriended John Wycliffe* in Bible translation. Thought to be the translator of the 1380 version of Wycliffe's Bible* up to the point where there is a break in the translation, because the Bodleian Library, Oxford*, has a ms., written under Hereford's direction, broken off abruptly at Bar. 3.20 in the middle of a sentence, and another ms. (copied from it and also at Oxford) ends at the same place, adding a note assigning it to Hereford. This may mark the point in 1382 when he was summoned to London to answer for his opinions, as a result of which he was excommunicated. He set out for Rome to plead his case but was ordered by the Pope to be imprisoned for life. He escaped and returned to England in 1391, was imprisoned, recanted, and was made Chancellor of Hereford Cath-

edral. From 1417 he lived in Coventry as a Carthusian monk.

Nida, Eugene Albert (1914–). An American biblical scholar, who majored in Greek combined with linguistics at the University of Michigan, where he received a doctorate, 1943, while working with the Wycliffe Bible Translators*. As a student of cultural anthropology he recognized the importance of local culture and these skills led him and enabled him to design ways of improving Bible translation. (See Cultural Differences, above.)

He drew up an eight-point plan for translation, which included growing cooperation between the Bible Societies*, Roman Catholic and Orthodox churches, text projects in Hebrew and Greek (aimed particularly for translators), popular translations, helps for translators and readers, and a programme of translation consultants to help in projects around the world, and actually started *The Bible Translator*, 1950, to explore some of the problems and solutions to translation problems.

For many years secretary for translation work in the American Bible Society* and the United Bible Societies*, UBS Translation Research Co-ordinator, 1971–80, and originator of the idea of dynamic equivalence*, first put to good effect in Today's English Version*, 1976.

Norlie, Olaf Morgan (1876–1962). Translator of the Simplified New Testament*, 1961. Minister of a Norwegian Lutheran congregation in the USA, editor of the Augsburg Publishing House and founder of the Norlie Reference Library.

Norton, Andrews (1786–1853). A Unitarian, Harvard professor and outstanding American biblical scholar whose *Translation of the Gospels, with Notes** was published in two volumes in 1855.

O

Ogden, Charles Kay (1889–1957). An English linguistic reformer who studied classics at Cambridge, where he became founder and editor of the *Cambridge Magazine*, 1912–22, founder of the Orthological Insitute,1917, and the originator of Basic English, thus facilitating the Bible in Basic English[*], 1949.

Old Cairo, Egypt. Home of the only complete Coptic[*] translation of the *Gospel of Thomas*[*] found at Nag Hammadi[*].

Old Latin. A late-second-century translation, direct from the LXX[*], which first appeared in the Roman Province of North Africa, associated with Tertullian[*], and of which only fragments remain. Called 'Old' to distinguish it from Jerome[*]. Sometimes known as the African version it was circulating in Carthage c. 250 CE. As it spread it underwent various adaptations. Valuable as a guide to the content of the LXX at a very early date, but (like the Coptic[*]) with a richer and more varied text than the Greek tradition.

A European version, in the vernacular, appeared in Italy, Gaul and Spain towards the end of the fourth century and versions and codices multiplied to the point of textual confusion, which was what led Jerome to make a new translation.

More valuable in the NT than in the OT because the NT translation was made from the original Greek whereas the OT was translated from the LXX[*], but no single ms. contains the entire NT in the Old Latin Version, there is no single translator of the 27 books and the result is not uniform. One probability is that the earliest translations were oral to accompany the reading of the LXX (OT) and the Greek (NT), leading to many translations in many places. The date is uncertain but NT mss. run from the fourth to the thirteenth centuries, reflect a Western[*] Greek text, marked by literalism and a popular speech and style.

Early translations were interlinear and the best copies fragmentary and palimpsest[*]. Mss. are listed according to their contents, usually designated by a lower case italic letter, following a system adopted by Lachmann[*].

Old Syriac. The language of Mesopotamia and Syria, north-east and north of Palestine, similar to the Aramaic[*] commonly spoken in Palestine in the days of Jesus, and sometimes known as Eastern Aramaic.

The origins of the Old Syriac OT are unclear but go back to the second century CE, were made from a targum[*] and may well have been the work of Jewish Christians in the first century. The text was revised in the ninth century, continued in circulation and was later used for the Syro-Palestinian version.

The Old Syriac NT is derived from Tatian's Diatessaron*, providing a life of Jesus with all the details to be found in the four gospels, a work of literary quality, in a Western* text, and showing a good knowledge of the topography and customs of Palestine.

Of the many translations in the early years of Christianity the Peshitta* became the standard and held the field until the middle of the nineteenth century when a number of other Syriac mss. came to light providing insight into two Syriac traditions, the Curetonian and the Sinaitic. Both relate to the same version and both are of great antiquity but they represent two independent Syriac textual traditions.

The Curetonian consists of 80 leaves (out of a total of 188) of a fifth-century ms. found near Cairo* in 1842 and passed to the British Museum where William Cureton*, Assistant Keeper of Ancient Manuscripts, recognized a Syriac version of the gospels in a text completely different from anything previously known, edited it and made claims (subsequently substantiated) for a dating earlier than the Peshitta*.

The Sinaitic is a palimpsest* containing about three-quarters of the four gospels (142 leaves out of a total of 166) and was found in 1892 by two Scottish travellers, Agnes Smith Lewes* and Margaret Dunlop Gibson*, on a visit to St Catharine's Monastery*, Mount Sinai. Thought to be the same or a little earlier than the Curetonian and certainly earlier than the Peshitta. Possibly one of the earliest versions of the NT.

Because the Syriac versions are in a Semitic language and therefore closer than the other versions to the Hebrew and Aramaic they incorporate different textual and exegetical traditions, both Jewish and Christian.

Old Testament. A written version of OT texts as we know them dates from around the tenth century CE and came together as the Hebrew Bible* in three stages. First the Pentateuch*, Law, or Torah*. Second, the Prophets*. Third, the Writings*. The sacred text also went through three distinct stages of development. First, a consonantal text, developed in pre-Christian times and in common usage by the second century CE. Second, the addition of vowel points by the Masoretes*, c. 500–950. Third, the addition of diacritical marks, possibly to ensure correct reading in the synagogue but at the same time contributing to a fixed text prior to the invention of printing in the fifteenth century.

The title 'Old Testament' first appeared in Christian circles towards the end of the second century to parallel the emerging 'New Testament' in the writings of Irenaeus*, Tertullian* and Origen*, the word 'covenant' often being used to distinguish the books of the 'old covenant' which God made with Israel from those of the 'new covenant' inaugurated in Jesus. Eusebius*, describing the canon of Josephus*, refers to the Old Testament and later to the New Testament. A little later the Greek word for 'covenant' was translated into the Latin as *testamentum* to give the Old and New Testaments, but the words were not regularly used until the fourth century. This description has Christian implications and has led to terms like 'Hebrew Bible' becoming customary usage outside Christian circles.

Old Testament: An American Translation, 1927. A translation, somewhat similar to Goodspeed's New Testament: An American Translation*,1923, prepared by T.J. Meek*, Leroy Waterman, A.R. Gordon and J.M. Powis Smith*, though with four translators there are inevitably more variations in style and perhaps less enthusiasm for the language of the marketplace than are to be found in the NT. Subsequently united with Goodspeed to form The Complete Bible: An American Translation*, 1931.

Omissions. Single letters, words, phrases or even verses are occasionally missing from some mss. There are many possible causes of which haplography*, unclear copy or lapses on the part of the scribe are among the most common. (See Omissions, below.)

Onkelos Targum. The best known of the targumim* and the one with the greatest authority. A literal rendering of the complete text of the Pentateuch*, following the plain sense of scripture with many exegetical elements, especially in the poetic passages. Scholars are divided as to whether it dates from the first, third or fifth centuries, and as to whether it is of Palestinian or Babylonian origin, but if its origins are Palestinian the definitive version was Babylonian and if the date is late it was preceded by a written or oral

formulation. Thought by some to be the work of Aquila*.

Oral Tradition. The view that the current OT text had its origin in storytelling and a long oral tradition, possibly not being committed to writing until the exile, a view popular a few generations ago particularly among Scandinavian scholars, is now seriously questioned. Contemporary scholarship holds to the view that though stories may have been passed on by word of mouth anything recognizable as 'early biblical text' was certainly written, and probably at a later date than used to be thought.

In the case of the New Testament* oral tradition, insofar as it existed at all, is likely to have been shorter and confined to the gospels. Some evidence suggests that this is the teaching method of Jesus and that the stories of Jesus circulated orally among his followers and in the various churches, not always in precisely the same form and often with differing emphases and additions, for at

---

Omissions

Gen. 4.8. 'Let us go into the field' (found in the older versions) appears to be a random omission from the MT.

1 Sam. 2.20. Are we to read יִשֵׁם (yšm) ('will give') or יִשְׁלֵם (yšlm) ('will repay'), as in the Greek, and was the ל (l) omitted or inserted, and why?

2 Sam. 22.41 has the word תתה (tth) which is meaningless. Assume an initial (n) has been omitted so as to give נתתה (ntth) and you have 'thou hast given' which not only makes good sense but lines up with the parallel passage in Ps. 18.40.

Some mss. used abbreviations for plurals and proper names.

1 Sam. 20.38 has החצי (hḥsy) ('arrow'), where it so obviously should read החצים (hḥsym) ('arrows'), the final 'm' to make the Hebrew plural having been omitted.

least 20 to 30 years before being committed to writing.

Origen (c. 185–253). Head of the Catechetical School in Alexandria* in 203 and one of the outstanding scholars of the early church. Collated mss. of biblical texts, both Greek and Hebrew, to produce Origen's Hexaplar*, accepted the LXX* form for the OT and the NT in much the same form as we have it, seems to know only four gospels and was the first to make explicit reference to 2 Peter though (like 2 and 3 John) he regarded it as of doubtful authenticity. In addition to 1 Peter, 1 John and Revelation, he seems to have recognized and accepted 14 of Paul's letters (including Hebrews though he did not believe Paul wrote it) and indeed often quotes from him which might suggest that by the middle of the third century there was an increasing awareness of a Pauline Corpus*. In common with Eusebius* he had James and 1, 2 and 3 John on his 'disputed' list.

Origen's Hexaplar. One of the great achievements of early Christian scholarship, completed c. 240 CE at Caesarea*. A scholarly edition of the OT, prepared by Origen*, in six parallel columns, giving the Hebrew, the same text in Greek letters, a Greek translation by Aquila* (following the Hebrew very closely), a Greek translation by Symmachus*, the Old Greek (with a text corresponding to the LXX*) and a Greek translation by Theodotion*. The fifth (sometimes called 'Origen's Septuagint') is the most important, though it is not clear whether it is the LXX as he knew it or the LXX as he had revised it. The Tetrapla, consisting of the text minus the two Hebrew columns, is also attributed to Origen.

Orlinsky, Harry Meyer (1908–92). Born in Canada. Jewish biblical scholar and philologist. Professor of the Bible at the Hebrew Union College Jewish Institute of Religion, New York City, from 1943, and Chairman of the Society for Biblical Literature and subsequently President. The only Jewish consultant on the translation of the RSV* (OT). Co-translator of the five-volume English translation of Rashi's commentary on the Pentateuch, 1949–50, and Editor-in-Chief of the New Jewish Version*, 1962–81.

Ormulum. A poetical version of the gospels and Acts, with commentary, done by an Augustinian monk, Orm (or Ormin), c. 1215. One copy, possibly the original, survives in the Bodleian Library, Oxford*.

Ostraca. Broken pieces of pottery and ideal writing materials* in the earlier part of the first millennium. The Hebrews found pottery useful for scribal practice, notes, receipts, brief letters and other inscriptions. Their existence points to a widespread knowledge of writing in seventh-century BCE Judah. Some, from Samaria (mainly wine receipts), are of value because of what they teach us about the Hebrew language in the eighth century BCE, and others, from Lachish*, because they demonstrate the habit of writing as a normal and formal medium of communication. Other important finds are at Ezion-Geber, Masada, Elephantine* and Egypt in general.

Oxford, England. Home of Thomas Bensley, printer of the Murderer's Bible*, and location for the Bodleian Library, founded by the son of John Bodley*, whose archives contain many ancient Bible texts and versions, including Codex Laudianus*, some mss. from the Cairo Geniza*, a fragment of the Oxyrhynchus* Papyri, the Rushworth Gospels*, Ormulum*, one copy of the West Saxon Gospels* and the earlier Wycliffe Bible*.

Oxyrhynchus, Egypt. An ancient Egyptian city, 120 miles north of Cairo* now known as El-Bahnasa, excavated by Grenfell* and Hunt*, 1897–1907, where they discovered the largest ever collection of papyrus* texts, the Oxyrhynchus papyri*.

Oxyrhynchus Papyri. Twenty-eight papyrus* mss., all fragments, rarely more than a couple of leaves, dating from the third century, found at Oxyrhynchus*, beginning with excavations in 1897 by Grenfell* and Hunt*.

They chose Oxyrhynchus knowing that Christianity had taken a firm foothold there both before and after the Diocletian persecutions of 303 CE and believed that the citizens would have been wealthy enough to have libraries of texts, even if as a result of the persecutions some had been consigned to the rubbish heaps. They were right.

On the second day of the dig they unearthed the apocryphal 'Sayings of Jesus' ('Logia'), later identified as belonging to the *Gospel of Thomas**, and a papyrus fragment ($\mathfrak{P}^1$), written in Greek, containing verses from Matthew 1, at that time the earliest extant copy of any portion of the NT and at least a hundred years earlier than the Codex Vaticanus*. Another fragment, part of a codex* rather than a scroll*, contained on one sheet portions of the first and last chapters of John's Gospel.

In 1898 they published the first volume of Oxyrhynchus papyri and went on to make more discoveries over the next ten years, their work being continued by Italian archaeologists, 1910–13, 1927–34. Twenty-one mss. were published in 1922 and give a flavour of many verses from several NT books at an early date. Others appeared, published in 1941, 1957, 1968 and 1983. Many subsequently proved of limited value for NT study, but two stand out. One ($\mathfrak{P}^5$) contains Jn 1.23-31, 33-41; 20.11-17, 19-25. The other ($\mathfrak{P}^{13}$) contains Heb. 2.14–5.5; 10.8-22, 29–11.13, 28–12.17, written on the back of an epitome of Livy.

P

Packington, Augustine. A London merchant who bought up copies of Tyndale's Translation* from Tyndale* and sold them (with Tyndale's connivance) to Cuthbert Tunstall*, bishop of London, knowing he would burn them, but arguing that people would be outraged at the burning of the Bible, demand would be increased and the money raised could be used to meet it.

Palaeography. The study of ancient writings and inscriptions so as to date mss. by comparing the shape and stance of letters with external sources such as dated coins and other inscriptions. When applied to the DSS*, for example, these methods gave a date very similar to that arrived at by the Radio Carbon Dating* method.

Palimpsest. When writing paper was scarce or expensive, writers sometimes took a piece that had been used, rubbed off the writing as much as possible and then reused it by writing on it again at right angles to the original. The result is a palimpsest. Not suitable with papyrus* but increasingly practised with the arrival of vellum*. In some cases ultra-violet and infra-red photography has made it possible to rediscover the original writing. Codex Ephraemi* is a good example of a palimpsest ms. of the NT and the John Rylands Library, Manchester*, has a ms.

of 1 and 2 Peter where the original text was overwritten in places with prayers in Coptic*, though the earlier writing continued to be decipherable (just) and is now reproduced in some scholarly editions of these epistles. The Council of Trullo, 692, condemned the practice of using parchment from mss. of the scriptures for other purposes on pain of excommunication for one year, but the practice nevertheless continued and of the 250 uncial NT mss. 52 are palimpsests.

Palmer, Edward. An archdeacon and member of the NT panel of translators of the RV*, 1881, who subsequently produced a Greek text reflecting the translators' decisions, to which Souter* added a critical apparatus* to give what is commonly called a Souter text*.

Palmer, Edwin H. (1922–80). Born in Massachusetts and educated at Harvard, the Free University of Amsterdam and Westminster Theological Seminary, where he later taught Systematic Theology. A minister of the Christian Reformed Church, Executive Secretary of the New International Version*, 1968–80, and appointed General Editor of the NIV* Study Bible, 1979.

Panopolos, Egypt. Site for the discovery of a number of ancient papyrus mss., possibly including some of the Chester Beatty* and Bodmer* collections because of their similarity to texts known to have come from here.

Papias (c. 70–160). Bishop of Hierapolis in Asia Minor (c. 130) and the first to name a gospel ('Mark became Peter's interpreter and wrote accurately all that he remembered…'). He also refers to an Aramaic collection of the Sayings of Jesus, attributed to Matthew. But Papias still belongs to the age of oral tradition* and reflects the suspicion of many who still felt that 'the living voice of those that are still surviving' was preferable to written texts.

Papyrus. Writing material, made from the stems of the papyrus plant (or reed) that grew abundantly in the River Nile. The commonest writing material in the ancient world and the regular material for book production in the Greek world from about the fifth century BCE until the invention of paper in China and its spread throughout Syria and Egypt in the sixth to eighth centuries CE. Very cheap and readily available, a typical sheet would be 19 × 16.5 inches and 20 sheets would make a standard roll. Buried in dry sand or in cool desert caves papyrus mss. could remain intact for hundreds of years.

Writing* on papyrus tended to be in fairly small letters, sometimes joined together. Its use as a writing material is not specifically mentioned in the Bible but the scroll in Jeremiah 36 could be an early example. When Jews in Egypt in the third century BCE wanted a copy of their Scriptures in Greek it was probably written on papyrus; the first NT books were almost certainly written on it; and it continued to be used as writing material as late as the seventh century.

Papyrus fragments cover about 40 per cent of the NT text and provide some evidence that from an early date the NT writings were being collected together to form groups, such as the gospels, the gospels and Acts, and the letters of Paul, an obvious prelude to the formation of the canon*.

The first Greek papyrus to come to light was in 1778, but until almost the end of the nineteenth century only nine papyrus mss. of the NT were known. The period of discovery began c. 1894 with the Oxyrhynchus Papyri*, and today almost 100 have been catalogued though not all contribute to our understanding of the NT text. They are mostly fragmentary, tiny, and sometimes barely readable. Almost all come from Egypt, date from the second to the eighth centuries, with more than half coming from the third and fourth and so ante-dating previous Greek texts by up to 200 years.

Their impact was minimal to begin with but increased considerably with the discovery of the Chester Beatty* Papyri and the Bodmer* collection, which provide important ms. evidence of variant readings* in some biblical books, the results of which were embodied in critical editions* such as von Soden*, Souter* and Nestle-Aland*, and indicate a complex editorial process going back a long way. Recognizing their enormous value for textual criticism*, scholars evaluated, classified and published them, allocating to each the letter '𝔓' plus a number. The most important are $\mathfrak{P}^{45}$, $\mathfrak{P}^{46}$, $\mathfrak{P}^{47}$, $\mathfrak{P}^{52}$, $\mathfrak{P}^{66}$, $\mathfrak{P}^{72}$ and $\mathfrak{P}^{75}$.

In some instances they are also responsible for new translations of the texts into English, particularly in the ASV*, the RSV*, the NASB*, the NEB*, Today's English Version*, the JB*, the NIV* and the NRSV*, all of which benefited from them. (See Making and Using Papyrus, p. 132.)

Parablepsis. Lit. 'a looking by the side'. What happens when two words begin or end with similar syllables, two lines with

---

Making and Using Papyrus

The manufacture of papyrus* (or reed) which flourished to a height of 12–15 feet in the shallow waters of the Nile Delta was a major industry from as early as 3000 BCE into the early years of the Common Era, and was widely used for non-literary works including notes, bills, receipts and love letters.

The main stem, triangular in shape, was the thickness of a human wrist and could easily be cut into sections about a foot long, opened lengthwise and then further cut into thin strips. Several were then placed on a flat surface with the fibres all running in the same direction, followed by another layer on top with the fibres all running at right angles. Both layers were then pressed together, using water and glue, to form one fabric with a strength almost equal to that of a sheet of quality paper today. Once dried they were cut into smaller pieces 6–9 ins. wide and 12–18 ins. high and then fastened together to form long scrolls.

---

the same word or two paragraphs with the same phrase, and the scribe's eye, on returning to the ms. after copying, picks up the second rather than the first, thus accidentally omitting everything in-between and leading to haplography*, or picks up the first rather than the second, thus repeating it and leading to dittography*. Also known as homoioarcton* and homoioteleuton*.

Paragraphing. Before the Masoretes* divided the OT into chapters and verses, the Hebrew Bible was divided into paragraphs known as *parashiyyot* or *pisqa'ot*. Each new topic began on a fresh line and the end of the previous line had to be left blank after the last word of the previous unit.

Parallel Texts. Instances where there are two versions of the same story in the same book or in different books. Minor differences may be due to the same story being quoted from a different source, prior to being incorporated in the biblical text, or to changes which took place in later mss.

Paraphrase. A free translation in different words in order to convey the meaning more effectively. In biblical terms it may even alter the original cultural and literary setting, possibly even omitting or adding something in order to make the text more intelligible to the readers. Some translators argue that this is often necessary in order to convey the sense of the original to a different culture and so we have a translation which aims at dynamic equivalence* or 'sense for sense' rather than verbal equivalence* or 'word for word' representation, and a few maintain that this is what every meaningful and intelligent translation must be. A more precise definition retains 'paraphrase' for a modernization or updating of a translation, as against a translation which begins with the original, so that whereas the translation seeks to bridge the gap between the ancient text and the modern reader the paraphrase seeks to bridge the gap between the translated text and an even more modern reader.

Paraphrase and Commentary on the New Testament, 1703. An explanatory expansion of the AV* produced by Daniel Whitby*.

Paraphrase on the Epistles of St Paul, 1675. An anonymous production, subsequently edited by John Fell* and published under the names of the three original authors, Richard Allestry*, Obadiah Walker* and Abraham Woodhead* in 1708.

parashiyyot. See Paragraphing.

Parchment. See Vellum.

Paris, France. City where the Great Bible* was printed, possibly because France could supply better paper and more experienced workmen. But the Inquisition got busy and before the work was completed Coverdale* had to flee and the printer was arrested. Cromwell* then moved type, presses and workmen to London, where the printing was completed. Location of the Bibliothèque Nationale and home to a number of Bible texts and versions including Codex Claromontanus*, Codex Ephraemi* and an Ethiopic* version of the four gospels.

Paris Polyglot, 1629–45. Ten large volumes containing Hebrew, Greek, Latin, Syriac and Arabic (with a Latin translation) and the Samaritan Pentateuch* and targum*. Significant for its maps and plates. Followed the Antwerp Polyglot* rather closely and was superseded by the London Polyglot*.

Paris Psalter, 871–901. One of the oldest examples of biblical text in Old English, the other being the Vespasian Psalter*, consisting of 50 psalms in prose and the rest in verse.

Parker, Matthew (1504–75). Brought up as a gentleman and destined for Cambridge. Appointed Archbishop of Canterbury, 1559. Responsible for organizing and working with other biblical scholars on a revision of the Great Bible*, with their own marginal notes, to produce the Bishops' Bible*, unsuccessfully intended to become an official version to replace the popular Geneva Bible*.

Pau Bible, 1871. The French name for Darby's Translation*.

Pauline Corpus. Paul wrote a number of letters to the churches and some to individuals. Possibly, they were occasionally read in worship. Some scholars have suggested that one or two may even have been circular letters but little is known about their collection or canonicity. It is difficult to imagine a collection emerging without some significant individual or group but there is no evidence for any such collection in the first century and Luke seems to be unaware of any when compiling Acts. Similar uncertainty shrouds their canonicity except that by the Council of Carthage*, 397, 14 of them were attributed to Paul and accepted as part of the canon* along with the other books which make up the NT. For evidence of their growth in influence and importance and for the varied and somewhat chequered story which led to their recognition it is necessary to refer to the early church Fathers such as Clement of Rome*, Ignatius*, Polycarp*, Marcion*, Tatian*, Irenaeus*, Clement of Alexandria*, Tertullian*, Origen*, and documents like the Chester Beatty Papyri*, especially $\mathfrak{P}^{46}$, and the Muratorian Fragment*.

PC Bible. A pejorative name accorded by some to The New Testament and Psalms: An Inclusive Version*, 1995.

Pen. Originally a stylus of metal, ivory or bone for writing on waxed tablets. The reed pen, which arrived with papyrus and parchment, was a thick reed, sharpened to a point and with a slit in the middle, not unlike the traditional pen nib of today. The more versatile quill pen, suitable for vellum*, arrived about the fourth century CE.

Penguin Translations, 1952. Shortly after the Second World War Penguin Books planned a complete translation of the Bible and invited E.V. Rieu* to act as General Editor. When plans for the NEB* were announced the project was dropped but two translations already in hand were published separately, The Gospels, by Rieu himself and The Acts of the Apostles, by his son, C.H. Rieu*.

Pentateuch. The first of the three sections of the Hebrew Bible or OT, consisting of the first five books (Genesis, Exodus, Leviticus, Numbers and Deuteronomy), often known as the Law or Torah*, the other two being the Prophets* and the Writings*. For Jews, the most venerated section of the Bible.

Pergamon, Asia Minor. An ancient centre of learning in Asia Minor and the original source of vellum*.

Pericope. A short piece of text, such as a story or poem.

Peshitta. Lit. 'stretched-out', meaning 'simple' or 'clear', but often taken to mean 'simple', 'common' or 'current', similar to 'vulgate' in Latin. The name given to one of several translations of the Hebrew Bible into Old Syriac* to distinguish it from translations made from the

LXX*, and the accepted scriptures of the Syriac Church. In general use from the fifth century and still the authoritative biblical text of the Syriac churches (Syrian Orthodox, Church of the East, Maronite).

Its origins, probably during the first and second centuries CE and by translators who worked basically from the Hebrew with one eye on the LXX*, are shrouded in uncertainty, different books being translated by different translators, at different times, and in different places, and resulting in a version which varies from the literal to the paraphrase. Since it contains Christian elements some scholars have seen its origin with the early Christians in the first or second century, but a more cautious view leaves its Jewish or Christian origins an open question. It is of some critical value because it has affinities with the text of Isaiah in the DSS*.

Mss. fall into two categories, Eastern and Western, reflecting the division that split the Syrian Church in the sixth century. The oldest mss. go back to the fifth century CE though only five complete ones go back before the seventh century, the most familiar text being that found in the Paris Polyglot*.

Phillips, John Bertram (1906–82). Bible translator, writer and broadcaster who published an English translation of the New Testament epistles as *Letters to Young Churches*, 1947, with an introduction by C.S. Lewis*, arising partly from a desire to relieve the monotony of civilian duties during the Second World War and partly because he discovered that young people in his church youth club in southeast London simply did not understand 'Bible language'. His commitment to make truth comprehensible combined with his inner desire to do some translation led him to put Paul into language they could understand and he was rewarded beyond all expectation as they came to see for the first time not only that Paul made sense but also that what he said was 'extremely relevant to life as they knew it'. One of the first modern translators to provide brief introductory notes with cross-headings at the beginning of each letter or section, with text in paragraphs rather than verses and verse numbers only at the beginning of each section.

Phillips had five basic principles: the language must be as commonly spoken, the translation may expand to preserve the original meaning, the result should read like letters rather than theological treatises, the text should flow and the overall value should lie in its ease-of-reading. The result was more paraphrase* than translation.

He had a fourfold method. First, to rid his mind of the language of the AV*. Second, to make a rough but accurate translation of the Greek without reference to any other translations. Third, to ignore the Greek and put his rough translation into modern English. Fourth, to compare the re-written text with the Greek. For the 1958 edition he consulted no other translations, but for the revision in 1972 he had the benefit of criticisms of the 1958 edition, he did consult other translations and he also used a better Greek text, the (UBS) Greek New Testament*, 1966.

Like all dynamic translators he offers some memorable phrases but also occasionally some infelicitous expressions. 'Ring of authority' (Mt. 7.29) and 'wells without a drop of water in them' (2 Pet. 2.17) illustrate the former, 'you little-faiths' (Mt. 8.26) and 'serried ranks of witnesses' (Heb. 12.1) the latter.

Subsequently he produced *The Gospels*, 1952, *The Young Church in Action* (Acts), 1955, *The Book of Revelation*, 1957, all later revised and combined to give one volume, The New Testament in Modern English*, 1958, with a revision in 1972, followed by *The Four Prophets* (Amos, Hosea, Isaiah 1–35 and Micah), 1963. All the books have a contemporary look. Published by Geoffrey Bles, London.

pisqa'ot. See Paragraphing.

Pius XII (1876–1958). Pope, 1939–58, who changed the approach to Bible translation and biblical scholarship in the Catholic Church by his encyclical on Scripture Studies, *Divino afflante Spiritu*, in which he encouraged Roman Catholic biblical scholars to turn their attention to the ancient languages.

Plain English New Testament, 1952. An independent translation by Charles Kingsley Williams, Vice-President of Wesley College, Madras, and Vice-Principal of Achimoto College, Ghana, with the title, *The New Testament: A New Translation in Plain English*, published by SPCK, London, possibly with a view to helping readers whose native language was not English but who needed the Bible in English to share in common culture. Translated from the Greek text underlying the RV*. 'Plain English' is based on 1500 'fundamental and common words that make up ordinary English speech' as listed in *Interim Report on Vocabulary Selection* (London: P.S. King, 1936), to which Williams added a further 200 words which he explained in a glossary. He also used short sentences and changed or omitted conjunctions in accordance with modern English usage. Printed with paragraphs but retaining the verse numbers for reference and carefully laid out to encourage reading.

Polycarp (c. 69–155 CE). Bishop of Smyrna. Shows some awareness of Paul's writings in that he quotes Paul when writing to the Philippians and seems to be aware of Romans, Galatians, Philemon, Ephesians, Colossians (possibly) and 1 and 2 Timothy, which is thought by some to suggest an awareness at least of the beginnings of a Pauline Corpus*. He also quotes 1 Peter several times when writing to the Philippians and is the first to show acquaintance with 1 John.

Polychrome Bible, 1893. Popular name given to *The Sacred Books of the Old and New Testaments*, edited by Paul Haupt*, a Baltimore editor. A somewhat ambitious project, backed by British, German and American scholars, which began in 1893 but was never completed. Two volumes were to be devoted to each book of the OT, one containing a revised Hebrew text and the other a new English translation with commentary, but not all the volumes appeared and the scholars never got to the NT.

Polyglot Bibles. A Bible issued in several languages, mostly Hebrew* (Masoretic Text* and Samaritan Pentateuch*), Greek*, Aramaic*, Syriac*, Latin* and Arabic*, often with Latin versions of the non-Latin texts, sometimes with grammars and lexicons, and usually in parallel columns. Several appeared in the sixteenth and seventeenth centuries, the first being the Complutensian Polyglot* and the others the Antwerp*, the Paris* and London*. Of special value to scholars because of the amount of material they contain.

Porter, John (d. c. 1550). A Protestant, imprisoned in 1540 for reading the newly installed Bibles aloud in a London cathedral and so disrupting the services. Released fairly soon but then re-arrested for heresy in 1542 and died for his belief that the Bible contained pure doctrine and the priests were misrepresenting it.

Pratensis, Felix (d. 1539). A Christian, the converted son of a rabbi, who published a Hebrew OT at the famous press

of Daniel Bomberg* in Venice, 1516–17, followed by a second edition, in four volumes, edited by Jacob ben Chayyim, 1524–25, which was destined to become the standard Hebrew scriptures until 1937, when Kahle* went to an earlier text in the third edition of Kittel's *Biblia hebraica*. His chapter divisions* and the division of Samuel, Kings and Chronicles into two books have been followed in English Bibles ever since.

Pre-Samaritan Texts. Texts from the second century BCE, similar to the DSS*, and underlying the Samaritan Pentateuch*. Thanks to the DSS some scholars have thought it possible to distinguish two layers: the Pre-Samaritan, which lacks the ideology and suggests more freedom of copying, and the Samaritan, which is quite thin and can fairly easily be removed but which contains a number of ideological features and reflects an established, more fixed and rigid position.

Price, Thomas (b. c. 1700–72). A Cambridge scholar who played an important role as editor in the 1762 edition of the AV*.

Primitive New Testament, 1745. The work of William Whiston*, following the AV* except at those points where Whiston thought it ought to be brought into line with more recent discoveries such as the Western* text.

Prindele, William. A retired American attorney and publisher of The Twenty-first Century King James Version*, 1994, and The Third Millennium Bible*.

Printing. First achieved in Europe by John Gutenberg* of Mainz*, 1454. The first printed Bible was the Latin Vulgate* (c. 1454), followed by the Psalter in Hebrew (1477) and the Pentateuch* in

Hebrew (1482) in Bologna*, the Prophets* in Hebrew (1485–86) in Soncino*, and the Writings* (1486–87) in Naples. The first Hebrew OT, complete with vowels and accents but without comments, was printed at Soncino in 1488 and the first Greek NT at Basel* in 1516, the delay being partly due to the difficulty of achieving satisfactory fonts of Greek type. Over 100 editions of the Latin Bible appeared in various printing houses, 1450–1500.

Prophets, The. The second of the three main sections of the Hebrew Bible*, the other two being the Torah* and the Writings* and the second major section of the Hebrew Bible to be regarded as authoritative and inspired, possibly c. 250–150 BCE. In two parts:

> *The Former Prophets.* Joshua, Judges, 1 and 2 Samuel and 1 and 2 Kings, sometimes referred to as the Historical Books, though that would normally also include 1 and 2 Chronicles, Ezra and Nehemiah.
> *The Latter Prophets.* Isaiah, Jeremiah, Ezekiel and the Twelve (often called 'the Minor Prophets', which exist as one scroll in Hebrew).

Proto-Masoretic Text. The accepted Hebrew text in Judaism from the second century CE, on which most of the ancient translations (Vulgate*, Aquila*, Symmachus*, Peshitta* Targum* and Theodotion*) were based, and the starting text for the work of the Masoretes*.

Pseudepigrapha. (Lit 'false writings'). A collection of some 65 documents, written sometime between 250 BCE–200 CE by Jews and Christians, mostly under a pseudonym, often built round the name of an Old Testament character and regularly associated with the Scriptures

in certain places but which never found their way into the Hebrew, Latin or Greek canons. Variously described as intertestamental, deutero-canonical or non-canonical and to be distinguished from the Apocrypha* which consists of books in the Vulgate* and LXX* but not in the Hebrew. They are of four kinds:

> *legendary*, such as *Jubilees* and the *Testament of the Twelve Patriarchs*.
> *apocalyptic*, such as *Enoch*.
> *poetical*, such as the *Psalms of Solomon*.
> *didactic*, such as the *Magical Book of Moses*.

Pseudepigrapha is the name used by Protestant Christians. The Roman Catholic Church calls them 'Apocrypha'*, being more closely related to the Vulgate* and the LXX* and having already included what the Protestants call 'Apocrypha'* in their canon. (See Some Examples of Pseudepigrapha, p. 138.)

puncta extraordinaria. Dots placed by the Masoretes* over letters in ancient Hebrew mss. where the rabbis had doubts about their correctness.

Purvey, John (1353–1428). Educated at Oxford and worked as secretary to John Wycliffe* at Lutterworth*. Thought to be the person responsible for translating the latter part of the earlier version of Wycliffe's Bible*. Responsible for the later version, and for a thorough revision of the earlier one, thus producing a truly idiomatic translation, 1388–95. Suffered imprisonment for his translation activities.

Pyle, Thomas (1674–1765). One of a number of scholars who produced a paraphrase*, 1717–35, with bracketed explanatory material inserted into the text of the AV*.

Some Examples of Pseudepigrapha

The Apocalypse of Abraham

The Apocalypse of Baruch

The Apocalypse of Ezra (2 Esdras)

The Ascension of Isaiah

The Assumption of Moses

The Book of Jubilees

The Enoch Literature

The Life of Adam and Eve

The Lives of the Prophets

The Psalms of Solomon

The Sybilline Oracles

The Testament of Solomon

The Testament of the Twelve Patriarchs

3 and 4 Maccabees

Q

Q. The first letter of the German *Quelle*, ('source'), used in source criticism* to refer to material common to Matthew and Luke but not found in Mark, and therefore thought to come from 'an unknown source'.

Qere. See *Kethib*.

Qift, Egypt. The modern name for the ancient city of Coptos*.

Quentel, Peter. A printer in Cologne* who was intending to print Tyndale's Translation* in 1526 when some of Tyndale's enemies decided to stop the translation and Tyndale had to flee to Worms* where the first edition appeared.

Qumran, Israel. Site, 11 miles south of Jericho, on the shores of the Dead Sea, where the DSS* were found, in 1947. Occupied from the eighth century BCE to 135 CE, but principally 150 BCE–68 CE.

R

Rabbinic Bibles. The successors to the Polyglots*, sometimes known as 'extended Bible texts' because they included commentaries and translations. The first two were printed by Daniel Bomberg* in Venice, one edited by Felix Pratensis* (1516–17), the first to divide Samuel, Kings and Chronicles each into two books, and to divide Ezra into Ezra and Nehemiah, and the other by Jacob ben Chayyim (1524–25), the first printed edition to have the *Qere** printed in the margin and which became for a long time the Textus Receptus* or standard version of the Hebrew Bible*. It also contained several targumim*, including Onkelos*.

Rabbula (d. 435). Bishop and head of the theological school of Edessa who collaborated with others in the fifth century to produce the NT portion of the Peshitta* to replace the widely used Tatian's Diatessaron*.

Radio Carbon Dating. A technique, developed in Chicago, in 1946, by Willard F. Libby*, for dating the age of an object by examining the radio activity of minute segments of material. Applied to ancient mss. found at Qumran*, the technique enabled scientists to give a dating for some of the DSS* somewhere between 168 BCE and 68 CE.

Rahlfs, A. A distinguished German Septuagint* scholar who in 1914 edited a list of all the known mss. of the LXX* and edited the Göttingen Septuagint*, 1931 (with later editions); a critical edition* based on Codex Alexandrinus*, Codex Sinaiticus*, Codex Vaticanus* and other readings, which to some extent replaced the earlier edition by Swete*. Subsequently edited a two-volume handbook edition in Stuttgart, 1935.

Ras Shamra Tablets. A library of ancient documents on clay tablets, dating from c. 1500 BCE, found in 1929 at Ras Shamra on the north-west coast of Syria, the site of the ancient Phoenician city of Ugarit*, containing early Canaanite mythology and some names also found in the OT, in cuneiform* writing with only 30 signs and thus forming an alphabet, in a language closely akin to Hebrew*. Important for what they tell us about ancient Canaanite religion and the origins of the Hebrew language.

Received Text. See Textus Receptus.

Recension. Sometimes used simply to describe a text or ms., but more often used for a particular edition of an earlier text and the result of some editorial activity.

Prior to the discovery of the DSS* in 1947, the Masoretic Text*, the Samaritan Pentateuch* and the LXX* were regarded as the three main recensions for the

Torah*, and the Masoretic Text and the LXX for the Prophets* and the Writings*; at this time it was also common to refer to the Masoretic Text in its Babylonian, Samaritan and LXX (Egyptian) forms. Since 1947 we know that these three recensions were only three of very many, some of which, like the Leviticus Scroll*, seem to represent an independent tradition; we also now know that they too had reached their present state after many years of editing and that, although the Masoretic Text predominates, all three recensions which underlie the Hebrew Bible are reflected in the DSS*.

According to Jerome* at the end of the fourth century there were three main recensions (or kinds of Bible mss.) in circulation: those resulting from the recensions of Hesychius*, mainly in Egypt, those from the recensions of Lucian* in Syria and Constantinople*, and those in Palestine, the work of Pamphilus, a disciple of Origen*.

Redaction Criticism. A method of textual criticism* which concentrates on identifying the hand of the compiler or editor with a view to understanding his own particular beliefs or interests, the background against which he worked, the culture to which he belonged, and anything else that might have led him to make changes or adjustments in the text or to arrange it in a particular way.

Revised Authorized Version, 1982. A revision of AV*, 1611, which concentrates on modernizing the language but pays no attention to the many texts and resources made available since 1611. Best known in America, where it first appeared and is often referred to as the NKJV*.

Revised English Bible, 1989. A revision of the NEB* maintaining the principle of dynamic equivalence*. Like its predecessor it was planned and supervised by senior representatives of all the major British churches, this time with full participation by the Roman Catholic Church, the Moravian Church and the Salvation Army. Building on the accuracy and scholarship of the NEB, it set out to serve a wider readership and to meet the needs of liturgical use, private reading and students. It also departed from the eclectic text of the NEB in favour of the 1979 Nestle-Aland* text. Whilst trying to preserve language of dignity and beauty, it made a number of significant changes, especially inclusive language (though somewhat sporadic and quite limited), addressing God as 'you' and avoiding technical, flowery and traditionally religious expressions. Printed in more traditional style with two columns and published by the University Presses of Oxford and Cambridge.

Revised Standard Version, 1946 (NT), 1952 (OT), 1957 (complete). A thorough revision of the ASV*, authorized in the mid-1930s by 40 major Christian denominations in Canada and the USA, who had assumed copyright and ownership of the ASV through the International Council of Religious Education and the National Council of Churches, USA, begun in 1937 and published in Britain by Thomas Nelson and Sons, Edinburgh. The object was to produce a more flexible verbal equivalence* translation, not always translating Hebrew and Greek words by the same English word as in the RV* and the ASV*. Based on the best modern scholarship, in English, suitable for private and public use, and preserving something of the quality of Tyndale's* work and the AV*.

The Revision Committee consisted of 15 members, appointed as early as 1928 by Luther A. Weigle* of Yale University and chairman of the ASV, to revise the ASV. The delay was due to the depression of the 1930s and the number was later increased to 22, with Weigle as chairman. James Moffatt* of Union Theological Seminary served as Executive Secretary and was a member of both sections. Not more than five and not less than three were chosen for their competence in English literature, the conduct of worship and religious education. Not more than 12 and not less than 10 were chosen for their biblical scholarship. Thirty-two scholars were involved in the work, from 20 universities and seminaries, and (with the exception of Harry M. Orlinsky*, a Jewish member with a specialised knowledge of the LXX*), all were active members of Protestant communities. There was an Advisory Board of 50. They worked in two sections (OT and NT) with a smaller body on the Apocrypha*, using the English versions of 1611 and 1895 as a basis. Hopes of including British scholars were dashed by the 1939–45 war but there was partial collaboration in the case of the OT.

Their commitment was to revise the ASV*, not to undertake a new translation, so a scholar would begin by offering his own revision. The appropriate Section then discussed it in every detail to achieve a revised draft, which was the work of the Section. This was later revised and had to be accepted by the whole Committee. After 14 years and 81 meetings, often working from 9 in the morning until 9.30 in the evening, the NT was completed; the OT Section met more frequently and spent 148 days together in the last three and a half years to hasten the completion. They received no payment for their work.

Following the Second Vatican Council* a 'Catholic edition' of the RSV* and including the Apocrypha*, edited by a Catholic Committee but containing very few alterations, was approved for use by British Catholics in 1966, fol-

lowed by The Common Bible*, 1973.

Based on the Hebrew consonantal text and the ancient versions for the OT and the seventeenth edition of the Nestle* text (1941) for the NT, and able to take account of advances in our knowledge of biblical languages, historical criticism and the various papyrus* mss. which had been discovered since the RV*, including the Chester Beatty Papyri* and the DSS*. This led to some passages not in the best early texts being printed as footnotes and to a few other verbal changes. For example, 'virgin' in Isa. 7.14 became 'young woman', and the longer ending of Mark (16.9-20) and the woman taken in adultery (Jn 7.53–8.11) were included only as footnotes.

The version, which attempted to eliminate old-fashioned language while at the same time retaining a text that was suitable for public worship, proved very popular in Britain. Older forms, such as 'saith' and 'doth' were replaced by their modern English equivalents, 'says' and 'does', and 'you' replaced 'thou' except when addressing the deity. Other features included poetry printed as poetry, modern paragraphing, punctuation and quotation marks for direct speech, a single-column page and verse numbers made less conspicuous.

Nelson held exclusive publishing rights for ten years but from 1962 other editions began to appear, including The Oxford Annotated Bible, edited by May and Metzger*, 1962, which included chronological tables, weights and measures, maps and notes, and (in the 1966 edition) the Apocrypha, The Common Bible, 1973, and the New Oxford Annotated Bible with the Apocrypha, 1977, which may claim to be the first truly ecumenical edition of the Bible in English in that it had the support of Protestants, Roman Catholics and the Eastern Orthodox.

Revised Version, 1881 (NT), 1885 (OT), 1896 (complete). A revision of the AV* made in the light of fresh knowledge and the discovery of new mss. and versions.

The Convocation of Canterbury agreed to undertake a revision of the AV*, 10 February 1870. They followed a familiar pattern as for the earlier version: two panels (one, under the chairmanship of C.J. Ellicott*, for the OT and one, under the chairmanship of E.H. Browne*, for the NT), each consisting of 24 people, and of the 65 scholars who worked on the translation (due to changes of personnel) 48 were Anglicans, the rest coming from other traditions. On completion it was submitted to other scholars, including literary people, at home and overseas. There were separate arrangements for the revision of the Apocrypha* which appeared in 1896.

Possibly the first major translation in which principles of scholarship took precedence over ecclesiastical allegiance, particularly in the selection of translators, in that both John Henry Newman, the most eminent Roman Catholic theologian in the English-speaking world, and G. Vance Smith, a distinguished Unitarian scholar, were both asked to join in the work. Smith agreed but Newman declined.

The OT panel met five times a year for ten days at a time, the NT panel four days every month except August and September. The work was to be a revision (not a translation). Each panel was to go over every passage twice, alterations were to be as few as possible and only if approved by two-thirds of those present. Some of those which did not command such assent were printed as marginal notes. Two parallel panels were set up in the USA and at one time it was hoped to produce one translation but when that proved impracticable the Americans eventually came out with the ASV*, 1901, without the Apocrypha*. Costs were borne by the Oxford and Cambridge University Presses, who published the work, and revisers made no charge for their work.

Each verse was no longer presented as a paragraph; instead, paragraphs were formed according to sense, though verse numbers were retained for reference. The revision also included chapter and page headings, paragraphs, italics and punctuation, and in the course of the work marginal notes included variant readings* in the Greek. In 1898 a version appeared with full cross-references and the marginal notes became footnotes. Alterations were mainly due to situations where the AV* seemed to be wrong, or ambiguous, or inconsistent within itself in the rendering of two or more parallel passages, or were the result of adopting a different text from that which underlay the AV, or became necessary as a result of changes already made.

In the NT it was a much better rendering of the Greek text than the AV, benefiting from the more recently discovered Codex Sinaiticus* and Codex Vaticanus* and the researches of Westcott* and Hort*, two of the translators who published their own epoch-making edition of the Greek Testament five days before the appearance of the RV. It was however, never, regarded as a wholly satisfactory translation because it tended to be too literal, a defect which made it particularly beneficial for students of NT Greek.

The OT, on the other hand, was judged an excellent achievement, probably because the translators used the same text as the AV but knew their Hebrew better than their seventeenth-century counterparts. Poetical passages in the ancient mss. were printed as verse for the first time, the translation of proper names was systematized and particular words in the ancient texts were translated by the same English word as far as possible.

As with the ASV[*], which copied it, the underlying Greek text for the NT is Codex Sinaiticus[*] and Codex Vaticanus[*], reflecting the work of scholars like Tischendorf[*], Westcott[*] and Hort[*]. Little influence from papyrus[*] mss. because most of them had not then been discovered.

Reynolds, John (1549–1607). President of Corpus Christi College, Oxford, a Greek scholar and a leader of the Puritan side in the Church of England. Present at the Hampton Court Conference[*], 1604, where he made a proposal for a new translation of the Bible, which resulted in the AV[*]. Insisted that the work of revision should be left to the universities and should not be prejudiced by any notes.

Rheims-Challoner. See Douay-Rheims Bible.

Rheims, France. Home of an English College for Roman Catholics founded by William Allen[*] where Gregory Martin[*] translated the New Testament into English, later becoming part of the Douay-Rheims Bible[*].

Rich, Jeremiah (d. 1660). Compiler of the first Shorthand Bible[*], 1605, in London.

Rieu, Chares Pierre Henri H. (1920–1992). Son of E.V. Rieu[*], born in Geneva, studied Arabic[*] and Sanskrit in Bonn, Keeper of Oriental Manuscripts in the British Museum and Professor of Arabic at Cambridge. Lay reader and translator of *The Acts of the Apostles* (Penguin, Harmondsworth, 1957), one of the early modern translations with a thoroughly modern appearance, easy to read and preceded by 30 pages of introduction and 60 pages of notes, using a Nestle[*] text with some preference for the Western[*] text. Critical of the AV[*] and RV[*], and, following J.B. Phillips[*], he arranged his material in

paragraphs, put bold, clear headings to each page, using italics for quotations and small capitals for emphasis. (See Penguin Translations.)

Rieu, Emil Victor (1887–1972). Classical scholar, educated at St Paul's and Balliol College, Oxford. Joined Oxford University Press in 1910. Translator of Homer and editor of Penguin Classics. Translator of *The Four Gospels* (Penguin, 1952), with an introduction discussing some of the problems of translating the gospels. Puts Mark's Gospel first because it was commonly thought to have been the first to be written, retains the chapter[*] divisions but not the verses. (See Penguin Translations.)

Riverside New Testament, 1901, revised 1934. A modern dynamic equivalence[*] translation by W.G. Ballantine[*], made directly from the original Greek, following Nestle[*], with a phrasing which neither sought nor shunned originality. The format is that of a modern book, without verses, well spaced and easy to read but it was always somewhat overshadowed by Goodspeed's Translation[*].

Roberts, Colin Henderson (1909–90). Classical scholar and papyrologist, and Fellow of St John's College, Oxford, who in 1934 was sorting through some unpublished papyrus[*] fragments at the John Rylands Library in Manchester[*] when he recognized one scrap as containing some verses from John's Gospel (18.31-4, 37-38) later known as the John Fragment[*].

Robertson, James Alexander (1880–1955). Responsible for revising Weymouth's New Testament[*], 1924.

Robinson, Theodore Henry (1881–1964). Professor of Old Testament Studies in the University of Wales and Convenor of the panels for the OT and the Apocrypha[*] for the NEB[*].

Rogers, John (c. 1500–55). English Protestant reformer, friend of William Tyndale* and first of the Marian martyrs to be burned at the stake, 1555, in the period of reaction that followed the accession of Mary* to the throne. After graduating in 1525 he moved to Antwerp* to become chaplain to the Merchant Adventurers where he met Tyndale. Thought to be the translator of Matthew's Bible*, using Thomas Matthew as a pseudonym.

Roll. See Scroll.

Rolle, Richard (1300–49). Hermit, mystic and poet. Translated the Psalms in the first half of the fourteenth century at Hampole, near Doncaster, into his northern dialect and included a verse-by-verse commentary. Its popularity may be judged by the fact that it subsequently appeared in other dialects.

Roman Catholic Canon Law. Prior to the Second Vatican Council*, 1962–65, Roman Catholics were forbidden to use any version of the Bible other than those produced by Catholics, except for the purposes of biblical or theological study (and the general public were scarcely aware of the exception), on the widespread feeling that access to the Bible should be made difficult rather than easy, and on the assumption that all biblical translation would be from the Vulgate*. (Canons 1399, 1400 and 1391).

Rotherham, Joseph Bryant (fl. 1828–1906). A scholar well-versed in Hebrew and Greek, author of The Emphasised Bible*, 1902, and unfairly dismissed by some as being more of an elocutionist than a translator because of the way he used various signs to convey the finer points of the original text.

Rufinus, Tyrannius (345–410). Born in North Italy. Monk, historian and translator, mainly of Greek theological works into Latin. Set out a list of OT canonical books similar to that of Jerome* but added Maccabees to those described by Jerome as 'edifying but not canonical', and called them 'ecclesiastical books'.

Rushworth Gospels. A ms. of the four gospels which came to light in the tenth century, written in Latin by an Irish scribe, three of them being virtually the same as the Lindisfarne Gospels* but the fourth (Matthew) being an independent work in the Mercian dialect by a priest named Faermon. Now in the Bodleian Library, Oxford*, it takes its name from Mr Jack Rushworth who held it for many years,

Ruthwell Cross. An ancient cross near the Solway Firth on the old pilgrim way between Iona and Lindisfarne* depicting incidents from the gospels. Under each panel is a text from the Vulgate* and travellers unable to read were able to study the gospels in pictures.

S

Sacred Books of the Old and New Testaments, 1893. More popularly known as the Polychrome Bible*.

Sahug (390–439). Armenian Patriarch, *alias* Isaac the Great. Joint translator with Mesropius* of the Armenian Version* and liturgy.

Samaritan Pentateuch. A Hebrew version of the first five books of the OT, in a purely consonantal text, written in the old Hebrew characters rather than the square ones adopted by the Jews at a later date. The Samaritans also developed vowel signs but their use is spasmodic and late, and the Samaritan Masorah relates more to paragraphing*, the fixing of sections and musical directions.

Differences from the Masoretic Text* number about 6000, mostly variations in spelling and of little significance. The major difference is the substitution of Mount Gerizim for Jerusalem as the central place of worship, whilst the fact that the scroll contains only the Pentateuch is a reminder of what is regarded as scripture by the Samaritans, an illustration of the conservative nature of the group and a rejection of anything that suggests innovation or modernization.

When first discovered the ancient script gave the impression that the text was much earlier than the more familiar Hebrew and for this reason it was thought to be valuable for the picture it provided of the text of the Hebrew Bible at the point of separation, the argument being that where the Samaritan Pentateuch, the LXX* and Hebrew were in agreement there was good reason to believe that they represented the earlier text on the grounds that the Samaritans were unlikely to have accommodated themselves to the Jewish version after the split. Closer examination suggests this not to be the case and as a result of revised datings for the split between Jews and Samaritans the Samaritan Pentateuch is now thought to be much later. Scholars are divided as to its date; it may have been based on earlier, Pre-Samaritan texts* similar to those found at Qumran*, though if it is there is very little difference between them. One thing they have in common, however, is that with their frequent explanatory notes and glosses they offer a more expanded form of the received Hebrew text and it is this which makes them important for textual study.

What brought about the separation of the Samaritans from the Jews, and whether it was because the Jews refused to allow them to take part in the re-building of the Temple at the beginning of the sixth century BCE (as is often said) is debatable. The separation is variously dated in the fifth, fourth or second centuries BCE, the current preference being for the last, though some scholars suggest it was as late as the destruction of the temple by John Hyrcanus in 128 BCE, but whatever it is does not have much significance for the Samaritan Pentateuch.

No current ms. goes back earlier than the tenth century, the oldest and most complete version dating from 1149–50 (Cambridge). The first copy came to light in 1616, when Pietro della Valle obtained one in Damascus. The first printed version appeared in the Paris Polyglot*, followed by the London Polyglot*, both regarding it as more faithful to the original than the Masoretic Text*. In 1815 Gesenius* rejected it as being of minimal critical value and Geiger thought it to be one of the traditions rejected by the rabbis in the first century CE. Kahle* regarded it as one of the many 'common' translations and attributed its agreements with the LXX* to the fact that many early Greek translations came from the same tradition. There is an Aramaic version, also printed in the London Polyglot, and a Greek version known as Samariticon*. An eclectic edition edited by Von Gall (1914–18) is the one used most.

The DSS* have been thought by some to relate to the Proto-Samaritan text tradition and to offer new data on the relationship between the Samaritan Pentateuch, the Masoretic Text and the LXX. According to the traditional view the Samaritan Pentateuch reflects the Palestinian tradition from which we get the LXX and differences between them are due to their respective text traditions, Palestinian in the Samaritan Pentateuch and Babylonian in the Masoretic Text. Agreements suggest that the Samaritan Pentateuch was reworked on the basis of the Babylonian tradition which must have happened before the schism between Jews and Samaritans. The DSS discoveries suggest that the editing of the Samaritan Pentateuch cannot be earlier than the second century CE.

Samaritan Recension. See Recension.

Samariticon. A Greek version of the Samaritan Pentateuch* which sometimes followed the LXX* more than the Samaritan Pentateuch itself and is quoted by Jerome*.

Scarlett, Nathaniel (1753–1802). Bookseller, shipwright and accountant. Author of A Translation of the New Testament from the Original Greek Humbly attempted by Nathaniel Scarlett, Assisted by Men of Piety and Literature: with Notes, 1798. Scarlett divides the text into two sections, each with a title, personifies it by putting the names of the speakers as in the text of a play and assigning narrative portions to the 'Historian', and uses 'immerse' instead of 'baptize', the forerunner of other 'immersion versions'*.

Schaff, Philip (1819–93). A Reformed Church historian, born in Switzerland and educated at Tübingen prior to moving to the USA where he became a professor at Union Theological Seminary and President of the American Revision Committee for the ASV*.

Scheil, John Vincent (b. 1858). French archaeologist, discoverer and translator of the Code of Hammurabi, Joint Editor of *Revue Biblique*, and one of the first scholars to discover papyrus* mss., including one in 1889, on a visit to Coptos*, Egypt, dated c. 200, containing portions of Luke 1–4, and found in a jar walled up in a house and used as stuffing for a third-century codex of Philo.

Scholz, Johann Maretin Augustine (1794–1852). A pupil of J.L. Hug* and a professor at the University of Bonn. Published the first comprehensive catalogue of NT mss., which included 26 uncials*, and 469 minuscules* of the gospels, 8 uncials and 192 minuscules of Acts and the Catholic Epistles, 3 uncials and 88 minuscules of the Book of Revelation, plus 239 collections of lessons for reading in church, and listed over 600 other mss. to those already known, as well as a two-volume edition of the Greek Testament, 1830–36, marking something of a return to the Textus Receptus* while following in the traditions of J.A. Bengel* (with his division into two families*, Alexandrian* and Constantinopolitan), J.J. Wettstein* and C.F. Matthaei*. The first to appreciate the geographical location of several mss. and the forerunner of B.H. Streeter* with his emphasis on 'local texts', though Scholz's interest lay not so much in similarity of readings as in palaeography*, notes, colophons*, local saints and iconography.

Schonfield, Hugh Joseph (1910–88). A distinguished Jewish NT scholar, with an intimate knowledge of the Jewish environment in NT times, whose translation of the NT was published as The Authentic New Testament*, 1955. Author of a series of controversial works on early Christianity and its Jewish roots. Believed to be the first Jew to translate the NT into English and claimed that because of his Jewish background and learning he was better equipped to do so than a Gentile.

Scofield Reference Bible, 1909. See New Scofield Reference Bible, 1967.

Scribal Changes. Through the long period of copying* and textual transmission, besides additions* and harmonizations*, common scribal changes tended to be the result of familiarity with the same text in other places or for linguistic, stylistic, or exegetical reasons. (See Scribal Changes, p. 149)

scriptio continua. Lit. 'continuous script'. Used to describe the scribal habit of pro-

ducing text without word division*. Some dispute whether writers of OT texts practised it or whether word division was always present. One view is that it was but that scribes were not very consistent about it.

scriptio defectiva. The Latin term (sometimes referred to as *lectio defectiva*) for defective reading*.

scriptio plene. The Latin term (sometimes referred to as *lectio plene*) for full reading*.

Scripture Gift Mission. An international literature organization, founded at the end of the nineteenth century to produce Bible booklets and leaflets for distribution all over the world and currently working in more than 850 languages, with a special focus on minority languages.

Scrivener, Frederick Henry Ambrose (1813–91). Born in Bermondsey, son of a tradesman, with a flair for classical languages, who studied at Trinity College, Cambridge, taught at Sherborne School, and was Head of Falmouth School when he became interested in Codex Sinaiticus*. A NT scholar who published the text of 20 mss., listed all known mss. and devised a method classifying them, together with several other technical works on the text of the NT. Author of the Cambridge Paragraph Bible*, 1873, and one of the translators of the RV*, often adopting a conservative stance and preferring a Byzantine* to a Neutral* text.

Scroll. The normal form for a book from the great days of classical literature in Greece to the beginnings of the fourth century CE. Usually made of papyrus* or parchment* by glueing together a number of sheets and winding them round a long stick to produce a 'volume' (from the Latin *volumen*, meaning 'something

Scribal Changes

Scribes sometimes substituted more common words for rare ones, though this did not always add to clarity.

Isa 47.2. *šobel* (not found anywhere else in the Bible or in rabbinic Hebrew) is sometimes translated as 'leg' (AV) and sometimes as 'train', but one ms. has the more familiar *šolik* (skirt) which appears in Jer. 13.22, 26, Lam. 1.9 and Nah. 3.5.

Synonymous readings sometimes meant using a similar word, apparently interchangeable, but not necessarily with precisely the same meaning, a practice which easily gives place to doublets*.

'Palm', for example, sometimes substituted for 'hand', is not quite the same though it often works, as does 'house' for 'kingdom'.

Exegetical changes, very few in number, were sometimes made for theological reasons.

LXX*, Samaritan Pentateuch* and Syriac* have Yahweh completing creation on the sixth rather than the seventh day (Gen. 2.2), presumably to avoid any suggestion that he worked on the seventh.

Anti-polytheism led to names with Baal in their root being changed, as is evident when you compare the 'corrected' names in Samuel with those in Chronicles which, though written later, retained the older form. So, Saul's fourth son, Eshbaal (1 Chron. 8.33 and 9.39), appears differently in Samuel, first as Ishvi (1 Sam. 14.49) and then as Ishbosheth (2 Sam. 2.8-12, 3.8-15 and 4.5-8).

Most doctrinal changes alter or eliminate something which is doctrinally unacceptable or add something to make, prove, establish or defend a principle or practice.

Gen. 18.22 has 'Abraham still stood before Yahweh' though he was sitting when the story started (v. 1), a change made perhaps to stress awe and respect.

LXX* has 'the ephod' in 1 Sam. 14.18 whereas MT has 'the ark of God', a change possibly made once the ephod came to be considered idolatrous.

Did Scribes have difficulty reconciling the divinity of Jesus with his apparent ignorance on certain topics and so see fit to omit the words, 'nor the Son', in Mt. 24.36 and Mk. 13.32? And when they came to Lk. 1.3 was it not enough that 'it seemed good' to Luke so that some mss. add 'and to the Holy Spirit'? Something similar may have happened in Acts 15.28.

Instead of 'his parents' in Lk. 2.41, 43 some mss. read, 'Joseph and Mary', possibly to safeguard the doctrine of the virgin birth, while some substitute 'Joseph' for 'his father' in vv. 33 and 48 or omit v. 48 altogether.

Some mss. of Lk. 23.32 literally read, 'And also other criminals, two, were led away with him to be crucified'. Possibly to avoid any suggestion that Jesus was a criminal most other mss. read, 'And also two others, criminals, were led away with him to be crucified'. Two Old Latin mss. omit the word 'others' altogether.

rolled up'), with a second stick at the other end to facilitate winding. The reader held the rollers one in each hand, unwinding it from side to side, not from top to bottom, as required.

Ruling, to ensure straight lines and margins, was common, sometimes with ink* and therefore visible but sometimes with a pointed instrument and not afterwards clear to the naked eye. Normally papyrus was used on one side only with the horizontal lines as a guide; writing across the vertical lines on the other side was difficult. There was no ornamentation, no punctuation and no spaces between the words.

Size varied. Some are 15 inches high but 10 inches is more normal. Length also varied, some being as long as 50 feet, with 30-35 feet (about the length of a single gospel) being more normal. Anything larger was unmanageable. Evidence from the DSS* suggests that most scrolls contained only a single book, longer ones tending to be divided into two or more, which may explain why Luke and Acts (each about 30 feet in length) appear as two books rather than one, though the Minor Prophets appear to have come together in one scroll and it is possible that larger scrolls existed to contain all the Torah*.

The Torah* Jewish Scriptures were written either on skins or on pieces of papyrus*. Measurements varied but 10-20 inches in height with two, three or four columns of writing, 2.5 to 3.5 inches wide with 0.5 inches between them appear to have been common.

Not generally convenient, in that a scroll needed both hands, and locating particular passages was not easy. Gradually replaced in the second century CE by the codex*.

Second Vatican Council, 1962–65. Prior to the Second Vatican Council Roman Catholic Canon Law* forbade the use of Bibles, other than Catholic ones, except for biblical or theological study, but change was coming as a result of the efforts of people like Walter M. Abbott* and Cardinal Carlo Maria Martini*, subsequently Archbishop of Milan*, who pointed out that the current trend of distancing the laity from the Bible was comparatively recent and that well into the Middle Ages the Bible was regarded as the basic book for the formation of faith. The affirmations in *Dei Verbum*, therefore, were not new, the change in attitude being due to the increasing liturgical sense of the church (clergy and laity) as a growing community and the realisation of itself as a body of believers with frequent spontaneous communication between its members. Martini then quoted from *Dei Verbum*, 'Just as the life of the church grows through persistent participation in the eucharistic mystery, so we may hope for a new surge of vitality from an intensified veneration for God's word, which lasts for ever'. The New American Bible*, 1970, and The Common Bible*, 1973, were two early and positive results of the change.

Semitic Languages. A group of ancient languages, including Hebrew*, Aramaic* and Arabic*, so-called because an eighteenth-century linguist identified them as the languages of the sons of Shem (Gen. 10). Today there are several classifications, one of which divides them into North-West Semitic, which is Canaanite and sub-divides into Hebrew, Moabite and Edomite on the one hand and Ugaritic, Phoenician and Punic on the other, and North Semitic, which is basically Aramaic and can also be subdivided into Western (biblical and Palestinian) and Eastern (Babylonian). A common characteristic is that they are consonantal texts and the root form of most words consists of no more than three letters. In this respect the Semites may claim to be the originator of the alphabet (as distinct from signs and syllables) probably dating from c. 1600 BCE. The oldest Hebrew and Aramaic inscriptions, such as the Gezer Calendar*, go back to the tenth century.

Semler, Johann Salomo (1725–91). In 1767, seeing that even our oldest mss. were the result of recensions*, Semler took the classification of ancient NT mss. made by J.A. Bengel* and extended it into three groups:

Alexandrian, to which he assigned the earliest Greek mss., the Syriac*, Coptic* and Ethiopic* versions.
Eastern, with its centres at Antioch and Constantinople*, and including the main mass of authorities.
Western, to be found in the Latin versions and Fathers. This clarification was taken further by his pupil, J.J. Griesbach*.

Septuagint (LXX). The most important of all the old translations, the Bible of the early church and still the authoritative biblical text of the Greek Orthodox Church. Most of the OT quotations in the NT reflect this text.

Strictly speaking, a Greek version of the Torah*, expanded in the first century to include all the Jewish-Greek Scriptures and therefore may be loosely described as a translation of the OT from Hebrew into Greek. Begun in the third century BCE in the Greek city of Alexandria*, for the benefit of Jews of the Dispersion, some of whom were descendants of Jewish exiles and others who were travellers and traders, growing up with no knowledge of Hebrew and requiring their scriptures in their own language.

According to the Letter of Aristeas*, the LXX owes its origins to Ptolemy II, king of Egypt (285–46 BCE) who, having heard of the existence of the Jewish Scriptures through a large colony of Jews in Alexandria and being urged by his librarian to secure a copy for the library, sent a request to the 'high priest in Jerusalem asking for a copy and some capable translators. An alternative version agrees that a Greek translation of the Pentateuch was made in Alexandria c. the third century BCE, but attributes it more to the needs of the Jewish community (who had either forgotten their Hebrew or grown up without it) than to the monarch. Differences of style, its diverse character and uneven merit make it unlikely that it was the work of any particular group and there is some doubt as to whether there ever was one single Greek translation or whether the LXX was the result of a merging of several attempts to render the Hebrew in Greek.

A more likely view is that it was spread over a period of 150 years or more, beginning in the last quarter of the third century BCE with the Torah*, followed by the Prophets* and the later addition of other books, including 1 Ezra, Wisdom of Solomon, Ecclesiasticus, Judith, Tobit, Letter of Jeremiah, 1 and 2 Maccabees and possibly even additions to Esther and the Psalter as well as the canonical Writings*, even up to the middle or end of the second century, and by different writers. Why it was known as the Version of the Seventy when there were apparently 72 translators is also unclear. The number is usually thought to relate to the translators though another possibility is that it referrs to the 70 members of the Alexandrian Sanhedrin.

It contains 24 canonical books and a number of Greek texts (some translations and some originals, known more usually in the English Bible as 'the Apocrypha'*), and was the Bible of Greek-speaking Jews. The arrangement of the books is also different. Whereas the Hebrew version has the Torah*, the Prophets* and the Writings[*] (i.e. the three main sections as they came together), the LXX has them grouped according to their literary genre (i.e. legal and historical, poetry, and prophecy) and with the apocryphal books placed according to their genre.

Found in papyrus[*] (scroll[*]) and vellum[*] (codex[*]) form, papyrus mss dating from the third century BCE to the seventh century CE and vellum mss. from the fourth to the tenth centuries, in uncials[*] from the fourth to the fifth centuries, and in minuscules[*] from the ninth to the fifteenth. One of the most significant papyrus presentations is the Chester Beatty[*] collection and the most important uncial mss. are the Codex Vaticanus[*], the Codex Sinaiticus[*] and the Codex Alexandrinus[*].

The early Christians adopted it as their OT, and NT writers found it a useful source for terms and concepts, contents and symbols to help them to express the Christian faith, thus forming a useful bridge between the two Testaments. Revisions took place, partly to correct mistakes, partly to improve and update language and style, and partly to adapt the Greek to the proto-masoretic Hebrew text, but mainly to enable Jews to have a Greek version which more adequately represented the original Jewish texts. When the early church adopted it to go alongside the Greek New Testament Jews increasingly produced other Greek translations, notably those of Aquila[*], Symmachus[*] and Theodotion[*]. From the Christian side Jerome[*] in 396 cites three recensions: Origen[*], Hesychius[*] and Lucian[*].

With many copies extant, some much older than the earliest available Hebrew mss., and with a greater variety of variant readings[*] than all the other translations put together, the LXX is invaluable in helping us to discover the state of the Hebrew texts at an early date, though whether there was ever just one translation or whether there were several different attempts is unclear. Prior to the discovery of the DSS[*], it was almost the only source for studying the history of the text of the Hebrew Bible. Their discovery led to a period of re-evaluation when it was realised that the text of some books and variant readings represented a different, and sometimes preferable, Hebrew original from the Masoretic Text[*].

Current editions of the LXX follow one of two patterns, the Cambridge[*] and the Göttingen[*]. (See Letter of Aristeas, p. 153.)

Sharpe, Samuel (1799–1881). A Unitarian Egyptologist who published a New Testament, translated from the Greek of J.J. Griesbach[*], 1840, essentially a revision of the AV[*] in the light of Griesbach's[*] Greek text, and Hebrew Scriptures Translated[*], 1865, a similar revision of the OT. Wrote a Hebrew history and grammar and represented the Unitarian Church in the production of the RV[*], 1870.

Shaxton, Nicolas (1485–1556). Bishop of Salisbury who in 1538 required his clergy to ensure that by Whit Sunday an English Bible was chained to the desk of every parish church in the diocese. Hence the name, 'Chained Bibles'[*].

Sheed, Frank (1896–1982). A Roman Catholic publisher (Sheed & Ward) who sensed the need for a readable and more scholarly version of the Bible for the Catholic world and, knowing that Sheed and Ward were unable to handle it alone, approached Michael Longman[*] of Longmans Green with a proposal to translate *La Bible de Jérusalem*.

Letter of Aristeas, c. 130–70 BCE

The Letter of Aristeas* to his brother Philocrates, in the reign of Ptolemy Philadelphus (285–46 BCE), describes in some detail how Ptolemy sent an embassy (including Aristeas) to the high priest in Jerusalem, with magnificent presents and a letter in which he reviewed his practice of setting free Jewish slaves who had come to Egypt under the Persians and under his father and begged him to send a copy of the sacred books and a body of men capable of translating them into Greek.

The letter goes on to say how 6 translators were selected from each of the 12 tribes and dispatched to Alexandria bringing with them a copy of the Law, written in letters of gold. They were splendidly received by the king and, after a banquet and a public display of their wisdom, they set about the translation in a quiet house by the sea, working separately to begin with, but then comparing their results, finally producing the Version of the Seventy (hence the designation LXX) or Septuagint.

Aristeas then describes how the translation was read before the Jewish population in the place where it was made and how it 'met with a great reception also from the people, because of the great benefits which they had conferred upon them'.

> After the books had been read, the priests and the elders of the translators and the Jewish community and the leaders of the people stood up and said that, since so excellent and sacred and accurate a translation had been made, it was only right that it should remain as it was, and no alteration should be made in it. And when the whole company expressed their approval, they bade them pronounce a curse in accordance with their custom upon anyone who should make any alteration either by adding anything or changing in any way whatever any of the words which had been written or making any omission. This was a very wise precaution to ensure that the book might be preserved for all the future time unchanged. (*Letter of Aristeas*, 308–11).

The writer of the book of Revelation would probably have agreed with him (22.18-19). Apparently Ptolemy was also greatly pleased and the scholars went home with princely gifts.

(cont.)

Letter of Aristeas (cont.)

Later generations improved the story until the legend ran that each of the 72 translators was shut up in a separate cell (or by pairs in 36 cells) and each produced a translation of the whole of the OT in exactly 72 days, and when their translations were compared it was found that they were identical, in every word and phrase, thus proving that the translation was directly inspired by God.

Philo, a Jewish thinker belonging to a priestly family in Alexandria in the time of Jesus, for example, writes,

> Sitting here (on the island of Pharos [the traditional site of the translation work]) in seclusion…they became as it were possessed, and, under inspiration, wrote, not each several scribe something different, but the same word for word, as though dictated to each by an invisible prompt… The clearest proof of this is that, if Chaldeans have learned Greek, or Greeks Chaldean and read both versions, the Chaldean and the translation, they regard them with awe and reverence as sisters, or rather one and the same, both in matter and words, and speak of the authors not as translators but as prophets and priests of the mysteries, whose sincerity and singleness of thought have enabled them to go hand in hand with the purest of spirits, the spirit of Moses (*Vit. Mos.* 37–40).

The idea and commitment also passed over into Christianity to the extent that we have Eusebius saying,

> Ptolemy, wishing to make trial of them in his own way, and being afraid lest they should have made some agreement to conceal by their translation the truth in the Scriptures, separated them from one another and commanded them all to write the same translation. And this they did in the case of all the books. But when they came together to Ptolemy, and compared each his own translation, God was glorified and the Scriptures were recognised as truly divine, for they all rendered the same things in the same words and the same names, from beginning to end, so that even the heathen who were present knew that the Scriptures had been translated by the inspiration of God (*H.E.* 5.8.11-14, LCL).

These adornments are now regarded as legend and there are in fact numerous differences between the two texts but the legend at least illustrates the importance of texts and Scriptures at this time, the care and attention given to them and the importance of their not being altered.

Shorter Bible: An American Translation, 1918. A modern English translation consisting of nine books in their entirety, the rest considerably reduced, and a few verses from the Apocrypha*, arranged in chronological (historical) order and each with a short introduction. Included some selections from Goodspeed's Translation* following its publication as *The Bible: An American Translation*, 1931.

Shorthand Bibles, 1605 and 1904. The first was prepared by Jeremiah Rich*, based on his own version of shorthand, the second by Isaac Pitman and Sons, using the Pitman method.

Siloam Inscription. An inscription in an archaic Semitic dialect similar to that found in the Gezer Calendar*. An example of early Hebrew writing, discovered in 1880, traditionally believed to be a description of how Hezekiah's tunnel was dug under Jerusalem, between the Gihon Spring and the Siloam Pool, to ensure the water supply for the city when the Assyrians threatened siege in 701 BCE, and referred to in 2 Kgs 20.20. It tells how the tunnel was completed when two groups of workmen who had started at opposite ends each heard the sound of the other's tools in the heart of the rock and so cut through to meet them, and the very slight bend at that point, in an otherwise straight tunnel, indicates the precision with which they had worked towards each other. A good deal of recent archaeology, however, questions this dating.

Silver Codex. Another name for the Codex Argenteus*.

Similar Letters. Errors sometimes creep into textual copying* as a result of letters which look alike and are easily miscopied, particularly where the miscopying still makes good sense. In OT texts allowance must be made for similarities both in the early Hebrew script and in the later Hebrew square characters, as well as for a slightly different style of writing in the Samaritan script or at different times of writing, as, for example, in the DSS*. In NT texts allowance must be made for similarites in uncial Greek, which was used in ms. production down to the ninth century CE, and in minuscule mss. to a lesser extent because most of the variations crept in prior to their arrival on the scene. (See Similar Letters in Hebrew, Similar Letters in Uncial Greek. pp. 156-57.)

Similar Sounds. Sometimes when copying* a scribe may mishear, particularly where words, syllables or letters sound alike, or lose concentration, perhaps as a result of working long hours or trying to hold too much in his mind, leading to transposed letters, changed words or itacisms*.

Simonides, Constantine (b. 1825). An ingenious Greek who, in the middle of the nineteenth century, caused some sensation with quantities of Greek mss. claiming to be of considerable antiquity, including portions of the NT dating from the first century and a copy of Matthew on papyrus* said to date from 15 years after the ascension. One of the scholars who was responsible for exposing them as forgeries was Tischendorf*, so when Tischendorf triumphantly published Codex Sinaiticus* Simonides retaliated by stating that that was in fact the one forgery for which he was responsible, but his claims were quickly proved to be false.

Simplified New Testament, 1961. A translation by Olaf M. Norlie* using simple words and short sentences, including a translation of the Psalms by R.K. Harrison.

Similar Letters in Hebrew

ת and א taw and aleph (*t* and *'*)

The similarity of these two letters in the early Hebrew script explains why the LXX[*] has 'Thasoban' for 'Ezbon' (Gen. 46.16), 'Thasirite' for 'Ashurite' (2 Sam. 2.9) and 'Thoue' for 'Ahava' (Ezra 8.21, 31).

ד and ר daleth and resh (*d* and *r*)

In the square Hebrew characters, MT has וירק (*wyrq*) ('he armed his followers') whereas the Samaritan Pentateuch[*] has וידק (*wydq*) ('he crushed his followers') in Gen. 14.14 and אחר (*'ḥr*) ('behind him') when the Samaritan Pentateuch has אחד (*'ḥd*) ('one') in Gen. 22.13.

    2 Sam. 22.43 has אדקם (*'dqm*) ('I crushed them') whereas the parallel passage in Ps. 18.42 has ארקם (*'rqm*) ('I emptied them').

    Isa. 9.9 has ידעו (*yd'w*) ('knew') though one ms. has ירעו (*yr'w*) ('shouted').

    Isa. 14.4 has מדהבה (*mdhbh*) ('the golden city') where מרהבה (*mrhbh*) ('the boisterous city') is thought by some to be more appropriate.

    In Jer. 2.20 *Kethib*[*] has אעבד (*'bd*) ('work') whereas *Qere*[*] has אעבר (*'br*) ('transgress').

י and ו yod and waw (*y* and *w*)

In Prov. 17.27 *Kethib*[*] has וקר (*wqr*) ('cool') whereas *Qere*[*] has יקר (*yqr*) ('precious'), translated as 'excellent' (AV).

ב and ד beth and daleth (*b* and *d*)

In Josh. 11.2 MT has נגב (*ngb*) ('south') whereas LXX[*] has נגד (*ngd*) ('opposite').

ב and מ beth and **mem** (*b* and *m*)

1 Kgs 12.2 has Jeroboam במצרים (*bmṣrym*) (*settled in* Egypt') whereas the parallel passage in 2 Chron. 10.2 has him ממצרים (*mmṣrym*) (*returned from* Egypt'). The preceding verb ישב (*yšb*) can be vocalized to mean either 'stayed' or 'returned' to fit the different readings.

    This may also explain why the same name sometimes begins with a 'b' and sometimes with an 'm', as in Berodach and Merodach, and other cases.

ב and כ beth and kaph (*b* and *k*)

1 Kgs 22.20 has בכה (*bkh*) ('and one said *one thing*, and another said *another*') whereas the parallel passage in 2 Chron. 18.19 has ככה (*kkh*) ('and one said *thus* and another said *thus*').

    In 2 Kgs 3.24. *Kethib*[*] has ויבו (*wybw*) ('they went in'). *Qere*[*] has ויכו (*wykw*) ('they hit it').

Similar Letters in Uncial Greek

Uncial letters often confused are

Ε Ο Θ and Σ
Π Γ Ι Τ
Γ Π Τ
Μ ΛΛ
Α Δ Λ
Η Ν
Π Φ

In Lk. 6.42 most mss. have ΚΑΡΦΟΣ ('log') but one has ΚΑΡΠΟΣ ('fruit'), confusing Π and Φ.

In Rom. 6.5 most mss. have ΑΛΛΑ ('but') but some have ΑΜΑ ('together'), confusing Μ and ΛΛ.

Is 2 Pet. 2.13 ΑΠΑΤΑΙΣ ('dissipation') or ΑΓΑΠΑΙΣ ('lovefeasts')?

Final Letters

Some Hebrew letters (e.g. *k*, *m*, *n*, *p* and *ṣ*) are written differently when they are at the end of a word, e.g., the final form of כ is ך, of מ is ם, of נ is ן, of פ is ף and of צ is ץ. This custom should be a help when it comes to word division*, but can also lead to corruptions*, particularly because the distinction between final and non-final forms was introduced fairly late, partly because sometimes they appear in their final form when they are not final, and partly because not every scribe used the final form even when they were.

Slavonic Version. The first version (gospels, psalms and other texts prepared for the liturgy) was the work of Cyril (d. 869) and Methodius (815–85), apostles to the Slavs. To achieve it Cyril devised an alphabet consisting of 38 letters and began with the gospels. The version was completed towards the end of the ninth century and there were several recensions. A ms. from 1499 follows the Byzantine* Greek text and has become the text for church purposes. The current text of the Slavonic Bible is the St Petersburg* edition, 1751. The language is now commonly called Old Church Slavonic.

Slimbridge, Gloucestershire. Birthplace of William Tyndale*.

Smith, John Merlin Powis (1866–1932). One of four translators of The Old Testament: An American Translation*, 1927, subsequently revised by T.J. Meek* and part of The Complete Bible: An American Translation*, 1931.

Smith, Julia Evelina (1792–1886). An American, one of few women Bible translators, who produced a very literal translation of the Bible in 1876, sometimes called a 'pony' of the original text because she ignored context and translated every Greek or Hebrew word and phrase with the same English word each time it occurred, thus giving some unusual results and finishing up more with a crib than with a translation.

Smith, Miles (c. 1568–1624). Born in Hereford, the son of a butcher, and educated at Corpus Christi and Brasenose College, Oxford. Classical scholar and orientalist. Canon of Hereford and later Bishop of Gloucester. Worked with John Reynolds* on a translation of the prophetic books for the AV* and was responsible, with Thomas Bilson*, for the Preface, 'The Translators to the Readers', of the AV, 1611, and for seeing it through the press.

Soden, Hermann Freiherr von (1852–1914). A German scholar who developed a new theory of the history of the texts, a new classification system for mss., and his own system of ms. symbols which, though ingenious, proved too complicated for most scholars. Arising from them he divided the witnesses into three main groups (the *Koiné* Greek*, the Hesychian and the Jerusalem recensions) and developed a theory of text history to produce his own critical edition* of the Greek NT, 1913, featuring an enormous number of minuscule mss. In general his work has not found acceptance among scholars though Moffatt* used it as the basis for his English translation.

Soldiers' Pocket Bible, 1643. Extracts from the Geneva Bible* issued for the use of Oliver Cromwell's army.

Solway Firth, Scotland. Site of the Ruthwell Cross* on the old pilgrim way between Lindisfarne* and Iona.

Soncino Edition, 1494. The first printed edition of the complete Hebrew Bible*, so-called after the small town near Milan* where it took place. Very accurate in its masoretic notes. Once revised it was used for the first rabbinic edition and also for the later ones of Stephanus*, 1539 and 1544–46, and Münster, 1535, and was the one Martin Luther used for his translation of the Bible into German.

Sopherim. Forerunners of the Masoretes*, authorities in the textual transmission of the OT, who are traditionally supposed to have emerged during the exile and flourished in the fifth to the fourth centuries BCE. They derived their name from the fact that they used to count (Heb. *saphar*) all the letters in the Torah* to ensure accuracy and consistency, a task handled later by the Masoretes*. Another of their tasks was to draw attention to errors or omissions and this led to the development of the *kethib** and *qere*.

Source Criticism. A method of biblical criticism* which concentrates on identifying the written documents or sources which later compilers used to produce the texts as they have come down to us.

Souter, Alexander (1873–1949). Scottish NT and Patristic scholar, educated at Aberdeen and Cambridge universities and Professor of New Testament Greek at Mansfield College, Oxford. Author of several technical works on NT Greek, including the provision of a special critical apparatus* presumed to underlie the RV* in the Oxford Greek Testament, 1910 (rev. 1947), often known as the Souter text*.

Souter Text. The Greek text of the NT as found in Alexander Souter's* Oxford Greek Testament, first published in 1910 and reissued, unchanged, in 1947, reflecting British textual scholarship as it was in 1881. The work of Edward Palmer*, a member of the NT panel of translators of the RV*, 1881, and therefore (by inference) the Greek text behind that translation. Based on the third edition of Stephanus*, 1550. Palmer produced a continuous Greek text reflecting the decisions of the revisers, while staying close to the Textus Receptus* even when the RV represented correctly either of two competing readings. Souter's contribution was to supply a critical apparatus*, the chief strength of which lies in its quotations from the early church Fathers, particularly the Latin ones. In the 1947 edition the apparatus was enlarged with evidence supplied by the Chester Beatty Papyri* and other mss. discovered after 1910.

Southwark, London. Site for the printing of the first edition of the whole English Bible to be published in England. It was Coverdale's*, 1537.

Spencer, Francis Aloysius (1845–1913). An American Roman Catholic who published The Four Gospels*, 1898, and whose complete NT was published posthumously, 1937.

Sperry, Willard Leonyd (1882–1954). Faculty member of Harvard University and Vice-Chairman of the committee which produced the RSV*.

Spurrell Translation, 1885. A less-than-satisfactory translation of the OT by Helen Spurrell, a painter, sculptor and musician, who learned Hebrew and translated the whole of the OT when she was over 50 to produce *Translation of the Old Testament Scriptures from the Original Hebrew*. By 'original Hebrew' she meant the unpointed Hebrew, consonantal text, refusing to accept the vowels on the grounds that they had been put there by humans. She also had headings, printed in italics at the top of every page, with Hebrew textual and explanatory notes printed at the bottom. Poetry was in verse form.

St Catharine's Monastery, Mount Sinai. The place where Tischendorf* found Codex Sinaiticus* while visiting in 1844 and where Agnes Smith Lewes* and Margaret Dunlop Gibson*, twins from Castlebrae*, found an Old Syriac* ms. in Sinaitic Syriac.

St Mark for Children, 1951. Popular title given to *The Gospel of St Mark: A New Translation in Simple English*, by Edward Vernon, arising from his conviction that the second gospel at least should be capable of being translated, without notes, so as to be understood by a twelve-year-old of average intelligence.

St Paul from the Trenches, 1937. A translation of 1 and 2 Corinthians and part of Ephesians by Gerald Warre Cornish*, a soldier in the First World War.

St Paul's Cross, London. Site of the public burning, on the authority of Cuthbert Tunstall*, the Bishop of London, of Tyndale's Translation*, which was entering the country with the help of merchants such as Humphrey Monmouth, a wealthy cloth merchant who befriended Tyndale* by taking him into his house for six months so as to give him leisure to translate the Bible, a kindness for which he paid some years later.

St Petersburg, Russia. Home of Codex Leningrad*, Codex Petersburg*, three fragments of the OT of Codex Sinaiticus* and some mss. from the Cairo Geniza*.

Stanton, Elizabeth Cady (1815–1902). American social reformer and a leading suffragette. Translator and editor of the Women's Bible*, 1895.

Stead, William Thomas (1849–1912). English journalist, author, editor of *Northern Echo*, and a reformer. Founding editor of *The Review of Reviews* who received two letters from writers with no awareness of each other's existence. Mary Higgs, wife of a Congregational minister, was one. Ernest Malan, a signal and telegraph engineer in Hull and grandson of an eminent Swiss divine, was the other. Both felt the inadequacy of all current translations, both were concerned about young people, and both wanted to do something about it. Stead introduced them to each other and so paved the way for The Twentieth Century New Testament*, 1902.

Stephanus, Robert (1503–59). A French printer (Robert Estienne) who produced a Hebrew OT in quarto size (1539-44) developed from the Soncino* edition and an edition of the Greek NT in 1550 which continued to be printed for the next 300 years and is still found in many Greek Testaments. Substantially the Textus Receptus*. The fourth edition (1551) introduced a system of verse division*, subsequently adopted by Whittingham*, used for the first time in the Geneva Bible* and copied from then onwards in every edition. Mainly the text of the fifth edition of Erasmus*, with some help from the Complutensian Polyglot* and from 15 mss., one of which was Codex Bezae*. The rest were late tenth to fifteenth century mss. Two Dutch printers, often wrongly described as the Elzevir* Brothers, published 7 editions based on Stephanus and Codex Bezae, 1624–78, the second (1633) achieving recognition as the Textus Receptus except in Britain which retained the term for the 1550 edition, as in the London Polyglot*.

Strasbourg, France. City where Coverdale* lived for several years in exile and where he translated books from Latin and German into English.

Streeter, Bernett Hillman (1874–1937). A biblical scholar, educated at Kings College, London, and student, Fellow and Provost of Queens College, Oxford. Responsible for picking out the Caesarean text* as found in Family Theta*, who in 1924 posited a theory of local text types at each of the great Christian centres: Alexandria*, Antioch, Caesarea*, Carthage, Rome and (later) Constantinople*.

Stuttgart, Germany. Home of the Württemberg Bible Society (founded 1812) which made a notable contribution through the publication of scholarly Bible texts, including Nestle's* Greek NT, 1898, revised by Aland, 1979, Kittel's *Biblia hebraica**, 1937, revised by Elliger and Rudolph, 1977, Rahlfs's* Septuagint, 1935, and Weber's Vulgate*, 1969.

Swete, Henry Barclay (1835–1917). A biblical scholar at King's College, London, and Cambridge, founder of the *Journal of Theological Studies*, whose major work was a three-volume edition of the LXX*, published by Cambridge University Press, 1887–94 (with later editions), basically Codex Vaticanus* using Codex Sinaiticus*, Codex Alexandrinus*, Codex Ephraemi*, Codex Bezae*, and other well-established mss. to fill the gaps. Subsequently superseded by the Cambridge Septuagint* in the Cambridge tradition and by a larger two-volume edition by Rahlfs*, more in the Göttingen* tradition.

Symmachus (c. 170 CE). Possibly a Samaritan convert to Judaism or an Ebionite who translated the OT into Greek c. 193–211. Remarkable for its faithfulness to the Hebrew, for its pure and elegant Greek and for its literary quality, with the emphasis on the sense of a phrase or passage rather than a literal translation, but it has survived only in fragments. Found in Origen's Hexaplar*. Had some influence on the English Bible through Jerome* who had a high regard for Symmachus and used it in translating the Vulgate*.

Synoptic Gospels. The name given to Matthew, Mark and Luke because they provide an overall conspectus or general survey, are similar in style and content, and can readily be compared with each other. The distinction between these three and the Fourth Gospel was first recognized by Clement of Alexandria*.

Syriac Version. Possibly the earliest translation of the NT, in the latter half of the second century, was into Syriac, an Aramaic dialect spoken in north-west Mesopotamia from before the Christian era. Most Syriac versions contain only 22 books (omitting 2 Peter, 2 and 3 John, Jude and Revelation) reflecting the canon of the Syriac Church in use at Antioch in the fourth to fifth centuries, but one edition in the John Rylands Library, Manchester*, has all 27, including Revelation in a form found in no other Syriac mss., the missing five coming from a later version. By the end of the sixth century there were five or six Syriac versions of which one, the Peshitta*, was claimed as a standard version similar to Jerome's Vulgate*, but it was never literal enough for some scholars and other versions followed. An edition of the entire Syriac text of the New Testament was published in 1929 by the British and Foreign Bible Society*.

Syrian Text. The name given by Westcott* and Hort* to those many readings of the Greek NT which were not known to be Neutral*, Alexandrian* or Western*, and therefore a somewhat vague description and not always reliable. Westcott and Hort regarded it as a conflated text and believed that it originated with the Greek and Syrian Church Fathers in the late fourth century as an attempt to make a smooth, easy and complete text. The furthest from the originals, it was taken to Constantinople* and spread widely throughout the Byzantine empire, its latest form being the Textus Receptus*. Found today in the gospels (but not Acts and epistles) of Codex Alexandrinus*, the later uncial* mss. and the great mass of minuscule* mss.

T

Talmud. An accumulation of rabbinic interpretation and commentary on Torah* and Mishnah*, dating from the second to the sixth centuries CE, in two forms: a Palestinian, and a much longer and more highly regarded Babylonian which has continued to form the basis of Jewish religious education.

Tanakh, 1985. A one-volume edition of the *New Jewish Version** previously published in stages. Tanakh is a Jewish acronym for what Christians call the Old Testament, formed from the initial letters of the three main sections, Torah (law), Nebiim (prophets) and Kethubim (writings), with the vowels added for vocalization.

Targum (Heb. pl. Targumim). The word means an explanation, commentary or even a translation, and eventually came to mean a translation of the Hebrew Bible* into Aramaic*. Targumim emerged in the Persian period as Aramaic became the language of the Near East and Aramaic paraphrases* of scripture appeared to clarify the text for the benefit of Jews who no longer spoke Hebrew. All targumim have a tendency to paraphrase, though some have a fixed text with uniform transmission whilst others have a more free text with notes, explanations, interpretations, commentary, and sometimes even legends inserted. Oral at first, and used to accompany the reading in the synagogues, they became more complex and more literary as they were committed to writing and were used increasingly outside the synagogue.

Targumim hold a special place in Judaism, their texts being printed side by side with the Hebrew, and mediaeval commentators often quoted from them. They covered almost every book of the Hebrew Bible, though not Ezra, Nehemiah or Daniel, and increased in popularity with a decline in the knowledge of Hebrew during the period of the Second Temple. Today they often help scholars to determine the language of scripture or the way in which the early texts were read and understood, sometimes helping to fill gaps or to make sense of difficult passages.

There are many in existence. The oldest is the second-century Palestinian Pentateuch Targum and one of the most useful is the Babylonian Targum on the Pentateuch*, known as Onkelos*. There are large fragments of a Job Targum dating from the end of the second century CE and found at Qumran*, containing a literal translation from a Hebrew original close to the Masoretic Text* which sometimes deviates from the other textual witnesses and may lack the ending (42.12-17). There exist also a Targum to Leviticus, two Esther Targumim, one known as a First Targum and the other as a Second Targum, both midrashic* in nature.

Tasker, Randolph Vincent Greenwood (1895–1976). New Testament scholar and member of the NT panel of translators of the NEB* who subsequently set out the Greek text on which the translation was based.

Tatian (c. 110–180). A native of the Euphrates Valley, a pupil of Justin Martyr* and a convert to Christianity who lived in Rome. Compiled a harmony of the gospels which became known as Tatian's Diatessaron* and which was used in Syria till the fifth century and persisted among Christians as a life of Jesus in various Western languages up to the Middle Ages. Seems to have recognized and accepted most of Paul's letters, with the exception of 1 and 2 Timothy, and to have known the *Gospel of Thomas*￼* and the *Gospel of Philip*, but to have been aware that they were not generally used.

Tatian's Diatessaron. The earliest Syriac version of the gospels and evidence for the circulation of the four gospels by the middle of the second century. A composite or interweaving of all four, probably made first in Greek and then translated into Syriac. 'Diatessaron' is a Greek word meaning 'harmony of four'. Tatian* undertook the work for the benefit of the Syriac Church and the gospels circulated in this form from c. 175 until the fifth century when it was replaced by the fourfold gospel. All that remains of the Greek text is a small fragment of parchment* about 4 inches square and containing about 14 lines of Greek.

Taverner, Richard (1505–75). Greek scholar, educated at Cardinal College, Oxford, and at Cambridge, and protégé of Thomas Cromwell*. Translator of Taverner's Bible*, shortly before the Great Bible* but with little influence on subsequent editions.

Taverner's Bible, 1539. An independent revision of Matthew's Bible*, undertaken by Richard Taverner* and dedicated to Henry VIII*. More successful in the NT than the OT, possibly because Taverner was not a very good Hebraist. Almost immediately eclipsed by the Great Bible*. Influenced the 1582 Roman Catholic translation of the NT, which in turn was consulted by the King James translators of the AV*. The origin of the phrase in the AV which calls the Son of God the 'express image' of his person (Heb. 1.3).

Taylor, Kenneth Nathaniel (1917–). Born in Portland, Oregon. Publishing executive, first with Moody Press and Tyndale House and then Publishing Executive and President of Living Bibles International, Wheaton, Illinois, 1968–77. Author of the Living Bible*, 1971. Beginning with a paraphrase* of the New Testament epistles, *Living Letters*, 1962, for the benefit of his own children, he went on to produce a paraphrase of the whole Bible with a wide circulation and considerable popularity among young people.

Tbilisi, Georgia. Home of Family Theta*.

Tell el-Amarna Tablets. Three hundred clay tablets, written in cuneiform*, and discovered accidentally by a peasant woman in Egypt in 1887. Part of a correspondence between the king of Egypt (Amenhotep IV) and his officials in Palestine and Syria.

Tercentenary Commemoration Bible, 1911. An Oxford University Press publication to celebrate the tercentenary of the publication of the AV*. Reproduces the text of the AV with light corrections and improvements by a team of evangelical biblical scholars in North America.

Tertullian (c. 160–220). A native of Carthage, the Father of Latin Theology, one of the first to refer to Old Testament* and New Testament*, to acknowledge the authority of all four gospels and to indicate that they were written either by apostles or by associates of apostles. Seems to have recognized and accepted 13 of Paul's letters, Acts, 1 John, 1 Peter and Revelation, but appears not to have known 2 Peter. In common with Clement of Alexandria* and the general opinion of his day he accepted Jude, though this came to be challenged later by Eusebius* and Jerome* because of its use of apocryphal books.

Textual Criticism. The purpose of textual criticism is to locate or reconstruct the text that is closest to the original, and this calls for a study of the changes which a text has undergone in the course of transmission: how it was originally written, how mss. were copied and circulated, and how the text reached the form in which we now have it. It requires a study of early texts (with attempts at dating), of translations into languages, and of other sources such as the use made of the texts by teachers and leaders within the Jewish or Christian communities. Sometimes known as lower criticism*, to distinguish it from higher criticism*, though both terms are rarely used in contemporary scholarship.

Textual criticism has its origins in the early centuries of the Christian tradition when scholars began comparing mss., versions and translations. Origen's Hexaplar* is a good example from the third century.

Textual criticism as we know it today goes back to the seventeenth century and is to some extent the product of the invention of printing, the Protestant Reformation with its emphasis on the Word, the increasing interest in archaeology and the discovery of more ancient sources, and the capacity to study, compare and evaluate them. There have been three stages of development:

> the realization that the original text of the NT was to be found in Greek and not Latin, the Latin Vulgate* having been the dominant text in the West from the fifth to the sixteenth centuries.
>
> the realization that the Greek was different from other ancient versions and from the text of patristic quotations.
>
> modern textual criticism beginning with Griesbach* and the classification of mss.

In no case do we have an autograph* of a biblical book. What we do have is a collection of mss. in original languages, of translations, versions, commentaries and interpretations, coming from different times and places, with different editors. We have mss. meticulously copied from earlier mss. and it is sometimes possible to discern 'families' of mss. which appear to have the same parentage and which, like children and grandchildren, bear resemblances but are not identical. Differences are few, but they do exist, sometimes errors in copying*, sometimes deliberate changes on the part of an editor 'with a purpose', and sometimes the result of an editorial judgment where the ms. was unclear, or damaged, or both. Textual criticism seeks to establish an earlier (and therefore presumably more authentic) form of text, to understand why, and how, the changes crept in, and to make an evaluation. Once established, the text is then set out with the variant readings* in the margin to give a critical apparatus*.

The establishment of text types (or families) associated with Lachmann* helps in evaluating mss. For example, a ms. with a reading belonging to the Alexandrian* type will be given more credibility than one belonging to the Western* type, and one to the Western more than one to the Byzantine*. A reading found in several mss. and in line with both Alexandrian and Western has a strong claim to originality, and readings in the papyri* will always be given high credibility because of their early date. In view of the large number of mss. and variant readings the work of textual criticism is not as simple as it may sound and it is not always possible to stay with one family or type. All readings and variations have to be examined and evaluated on a one-to-one basis.

From the seventeenth century onwards scholars like Bentley*, Bengel*, Wettstein*, Lietzmann* and Streeter* tried to establish guidelines or general principles for textual criticism and interpretation, such as broad attestation, *lectio difficilior** and *lectio brevior**.

Textual criticism also helps to explain how some of the differences found their way into the English Bible, why different translations provide different meanings, and why fresh translations are always needed as more information comes to light.

Textus Receptus. An edition of the Greek Testament, partly the fruit of the work of Erasmus, which appeared in 1550, and became a standard text for the translation of the Bible into English and the Greek text underlying the AV* in the NT. The compilers also used the work of Robert Stephanus* and Codex Bezae*.

Two editions appeared in Leiden* (1624 and 1633), the work of two Dutch printers, often wrongly described as the Elzevir* Brothers, and in the second one the preface assures the reader that this is 'the text which is now received by all'. Hence the title 'Textus Receptus' or 'Received Text'. Printed regularly through the seventeenth and eighteenth centuries when better mss. were discovered, but

readings from those better mss. (like Codex Alexandrinus*, Codex Vaticanus* and Codex Sinaiticus*) were added to the Textus Receptus by way of notes or marginal readings, and the mss. themselves were tabulated and numbered for easy reference. Uncial* mss. were indicated by the capital letters of the Greek and Latin alphabets. Minuscule* mss. were indicated by arabic numerals. Eventually replaced as the basis for NT study by Souter* and Nestle-Aland* with their notes and critical apparatus*.

Theodotion (second century). A Jewish proselyte from Ephesus who translated the OT into Greek, 180–92 CE. A fairly free rendering, mostly following the LXX*, but with additional passages in Job and Jeremiah beyond what had become the standard Hebrew text, and occasionally adding things that in the LXX were abbreviated. It replaced the LXX in most of the mss. which have reached us and is the prevailing text for the book of Daniel. Found in Origen's Hexaplar*.

Third Millennium Bible. A product planned by William Prindele* to produce a modernized version of the Apocrypha* to accompany The Twenty-first Century King James Version*.

Thirty-nine Articles (Church of England), 1562, 1571. Article VI lists and approves books that belong to the canon (OT and NT), and includes the apocryphal books but says they are 'for example of life and instruction of manners' and not to be used 'to establish any doctrine'.

Thompson Chain Reference Bible, 1908. See New Chain Reference Bible, 1964.

Thomson, Charles (1729–1824). One of the founding fathers of the USA who produced an English translation of the OT from the Greek LXX*, 1808. Republished in Colorado, 1954.

Thomson, Lawrence. Secretary to Sir Francis Walsingham, Elizabeth I's Secretary of State. Produced a revised edition of the NT in 1576 which subsequently found its way into the Geneva Bible*.

Thumb Bibles. A name given to abridged Bibles, usually for children and therefore small and heavily illustrated or doctored. They appear to have originated early in the seventeenth century with *An Agnus Dei** and *Verbum Sempiternum** though the phrase was coined by Longmans who used it on the title page of an edition dated 1849, possibly borrowed from General Tom Thumb (Charles Stratton) who visited England in 1844. Thumb Bibles were also known in eighteenth- and nineteenth-century Europe and altogether over 300 such Bibles have been identified.

Two other miniature Bibles are noteworthy. *The Oxford Nonpareil Bible*, photographically reduced by Glasgow University Press in 1896 and printed in Glasgow* and London on 876 pages, 1.5 × 1 inches, in an edition of 25,000, complete with a pocket and magnifying glass inside the front cover, and an even smaller facsimile of the NT published the same year measuring 0.75 × 0.6 inches.

The phrase is also sometimes used to refer to Bibles with holes, suitable for inserting a thumb, in the outside of the leaves, each containing a small label with the names of the books of the Bible, to facilitate easy reference.

Tischendorf, Constantine (1815–74). A German, biblical scholar who followed Lachmann* in cutting free from the Textus Receptus* and relying more on the ancient mss. In May 1844, on a visit to St Catharine's Monastery*, Mount Sinai, he found some ancient mss., which turned out to be part of Codex Sinaiticus*, in a wastepaper basket. He set himself the task of searching out and publishing every fragment that he could find of uncial* mss. of either Testament, as well as many minuscules*. Discovered 18 uncials, including Codex Vaticanus*, and 6 minuscules and made new editions of 11 uncials of first-rate importance, including Sinaiticus* in 1862 and Vaticanus* in 1867. Published more uncials than anyone else, including 8 editions of the Greek NT, 4 of the Latin and 4 of the LXX*, and edited over 20 editions of the Greek NT altogether. Published the first papyrus* mss. ($\mathfrak{P}^{11}$) in 1868, dating from the seventh century and containing portions of 1 Corinthians. His final edition of the Greek NT (1869–72) based on Codex Sinaiticus and Codex Vaticanus, with a critical apparatus*, was the standard edition of scholars until the 1930s. Exposed the forgeries of Constantine Simonides*.

Titus Fragment. A papyrus ms. ($\mathfrak{P}^{32}$) found at Oxyrhynchus*, dating from c. 200 and containing Tit. 1.11-15 and 2.2-8. The oldest piece of Titus in existence, and now located in the John Rylands Library, Manchester*.

Today's English Version, 1976. First appeared as *Good News for Modern Man: The New Testament in Today's English Version*, 1966, published by the American Bible Society* at the request of the United Bibles Societies* and with the help of a consultant from the British and Foreign Bible Society*, and quickly sold 12 million copies. The first English translation to be based on the (UBS) Greek New Testament*. Seven translators were then commissioned to work on the same lines with the OT, using Kittel's Biblia hebraica*, to complete the Bible in 1976. A British edition, the Good News

Bible*, facilitated by the British and Foreign Bible Society with a team of British scholars advising on British usage and checking for Americanisms, was published by Collins.

Based on a new philosophy of translation, it owed its origins to Eugene Nida*, who in the 1950s had noticed a quality of Spanish translation for millions of Indians from Mexico to Chile, which was neither patronizing nor 'second-rate' and where the translators had paid as much attention to the language of the receivers as to the texts to be translated. Robert G. Bratcher*, a former Southern Baptist missionary to Brazil, with firsthand experience of such work, was therefore commissioned by the American Bible Society to produce a draft translation of Mark's gospel which proved so satisfactory that they asked him to direct a complete translation of the NT. The result was one of the first committee-produced translations to advocate the principle of dynamic equivalence* and to push it to its limits.

The language was to be natural, clear, simple and unambiguous. Each book began with a short introduction and outline and there were extensive notes, a chronological chart, an index, maps, and a list of words and phrases not easily understood. Words like 'centurion', 'mammon' and 'publicans' were modernized. A new feature was a list of NT passages, quoted or paraphrased from the LXX*, to help people who refer back to the OT only to discover that the translation from Hebrew differs from what they find in the NT because the latter has been taken straight from the LXX. Another distinctive feature was the line drawings by Annie Vallotton*, a Swiss artist, partly because of their novelty and partly because they often succeeded in conveying more than words could express. Some critics feel that at times the translation oversimplifies complex passages, is cavalier in its attitude

to gender inclusive language and is beginning to show signs of being dated.

Todd, John (b. 1918). Editor of Catholic books for Longmans Green and a key figure in the production of the Jerusalem Bible*.

Torah. Often translated 'Law' but more accurately 'teaching'. The name given to the first five books of the OT. Possibly a compilation of several traditions (if not actual documents), subsequently worked over by editors to produce the Pentateuch* in the form in which we now have it. By far the most important part of the Hebrew Bible for the Jews and the first part of the OT to achieve form and a sense of unity of recognition, by c. 400 BCE.

Torrey, Charles Cutler (1863–1956). A linguist who specialised in Aramaic*, Apocrypha* and Pseudepigrapha*, and professor of Semitic Languages at Yale University. First Director of the American School of Oriental Research in Jerusalem. Translator of The Four Gospels, a New Translation*, 1933.

Tothill Street, Westminster. Site of William Caxton's* printing press.

Transcriptional Probability. Textual criticism* often requires editors of ancient texts to choose between two or more variant readings* on the basis of which looks more probable. Hort* coined the phrase 'transcriptional probability'* for situations when he was appealing to what the copyists were likely to have made of it, as against 'intrinsic probability'* when he was appealing to what an author was likely to have written.

Translation of all the Apostolical Epistles, A, 1795. A popular eighteenth-century translation by James MacK-night*, similar to work by George Campbell* and Philip Doddridge*, subsequently used by Alexander Campbell* to produce his own translation.

Translation of the Gospels, with Notes, 1855. The work of Andrews Norton*, a Unitarian Harvard professor, in two volumes, in contemporary English using 'you' instead of 'thou'.

Translation of the Old Testament Scriptures from the Original Hebrew, 1885. More popularly known as the Spurrell Translation*.

Translations. Ancient translations of the Bible, mainly into Greek (the LXX*), Aramaic*, Syriac* and Latin*, exist and afford an excellent opportunity to study the text, relate to the original and evaluate the differences.

In the case of the OT respect for the 'word' and 'the original text' meant that these translations were usually very literal, or 'word for word' translations and where they differ from the Hebrew (or indeed from each other) it is sometimes possible to reconstruct the original text from which the translator was working, known as a *Vorlage*.

The NT similarly appeared in translation form, first in Latin*, Syriac*, Coptic*, and then later in Arabic*, Armenian*, Ethiopian*, Gothic* and Slavonic*, though possibly with a little more freedom than was accorded the OT. Such 'word-for-word' translations provided the norm for Bible translation until the Middle Ages.

Bible translation into English dates from the Reformation, beginning with Tyndale*, and until the start of the twentieth century (since when there has been considerably increased translation activity leading to a plethora of new ones) consisted predominantly of the AV* and

the RV*. Similar developments took place in other European countries and in the USA, and Bibles were also translated into many other languages all over the world as a result of missionary activity and the work of the Bible Societies*.

With increased translation activity came changes in translation method, possibly the influence of more literary translations from Greek to Latin, when 'word for word' or 'verbal equivalence'* gave place to 'sense for sense', or 'dynamic equivalence'*, and more recently to communication theory*, the intention being less to convey the words and more to convey the sense in another language and culture, thus giving the reader something very near to the impression created by the original on the first reader. Sometimes such translations step over into paraphrase*.

Translator's New Testament, 1973. Simple in vocabulary, uncomplicated in style, and avoiding over-simplification which fails to convey the full meaning of the original, this version of the NT was specially prepared by a team of 35 scholars, working under W.D. McHardy*, and published by the British and Foreign Bible Society* for the benefit of those whose knowledge of Greek was little or none but who were yet called upon to translate the English Bible into other languages. The original text is the (UBS) Greek New Testament*, 1966.

Tregelles, Samuel Prideaux (1813–75). Showed exceptional talent as a boy when, besides earning his living in an ironworks, he managed to devote his free time to learning Greek*, Aramaic*, Hebrew* and Welsh. Set himself in his early twenties to prepare a new critical edition* of the NT based on the evidence of the earliest witnesses. Travelled extensively in Europe, spent most of his time collating mss. and acquired an almost total knowledge of the known uncials* and many of the minuscules* of the day. Developed independently principles of criticism very similar to those of Lach- mann*, but used rather more ancient authorities and paid more attention to the versions* and the quotations found in the early church Fathers. Published two edi- tions of the Greek NT in full, 1857 and 1872, and collated many others. Ap- pointed one of the translators of the RV* but was prevented from participation by ill health.

Tunstall, Cuthbert (1474–1557). Bishop of London, an educated man with a good knowledge of Greek* and Hebrew*, to whom William Tyndale* applied unsuc- cessfully for help in translating the Bible into English in 1523. Disturbed when Tyndale's Translation* began to be im- ported and distributed in this country. He denounced it, said he could find 3000 errors in it and ordered everyone in his diocese to hand over any copies they pos- sessed for a public burning at St Paul's Cross*, 1526. When this failed to kill off demand he arranged with Augustine Packington* for the buying up of large quantities on the continent, a move which proved to be no more successful. Later, during his time as Bishop of Durham, his name appeared in the fourth and sixth editions of the Great Bible* lending his authority to a Bible translation which in fact is Tyndale's production more than anything else. (See Tunstall, Bishop of London, p. 170.)

Twentieth-Century New Testament, 1902. First widely accepted translation of the modern era, said to have had its ori- gin in the desire of a mother to translate the NT into language that her children could understand, and the result of an initiative by Mary K. Higgs and Ernest Malan who were introduced to each other in 1890 by W.T. Stead* and shared a common concern that children were unable to understand the English of the AV*. Beginning with Mark they worked together to translate the gospels and Acts and were later joined by others to do a full NT translation.

The work was divided into four sec- tions: the gospels (with Mark first) and Acts, Paul's letters to the churches in what was believed to be their chronolog- ical order, pastoral, personal and general letters, and Revelation. A tentative edition was issued in three parts, 1898–1901, and the final form appeared on the basis of the criticisms received. One of the consul- tants was Weymouth*. Published by Fleming H. Revell Co., New York. A later edition, printed by Moody Press, 1961, updated the English and restored the books to their canonical order.

A dynamic equivalence* translation from Westcott* and Hort's* Greek text into modern English, made by more than 30 translators, ministers and laity with a radical outlook on social and reli- gious matters but no outstanding linguis- tic experts, who set out nevertheless to go back to the original Greek and capture its freshness by conveying its force in idiomatic, modern English. A distin- guishing feature was the care with which it was undertaken and it was not really surpassed for half a century.

Modern paragraphing, quotation marks, titles and subtitles. Passages thought not to be original enclosed in square brackets. Chapter and verse nota- tions in the margin. Subject headings in black-faced type. Direct speech in quota- tion marks. Measures of time and space, values of coins and official titles given in their nearest English equivalents.

All the participants kept their identity secret until the last one died in 1933, when the relevant documents were deposited at the John Rylands Library, Manchester*, where they were studied in 1953 by Kenneth W. Clark*.

Tunstall, Bishop of London

Having rejected Tyndale's[*] appeal for help in 1523 Tunstall, Bishop of London, became anxious as he saw Tyndale's Bible[*] being imported from the continent and freely distributed. When his decision to buy up all the copies for a public burning seemed to inflame nothing more than the demand he concluded the only solution was to buy them up at source and this brought him into contact with a London merchant, Augustine Packington[*], whom he met in Antwerp.

Edward Halle, in his *Chronicle*, describes what happened:

> The bishop, thinking he had God by the toe, when indeed he had (as after he thought) the devil by the fist, said, 'Gentle Master Packington, do your diligence and get them, and with all my heart I will pay for them, whatsoever they cost you; for the books are erroneous and naughty, and I intend surely to destroy them all, and to burn them at Paul's Cross.'
>
> Augustine Packington came to William Tyndale and said, 'William, I know thou art a poor man, and hast a heap of New Testaments and books by thee, for the which thou hast endangered thy friends and beggared thyself; and I have now gotten thee a merchant, which with ready money shall dispatch thee of all that thou hast, if you think it so profitable for yourself.'
>
> 'Who is the merchant?' said Tyndale.
>
> 'The bishop of London', said Packington.
>
> 'Oh, that is because he will burn them', said Tyndale.
>
> 'Yea marry,' quoth Packington.
>
> 'I am the gladder,' said Tyndale; 'for these two benefits shall come thereof: I shall get money of him for these books, to bring myself out of debt, and the whole world shall cry out upon the burning of God's word. And the overplus of the money, that shall remain to me, shall make me more studious to correct the said New Testament, and so newly to imprint the same once again and I trust the second will much better like you than did the first.'
>
> And so forward went the bargain: the bishop had the books, Packington had the thanks, and Tyndale had the money.

Tunstall, Bishop of London (cont.)

In due course the bishop met Packington in London and complained that more copies than ever were coming into the country. Packington's defence was that he had kept his side of the bargain and if the bishop were not satisfied perhaps he should consider buying up the standing type.

Halle further suggests that the bishop had discussed his proposal with his colleagues, because he records how More tackled one called George Constantine and asked him who was financing Tyndale and his friends in Europe.

Halle continues,

'My Lord,' quoth Constantine, 'will you that I shall tell you the truth?'
'Yea, I pray thee,' quoth my lord.
'Marry I will,' quoth Constantine.
'Truly,' quoth he, 'it is the bishop of London that hath holpen us; for he hath bestoewed among us a great deal of money in New Testaments to burn them, and that hath been, and yet is, our only succour and comfort.'
'Now by my troth,' quoth More, 'I think even the same, and I said so much to the bishop, when he went about to buy them.'

Twenty-first Century King James Version, 1994. The project of William Prindele*, a retired American attorney, who formed a publishing company to produce, market and distribute a modern version of the KJV, 1611*. The wording is modernized on the authority of Webster's *New International Dictionary*, second edition, unabridged. Built on the foundations of the KJV* with some questionable readings. Claims to rescue the Bible from the ravages of modern translations but it may be more accurate to say it wishes to rescue it from 'modern liberal scholars'.

Tyndale, William (1494–1536). Born at Slimbridge, Gloucestershire. Educated at Oxford and Cambridge. Statue stands on the Victoria Embankment, London. Sometimes described as the Father of the English Bible. While at Cambridge he proved himself good at Greek* and dur-

ing a period in which he served as tutor to the children of Sir John Walsh in Gloucestershire, he translated Erasmus's* *The Christian Soldier's Handbook* (1502), which pleased his employers but not the ecclesiastical authorities who unsuccessfully called him to answer a charge of heresy. Tyndale wanted to have the NT in a language that people could understand. According to Foxe, though perhaps more accurately attributed to Wycliffe*, in controversy with a churchman he once said, 'If God spare my life, 'ere many years I will cause a boy that driveth a plough to know more of the scriptures than thou doest.'

He began his own translation and when he was opposed by king and church he left England in 1524 for Wittenberg and then moved on to Hamburg. He began printing at Cologne* the following year and when he met further opposition from Cochlaeus* he finished it at Worms*. Six thousand copies were printed. Copies began to reach England in 1526, many of them smuggled in bales of cloth or sacks of flour by friendly merchants, where they were eagerly bought for a few shillings a copy in English money. There were many editions, the 1534 edition becoming the foundation for the whole tradition of the English Bible, beginning with the AV* and continuing to the NRSV*.

He was betrayed, captured and thrown into prison on 21 May 1535 in Belgium, where he spent his closing years under the control of Charles V, Holy Roman Emperor. Cromwell* and Henry VIII* tried to secure his release but Charles was not in a friendly mood, partly perhaps because he was a nephew of Katharine of Aragon whom Henry had recently divorced. Tyndale was found guilty of heresy in August 1536, strangled and burnt at the stake on 6 October at Vilvorde*, with the final prayer on his lips, 'Lord, open the king of England's eyes.' Some months after his death a version of the Bible in English, based on Tyndale's work, was circulating in England with Henry's permission.

Tyndale's Translation, 1525 (NT).
First English NT to be printed, at Worms*, an earlier attempt at Cologne* having failed because the city Senate learned what was afoot and forbade the printer to continue.

An octavo edition, based on an edition of Erasmus's* NT with help from the Vulgate*. Revised several times, reaching its climax with a new edition, printed at Antwerp*, 1534.

Differs from previous translations in being from the original Greek and it may have been because the Greek gives different renderings from the Latin that Tunstall* accused Tyndale of error.

A deluxe copy, bound in vellum, with gold edges, now in the British Library, was presented to Anne Boleyn with the words '*Anne Regina Angliae*' still visible on the gold edges. Two other copies extant, one in the British Library (complete except for title page) and the other in St Paul's Cathedral (imperfect at the beginning and end).

Tyndale's attempts to translate the OT from the Hebrew started in Wittenberg but were never completed, partly because he had to undertake several revisions of the NT and partly because his knowledge of Hebrew was limited, but for the Pentateuch and the Historical Books he used the Hebrew text, the LXX*, the Vulgate* and Luther's German versions.

U

Udall, John (1560–92). Urged Cromwell*, with the publication of the Great Bible* in 1540, to persuade the king to make an order that all bishops should set up two or three Bibles in their cathedral.

Ugarit, Syria. An ancient city on the north coast of Syria in the fifteenth to fourteenth centuries BCE and a key Canaanite centre of industry, trade and culture. Site for the discovery of the Ras Shamra Tablets* in 1929.

Ulfilas, Bishop (311–81). Grandchild of a couple deported from Cappadocia to Dacia (Romania) c. 264 and probably the child of a Cappadocian mother and a Gothic father who gave him a Gothic name, 'Little Wolf'. He became known as the Apostle to the Goths of the Danube. He invented an alphabet for the Visigoths, reduced the spoken language to written form and translated the Bible from Greek into Gothic*. His translation was very literal (verbal equivalence*) but he was judged a competent translator.

Uncials. An ancient form of writing Greek, as against cursives*, dating from the third to the twelfth centuries, formal, usually kept for literary works, and found on vellum*. Fairly large, capital letters, not joined together. From the Latin *uncial* meaning one-twelfth, possibly used in this case because of the scribal habit of dividing a line into twelve characters and writing *scriptio continua**. Mss. written in this style are known as uncial mss. Prior to the tenth century only uncial characters appeared in NT mss. but by then they had become thick and ugly and were replaced with smaller letters called minuscules*, more suited to book production.

There are 268 uncial mss. of the NT extant, 4 of them (fragmentary) mainly from the third to the eleventh centuries, published between 1909 and 1935, and no more than about 60 anything like complete. Because of their age they are quite the most valuable of all early mss. for the reconstruction of the text of the NT, though the papyrus* discoveries of the twentieth century, because of their greater age, have called for a few corrections here and there. (Codex) Sinaiticus*, Alexandrinus*, Vaticanus*, Ephraemi*, Bezae* and Claromontanus* are regarded as the most significant.

When uncial mss. were tabulated they were each given a letter from the Greek or Latin alphabet for the purposes of identification and recognition. For example, Codex Alexandrinus is A.

Unitarian Version, 1808. The name often wrongly given to the translations of Gilbert Wakefield* and William Newcome*, neither of whom could be charged with issuing a sectarian version of the scriptures. The Unitarian Society for Promoting Christian Knowledge wanted a Bible devoid of technical theological phrases which had no basis in the Bible itself. Wakefield was approached, but his death in 1801 led them to look elsewhere, so they simply adopted Newcome's text (Newcome having died in 1800), got it edited and adapted by Thomas Belsham*, and published it in 1808 as *The New Testament in an Improved Version, upon the basis of Archbishop Newcome's New Translation; with a corrected text.* The fifth edition of 1819 simply bears the title Unitarian Version.

United Bible Societies. Founded in 1946, on an initiative in the Netherlands, as an international coordinating body for some 16 national Bible Societies which had sprung up around the world following the earlier initiative taken by the British and Foreign Bible Society* and the American Bible Society*. With the addition of other national Bible Societies the number quickly grew to over 100 and, as the larger societies withdrew from direct control of work in other countries and autonomous national societies developed, the work of the UBS became the provision of information, technical resources and funding.

Unknown Sayings of Jesus. Sayings attributed to Jesus in sources outside the four gospels and known as agrapha*.

Uppsala, Sweden. Location for the Silver Codex*.

Urtext. The original text of a book before copying* and transmission became operative. Interest in the possibility of arriving at such a text grew as a result of the work of Bauer* and de Lagarde* while some scholars, following Kahle*, do not believe that any such urtext ever existed and that from a very early date there were several texts all claiming equal authority. One of the purposes of textual criticism* was to arrive as near as possible at the urtext.

Uvedale, John. See Udall.

V

Vallotton, Annie (b. c. 1904). A Swiss artist, living in France, responsible for the line drawings in Today's English Version[*].

Variant Readings. Readings (that is, letters, words or phrases) which differ from what is regarded as the standard ms. In the case of the OT that would be the Masoretic Text[*], in the case of the NT or the English Bible, the Textus Receptus[*].

Wherever text is transmitted variations are likely to occur (on the principle that 'if something can go wrong, it will'). Some are accidental, some are deliberate. Accidental ones may be due to the absence of punctuation, to *scriptio continua*[*] leading to ambiguity, to the eye in copying[*], such as dittography[*], haplography[*], homoioteleuton[*] or homoioarcton[*], or to the ear in dictation, particularly where two words sound alike but may have different meanings.

As the text became standardized and editions of the OT (in Hebrew) and the NT (in Greek) were published variant readings were normally included in the margin, or at the foot of the text, together with the source, to produce a critical apparatus[*]. The first such systematic collection is to be found in the London Polygot[*].

Variant readings are just that—variants. They are not inferior or secondary. In some cases they may be superior.

Vellum. Parchment. Though it existed much earlier, Pliny attributed its popularity (if not its origin) to King Eumenes[*] of Pergamon (197–59 BCE), a city in Asia Minor, who wanted to establish a library to rival that of Ptolemy in Alexandria[*]. When Ptolemy realized what was happening he put an embargo on papyrus[*] exports, thus forcing Eumenes to turn to vellum which, because of its origins in Pergamon, was given the name of *pergamenē*, from which we get 'parchment'.

An ideal writing material (not to be confused with leather to which it is superior) made from the skins of certain animals, mainly sheep and calves, by soaking the skin in lime water, shaving off the hair from one side and the flesh from the other, stretching and drying on a frame, smoothing with pumice and dressing with chalk. The finest form, made from calf skin and kept for special purposes such as a deluxe edition, is the true vellum, though over the years the two terms came to be used interchangeably. Vellum leaves are fixed together to form a codex[*] or book as opposed to a scroll[*].

Used only for notebooks and cheap copies until the third century CE when its superior qualities were recognized: more widely available (papyrus being confined to the Nile Delta), more durable (especially in cool, damp climates), good writing surface, easier for making corrections, alterations and deletions, capable of being used on both sides and therefore more economical, able to contain much more writing than a scroll*, and sometimes capable of being used more than once thus giving a palimpsest*. Its disadvantages were that it was more costly, its edges easily became uneven, and because its shiny surface reflected more light it was thought by some to cause more eye strain.

Used increasingly for mss. of the scriptures from the second century CE, replaced papyrus by the fourth, and was the main writing material* until it was itself superseded in the twelfth with the arrival of paper and printing*.

Writing on vellum is usually uncial*. (See The Price of Vellum, below.)

Venice Edition, 1517–48. The first edition to divide Samuel, Kings, Chronicles and Ezra–Nehemiah into two separate parts respectively.

Venice, Italy. Site for the famous Bomberg* press and for the printing of the first two Rabbinic Bibles*.

Verbal equivalence. A method of translation* which aims at 'word-for-word' rather than dynamic equivalence* or 'sense for sense' and in its extreme form may retain the same English word for the same Hebrew or Greek word every time it occurs. Popular verbal equivalence translations are the AV*, the RV*, the NIV*, the NJB* and (to a lesser extent) the RSV* and the NRSV*.

Verbum Sempiternum, 1614. The second oldest and perhaps best-known Thumb Bible*, printed in London and reprinted well into the nineteenth century, containing summaries of OT and NT by John Taylor (1580–1653). The first American edition was published in Boston, 1786, measuring 2.5 × 1.5 inches. The first prose edition, 1727, ran to nearly 300 pages, with 16 engraved plates, and measured 1.5 × 1 inches.

Verkuyl, Gerrit (b. 1872). Professor of New Testament, Princeton University, and a member of the Board of Christian Education of the Presbyterian Church, USA. Translated The Berkeley Version* of the NT, 1945, and subsequently acted as Editor-in-Chief of a translation of the OT.

Verse Division. Verse division in the OT goes back to c. 200 CE and was finally fixed in the tenth century when Ben Asher divided the Pentateuch* into 5845 verses instead of the 5888 according to the Babylonians or the 15,842 according to the Palestinians. From c. 500 the divi-

---

The Price of Vellum

It took the hides of 4500 animals to make the vellum* for just 50 Bibles. Add to that the cost for the preparation of the parchment and the scribal fee and producing a Bible was a very expensive operation which only the wealthy could afford. Copy by dictation may have made materials more abundant and copies cheaper but even so it is estimated that a copy of Luke–Acts might cost as much as £100 or more in today's money. Books were clearly not for ordinary people.

sion is marked by the insertion of two dots. The criteria for determining a verse division are less clear. One suggestion is that it was the length of a line of poetry, another that it was the amount read out at one time for translation into Aramaic in the synagogue.

Verse division in the NT first appears in the Stephanus edition of 1551, made by Stephanus* himself while travelling from Paris* to Lyons, and the Stephanus Latin Bible (1555) was the first to show the present division in both Testaments.

Early editions of the English Bible were in paragraph form without any verse division. The first English NT to have verse division was that by Whittingham*, 1557, who adopted the division used by Stephanus* in his edition of the Greek NT. The first English Bible to adopt verse division was the Geneva Bible* which followed that introduced by Rabbi Nathan in 1448, first printed in 1524.

Version. A translation from the original language of a text into another one.

Vespasian Psalter. One of the oldest examples of biblical text in Old English, the other being the Paris Psalter*, dating from the ninth century, in Latin, with a very literal translation of the Psalms, possibly for use in monasteries by monks who knew no Latin. Located in the British Library.

Vilvorde, Belgium. A fortress, six miles north of Brussels where Tyndale was imprisoned, May to October 1535, after being kidnapped in Antwerp* and where he was first tied to the stake, then strangled by the hangman, and finally burned, 6 October 1536. (One record puts his imprisonment at 1 year plus 135 days.)

Vinegar Bible, 1717. An Oxford edition of the AV* which got its title because the chapter heading to Luke 20 had 'vinegar' for 'vineyard'.

Vocalization. The addition of vowels to the consonantal Masoretic Text* by the Masoretes* to assist and standardize vocalization, and to remove doubts as to the meaning of the word where the consonants alone allowed for more than one interpretation. The purely consonantal text persisted until the Middle Ages and even in the twelfth century there was still some opposition to adding vowels to assist vocalization on the grounds that they did not 'come from Sinai', but change had been coming much earlier. By the ninth century, three systems of vocalization had emerged: the Babylonian (eighth century), the Tiberian (780–930), and the Palestinian (700–850) which evolved until it gave way to the Tiberian, the one in current use and the one found in today's Hebrew grammars. Both Christians and Jews have tried to credit the system with divine authority which was not seriously questioned until the sixteenth century.

Vorlage. See Translations.

Vulgate. A Latin* translation produced as Christianity spread west into the world where Greek was not understood, and the Bible in general use throughout the Western world all through the Middle Ages. Change came with new translations from the Hebrew and the Greek, beginning with Tyndale*, and from the time of the Reformation Protestants adopted such translations for common use. The Council of Trent*, 1545–63, declared the Vulgate the authentic version of the church but this did not imply an indifference to the original Greek and Hebrew and the Vulgate, albeit in English translation, continued to be the Bible for Roman Catholics up to the middle of the twentieth century.

Its origins go back to the fourth century, by which time the Old Latin* text had reached such a state of corruption that, coupled with a growing appreciation of the Alexandrian* text and the Greek uncials* of the fourth century, it paved the way for a revision or fresh translation, undertaken by Jerome*, completed in 405 and given the title 'Vulgate', meaning 'public' or 'common'.

Jerome's principles of translation were sound, even if his work did not always follow a consistent pattern, and the translation had a literary quality about it. Besides the Hebrew text he also used the LXX*, Aquila*, Symmachus* and Theodotion*. His plan was to render the general sense of a passage rather than to achieve a word for word translation. There were revisions by Cassiodorus (d.

570) and Alcuin* and it replaced the Old Latin in the eighth to ninth centuries.

There are estimated to be over 10,000 mss. of the Latin Vulgate and they have been classified in families: Italian, French, Spanish, Irish, French, Alcuin and Theodulf. The most reliable extant ms. was made in England (at either Jarrow* or Wearmouth*), copied under the direction of Coelfrid*, presented to Pope Gregory II in 716 and now in the Laurentian Library at Florence, known as the Codex Amiatinus*. The first printed edition was the first printed book of any importance, the Mazarin Bible*, 1452–56, and the first critical edition* was that by Stephanus*, 1528. The definitive edition of the Vulgate NT is that by John Wordsworth published by the Clarendon Press, Oxford, 1889.

W

Wakefield, Gilbert (1756–1801). A dissenter*, in both theology and politics, educated at Jesus College, Cambridge, who rejected a free rendering of the AV* by Edward Harwood* and offered instead his own Translation of the New Testament, 1791, sometimes known incorrectly as the Unitarian Version*, which stayed much closer to the AV. Other editions appeared in 1795 and 1820.

Walker, Obadiah (1616–91). Fellow of University College, Oxford, and a Delegate of the Oxford University Press. One of three Oxford dons responsible for a Paraphrase on the Epistles of St Paul*, 1675.

Walton, Brian (1600–61). Bishop of Chester. Edited and published the London Polyglot Bible*, 1657–69, containing the readings of 14 previously unpublished mss. One of the first people to challenge the notion that there was only one Hebrew text, the Masoretic, underlying the Hebrew Bible* by pointing out that where there were two readings only one could be original. This then gave rise to the view that the text could be improved by comparison, first with other Hebrew texts, such as the Samaritan Pentateuch*, and then with other versions* such as the LXX*.

Walton's Polyglot, 1657. See London Polyglot.

Wand, John William Charles (1885–1977). Educated at St Edmund Hall, Oxford. Archbishop of Brisbane and (subsequently) Bishop of Bath and Wells and then of London. Produced The New Testament Letters*, 1943.

Wansbrough, Henry (1934–). Editor of the New Jerusalem Bible*, 1985. Born in London and educated at Ampleforth College and Oxford, with a First in Classics and Philosophy. Became a monk at Ampleforth, 1953, and studied at the Catholic University of Fribourg, Switzerland. Went to Israel to learn modern Hebrew and studied at the Ecole Biblique. Ordained a priest, 1964, and returned to Ampleforth. Master of St Benet's Hall, Oxford. General Editor of *The People's Bible Commentary*.

Wansburgh, Hans. See Henry Wansbrough.

Washington Codex. A group of four vellum* mss., two OT, two NT, discovered by Charles L. Freer* in Cairo*, 1906. 187 leaves, 5.5 × 8.25 inches, 2 columns to a page and dated c. sixth century. Usually known as W and located at the Freer Museum, Washington*. OT consists of 107 leaves of a Psalter, with a text akin to Codex Alexandrinus*. NT has 80 of an original 210 leaves, in fragmentary condition, containing the four gospels in the so-called order of the Western* text (i.e. Matthew, John, Luke, Mark) and portions from all Paul's letters (except Romans), with an Alexandrian* text and close similarities to Sinaiticus*.

Washington, USA. Home of the Washington Codex* in the Freer* Museum, and of the Mazarin* (Gutenberg) Bible in the National Library.

Way, Arthur Sanders (1847–1930). Classical scholar who wanted his readers to be able to understand Paul without reading a commentary and published a popular translation, The Letters of St Paul*, 1901.

Wearmouth. One of two possible sites for the copying of the Codex Amiatinus*, the other claimant being Jarrow*.

Webster, Noah (1758–1843). American lexicographer and publisher of various dictionaries and grammars, the forerunners of Webster's New International Dictionary of the English Language. A Congregational layman who had a high regard for the AV* but was also sensitive to the way some words had changed their meaning over 250 years, so he identified about 150 words and phrases which needed attention and produced *The Holy Bible, containing the Old and New Testaments, in the Common Version, with Amendments of Language, 1833*, with a second edition in 1841, so paving the way for many future revisions as later translators accepted his judgements.

Weigle, Luther, A. (1880–1976). Dean of Yale Divinity School and Chairman of the Standard Bible Committee of the National Council of the Churches of Christ in the USA and of each of the two sections which produced the RSV* and of that which revised the Apocrypha*.

Weiss, Bernhard (1827–1918). Professor of New Testament at Kiel and Berlin and editor of *The New Testament in Greek*, in three volumes, 1894–1900. Primarily an exegete with a detailed knowledge of the problems of NT translation and interpretation, Weiss avoided classifying mss. according to families and preferred to choose the one which seemed to him most suitable from the variety of readings available, working on the principle of intrinsic probability*. He also listed and evaluated different types of error found in variant readings*, including harmonizations* among the gospels, interchange of words, omissions* and additions*, word order and orthographical variations, and then evaluated mss. according to their freedom from such errors. His results were not very different from those of Westcott* and Hort*, including the priority of Codex Vaticanus*, but his work demonstrates how two different ways of working and assessing tended to reach the same conclusions.

Wells, Edward (1667–1727). Mathematician and theological writer, one of a number of scholars in the eighteenth and nineteenth centuries who attempted to incorporate the fruits of fresh knowledge into Bible translation, the first to produce a revised Greek NT text, with helps for the reader, 1707–19, largely based on the work of John Mill* but abandoning the Textus Receptus* in favour of readings from the more ancient mss.; and author of The Common Translation Corrected, 1718–24, a revised text of the AV*.

Wesley, John (1703–91). Published a translation of the NT with notes, 1755. Revised the AV*, 1768, based on a fresh and independent study of the Greek text, adding notes and arranging the material in paragraphs according to sense. An Anniversary Edition (1953) compares it with the AV, showing that he made 12,000 changes and that he was a good judge of the Greek text in that three-quarters of his changes were accepted by the revisers in the 1870s.

Wesley's New Testament, 1775. The name popularly given to *Explanatory Notes on the New Testament*, by John Wesley. A conservative revision of the AV* with the text in paragraphs to facilitate reading.

West Saxon Gospels. A translation, perhaps described more accurately as a paraphrase*, which appeared in the tenth century, attributed to Abbot Aelfric*, consisting of parts of the first seven books of the OT and some homilies on Kings, Esther, Job, Daniel and Maccabees. Two copies are extant, one at Oxford* and one in the British Library.

Westcott, Brooke Foss (1825–1901). An industrious Birmingham pupil who went to Trinity College, Cambridge, in 1844 and gained a First in Classics. Taught at Harrow, was ordained, became a Canon of Westminster and Peterborough, and, after a spell as a Cambridge professor from 1870, became Bishop of Durham in 1890. Worked with F.J.A. Hort* in their epoch-making edition of the Greek NT, *The New Testament in the Original Greek* (1881), a new text taking into account all the variations in the mss. that were available, which appeared five days before the RV* of the NT. Volume 1 contained the Greek text and volume 2 an introduction and appendix setting out the critical principles in detail. One of the key figures in the translation of the NT RV but was uneasy about the Textus Receptus* and stressed the superior value of Codex Sinaiticus* and Codex Vaticanus*.

Western Text. A text-type of the Greek NT, ancient (possibly dating from the first half of the second century) and widespread, identified by Westcott* and Hort* and most readily recognized in the gospels and Acts of Codex Bezae*, the epistles of Codex Claromontanus*, the Old Latin* and Old Syriac* versions, $\mathfrak{P}^{38}$ and $\mathfrak{P}^{48}$, and in quotations from the Latin Fathers up to 400 and Greek Fathers such as Justin*, Irenaeus*, Marcion* and Tatian* in the second century. The oldest known form of the NT text, but not necessarily therefore the best source because of its tendency to paraphrase and to go in for additions*, omissions* and harmonizations*.

Westminster Version of the Sacred Scriptures, 1935 (NT). A translation by English Roman Catholic scholars, based on the original Greek and Hebrew texts, under the editorship of Cuthbert C. Lattey*, with introductions and commentaries. Begun in 1913 and finished in 1935. Sold in parts until 1948 when it appeared as a one-volume edition with abridged notes. The OT was started in 1934 and appeared in parts but was never completed.

Wettstein, Johann Jakob (1693–1754). A native of Basle* with a flair for textual criticism* who became a professor of philosophy and Hebrew in Amsterdam* and established the principle of *lectio brevior*. Published a two-volume Greek text of the NT, 1751–52, very similar to the work of the Elzevir* printers but indicating in the margin which readings he felt to be correct. First to compile a list of mss. (21 uncials* and over 250 minuscules*) and to allocate letters to the uncials and numerals to the minuscules, 1751–52. List subsequently extended by C.F. Matthaei* and Caspar René Gregory* at the end of the nineteenth century.

Weymouth, Richard Francis (1822–1902). Born the son of a naval commander, a Baptist, in what was then Plymouth Dock, had a private education and studied in France for two years. Oxford and Cambridge being closed to Nonconformists he entered University College, London, where he studied Classics, graduating in 1843, and being the first to receive a Doctor of Literature from University College, 1868. The following year he became Head of Mill Hill School. Produced an edition of the Greek NT, *The Resultant Greek Testament*, reflecting the greatest measure of agreement on the Greek text among nineteenth-century scholars, with a critical apparatus* and an introductory note by J.J.S. Perowne, Bishop of Worcester. He then translated it into modern English to give *The New Testament in Modern Speech*, usually known as Weymouth's New Testament*, 1903. One of the consultants on The Twentieth Century New Testament*, 1902.

Weymouth's New Testament, 1903. A dynamic equivalence* translation of R.F. Weymouth's* *The Resultant Greek Testament*, made by Weymouth himself on the basis of some of the most recent ms. evidence available to him and published as *The New Testament in Modern Speech* by James Clarke & Co., London. There were many editions, including revisions by E. Hampden-Cook* and J.A. Robertson*.

Born of a strong desire to render the best Greek text into dignified, modern English, Weymouth's intention was to produce a translation without any specific theological viewpoint. A scholar of distinction but a free translator, he asked himself, 'how would the sacred writer have said this if he had been living in our age and country?' He then set out to help the reader to appreciate Paul by cutting down his long sentences into ones of more manageable size. He did not wish to replace the AV* or the RV* and had no desire to offer a version for read-

ing in church. Rather he intended 'a succinct and compressed running commentary (not doctrinal) to be used side by side with its older compeers'.

Distinguishing features include shorter, more manageable sentences, OT quotations in capital letters, extensive notes to support the translation in fine print at the bottom of the page, subject headings in black-faced type, chapter and verse numbers in the margin and direct speech in single quotes. Particularly valuable for its rendering of the Greek tenses in which Weymouth was a specialist.

Frequently re-printed. The fourth edition (1924) was thoroughly revised by J.A. Robertson who supplied introductions to the several literary divisions of the NT and replaced Weymouth's mis-translation 'life of the ages' by the more accurate 'eternal life'.

Whig Bible, 1562. The name given to the 1562 edition of the Geneva Bible* because of an error in Mt. 5.9 which read 'place makers' instead of 'peace makers'.

Whiston, William (1667–1752). Mathematician and theologian. Isaac Newton's successor at Cambridge and best known for his translation of Josephus. Published a Primitive New Testament*, 1745.

Whitby, Daniel (1638–1726). Rector of St Edmunds, Salisbury, a controversial writer and one of a number of scholars in the eighteenth and nineteenth centuries who attempted to incorporate the fruits of fresh knowledge into Bible translation, though he began to show signs of alarm lest the authority of the scriptures was in peril when John Mill* claimed to have identified 30,000 variant readings* in the Greek text. Produced Paraphrase and Commentary on the New Testament*, 1703, including an explanatory expansion of the AV*.

Whitby, Yorkshire. Home of an ancient monastery associated with Caedmon*.

Whitchurch, Edward (d. 1561). One of the printers of the Great Bible*.

Whitgift, John (1530–1604). Archbishop of Canterbury and leader of the Anglicans at the Hampton Court Conference*, 1604.

Whittingham, William (1524–79). Born in Chester, brought up as a gentleman, lover of music, educated at Oxford, Fellow of All Souls, Oxford, and Dean of Durham who married John Calvin's sister (or sister-in-law) and succeeded John Knox as pastor of the English church in Geneva*, where he and other exiles had fled to escape the Marian persecutions, and where they produced an English version of the New Testament and the Psalms, 1557, a revised Psalter, 1559, and the Geneva Bible*, Whittingham being personally responsible for the 1557 New Testament, often known as Whittingham's New Testament*, using Tyndale* as his basic text.

Whittingham's New Testament, 1557. A revision of the NT in English, produced by William Whittingham*, in small octavo form, with the text divided into verses. Soon superseded by a more comprehensive edition of the whole Bible, the Geneva Bible*. Uses the word 'church' for 'ecclesia' where Tyndale* and Coverdale* had used 'congregation'. Calls James, Peter, 1 John and Jude 'General Epistles' where they had been previously been called 'Catholic Epistles' and omits the name Paul from the title of the Letter to the Hebrews.

Wicked Bible, 1631. An edition of the AV* which earned its title by accidentally omitting the word 'not' from the seventh commandment (Exod. 20.14). The printers, Robert Barker* and Associates of Cambridge*, were fined £300 by Archbishop Laud and ordered to destroy the whole edition. Sometimes called the Adulterous Bible.

Wife-Hater Bible, 1810. An edition of the Bible which substituted 'wife' for 'life' in Lk. 14.26.

Wilberforce, Samuel (1805–73). Son of William Wilberforce, educated at Oxford and Bishop of Winchester. Proposed to the Convocation of Canterbury the setting up of a body of scholars to undertake a revision of the AV*, 10 February 1870.

Wilfrid (634–709). Educated at Lindisfarne*, Canterbury and Rome, Abbot of Ripon and Bishop of York, where he decorated the walls of the church with paintings and carvings as a way of teaching people the Bible, and so regarded by some as a forerunner of all Bible translators.

Williams, Alwyn Terrell Petre (1888–1968). Educated at Jesus College, Oxford, Bishop of Durham and (later) Winchester, Chairman of the Literary Panel for the NEB* and Chairman of the Joint Committee in succession to J.W. Hunkin* in 1950.

Witham, Robert (d. 1738). Biblical scholar, educated at the English College, Douay*. President of the Roman Catholic college at Douay and publisher of a revision of the Douay-Rheims Bible*, 1730.

Women's Bible, 1895. The work of Elizabeth Cady Stanton*, with help from a review committee, in the form of a commentary and revision of those portions of the Bible which related to women, particularly where women were conspicuous by their absence, as for instance when Sarah appears to be uninvolved in the sacrifice of Isaac or when the incidents connected with Abraham, Sarah and Hagar are presented as the story of a man rather than the story of two women.

Woodhead, Abraham (1610–78). Fellow of University College, Oxford, and one of three Oxford dons responsible for a Paraphrase on the Epistles of St Paul*, 1675.

Woolsey, Theodore Dwight (1801–89). Professor of Greek at Yale University and president till 1871. Chairman of the NT panel for the ASV*.

Word Division. Documents written in the Aramaic and Assyrian square scripts had spaces between the words from the seventh century BCE and many ancient Hebrew texts had words divided either by a vertical line or a dot, but there is also evidence that some early biblical texts had no word division at all, sometimes described as *scriptio continua**. This was the case with many NT Greek mss., particularly uncials*, sometimes leading to variant readings* where words could be divided differently or simply heard differently when read aloud. (See Word Division, p. 185.)

Worms, Germany. City where Tyndale's Translation* was first printed, 1526. There were six thousand copies on sale at a few shillings each until it was prohibited by Tunstall* in 1526 and by the king in 1530.

Worthington, Thomas (1549–1672), Educated at Brasenose College, Oxford. President of the Roman Catholic College at Douay*. Responsible for contributing the notes and printing of the OT of the Douay-Rheims Bible*, 1730.

Writing. Cuneiform* writing goes back to the ancient Sumerian invaders of Mesopotamia c. 3500 BCE. The earliest examples come from Uruk (the biblical Erech, Gen. 10.10), now Worka, south of Babylon, in the Tigris-Euphrates Valley. The earliest writing material* was clay, and the text consisted of pictures representing words, usually written in vertical columns starting in the top right-hand corner. As the Sumerians adopted the practice of their invaders it provided a basis for Babylonian cuneiform c. 2500 which later became the lingua franca of the Near East. From Egypt we have papyri* dating from c. 2000 BCE with evidence that writing was known there from 500 to 1000 years earlier, mainly hieroglyphics, with signs for consonants and no vowels, and usually found on stone inscriptions. Writing on papyri called for a more cursive* script.

From 1880–1900 thousands of clay tablets were found at Nippur, many containing writing which can be dated c. 2100 BCE or even earlier. Others from about the same period were found at Ur, containing temple records and accounts in minute detail. Some found at Kish are thought to go back about 1000 years earlier still, so that by the time of David and Solomon writing had been known in the Near East for close on 2000 years, and discoveries of Hebrew texts on stone, metal and pottery suggest that writing was widely known in the days of the kings.

By the time we get to to the New Testament there is ample evidence for literary activity in the libraries of ancient cities and centres of learning such as Nineveh, Babylon, Thebes, Athens, Alexandria* and Ephesus, whilst Rome had a reputation as a city of writers, publishers and book shops in the first century CE. The most famous library for early Christianity was that in Caesarea*, founded in 253 by Pamphilus, a disciple

Word Division

A good example in English of the difficulty of working without spaces is provided by the string of letters, GODISNOWHERE, which may be read as 'God is nowhere' or God is now here'.

Gen. 49.10. שׁילה (*šylh*) may be read as one word meaning 'until *Shiloh* come' or divided so as to give שׁי לה (*šy lo*), meaning 'so long as *tribute* is brought *to him*'.

Jer. 23.33. את־מה־משׂא (*'t mh mś'*) ('what burden') in the MT is contextually difficult because there is no other example of the Hebrew את (*'t*) being used in this way. Possibly as a result of a different word division*, אתם המשׂא (*'tm hmś'*), the LXX* and Vulgate* have 'you are the burden', which gives good sense. So was the MT scribe simply making a mistake or was he recalling a similar phrase in the first half of the verse?

Amos 6.12 reads בבקרים (*bbqrym*) ('does one plough *with oxen?*') The obvious answer is 'Yes', but the one required by the context is 'No'. By a different word division, however, we get בבקר ים (*bbqr ym*) ('does one plough *the sea* with an ox?'). Intended answer: 'No'.

1 Tim. 3.16 contains the letters ὁμολογουμενωσμεγα. Some mss. have three words (ὁμολογοῦμεν ὡς μέγα) meaning 'we acknowledge how great' whereas others have two words (ὁμολογουμένως μέγα) meaning 'confessedly great'.

---

of Origen*, while the finding of the DSS* suggests a significant collection of mss. there in the first century. It is also likely that many of the early churches and even some of the more well-to-do members had their own private collections.

Prior to the invention of printing in 1450 CE every copy of a book had to be copied by hand.

Writing Materials. Many ancient inscriptions, such as the Code of Hammurabi in Babylon, 1792–1750 BCE, appear in stone. Stone inscriptions are particularly prevalent in Egypt on the walls of temples and tombs or on stelae or rock faces. The Gezer Calendar* is the earliest known Hebrew inscription, alongside the Moabite Stone* and the Siloam Inscription*. Other ancient writing materials included wood and pottery, though none was really suitable for long texts. Clay, gold, silver, copper (one of the DSS* is on copper), bronze and lead were all used, as were ostraca*, papyrus* and vellum*, the most common and important for biblical texts being papyrus and vellum, particularly in the late centuries BCE and the early centuries CE. The use of papyrus as writing material spans about 3500 years, the oldest preserved papyrus writing going back to 2470 BCE in Egypt. The dry warm weather of Egypt was conducive to its preservation and explains why virtually no NT papyri have turned up anywhere else. Ninety-seven papyri of NT material exist, none of them complete and not necessarily the most reliable witnesses to the original text, the best known being the Chester Beatty* and the Oxyrhynchus*.

The tools of the scribe were pen* and ink*, a knife (for sharpening pens), a sponge (for wiping them and for erasing text), a whetstone, and some pumice stone for smoothing rough spots on vellum*.

Writings, The. The third of the three main sections of the Hebrew Bible*, the other two being the Torah* and the Prophets*.

Wuest, Kenneth Samuel (b. c. 1893). Translator of a three-volume Expanded Translation of the New Testament*, 1956–59.

Wycliffe Bible, 1380. The first complete English Bible. Wycliffe* was probably more the inspiration and driving force, the actual translation being done by his friends, two of whom were John Purvey* and Nicholas of Hereford*. Two versions, both based on the Latin Vulgate*, one (1380–84) before his death and the other (1384) after, the second necessary because of the inadequacy of the first which was very literal. The later version has more native English idiom and became the accepted one. Each copy had to be written by hand and large sums of money (the equivalent of four-figure sums today) were paid for it by the rich. A load of hay was the price for the use of the NT for one day. Condemned by the church, 1408, for fear of erroneous doctrine.

First printed edition (NT only) was not until 1731 because it pre-dated the invention of printing and when printing arrived there were newer translations to hand. A copy of the earlier version, perhaps the original, is found in the Bodleian Library, Oxford*.

Wycliffe Bible Translators. Founded in 1942 as a sending agency for the Summer Institute of Linguistics, formerly Camp Wycliffe, founded in 1934. Their Bible translation programme focuses on translation and literacy in vernacular languages, especially minority groups with languages previously unwritten. Their doctrinal statement includes divine inspiration and the authority of the whole of the canon.

Wycliffe, John (c. 1320–84). Born in Yorkshire. Master of Balliol College, Oxford. Rector of Lutterworth*, Leicestershire, 1374. Keen Bible student and preacher, scholarly commentator on the text and the most eminent Oxford theologian of his day. Concerned about the corruption of the church and interested in its reform. Organized a body of travelling preachers called Lollards*, each of whom carried a Bible in English from which they read to the people. The Wycliffe Bible*, 1380, a translation from the Vulgate*, published in 1382 (NT) and 1384 (OT), was the first complete English Bible and the first which the English people had in their own language, Middle English. Each copy took nine months to write and cost £40 at a time when a country parson with £10 pa from all sources was considered to have a tolerable income. Uncertain how much Wycliffe actually translated but he was certainly the inspiration behind it. Some of the work was probably done by Nicholas of Hereford* and Wycliffe's disciple, John Purvey*, continued the work after his death. Over 150 copies are still in existence, all of them hand-written mss. Held responsible for the Peasants' Revolt, 1381, and put on trial. Attacked in a sermon preached at Oxford, 1382, and, following a controversy in Oxford, his teachings were pronounced heretical.

X

Ximénez de Cisneros, Francisco (1436–1517). Archbishop of Toledo who in 1502 set in motion the preparation of an edition of the entire Greek Bible, which after many delays was completed in 1522 as the Complutensian Polyglot*.

Y

York, England. Home of Alcuin* and birthplace of Miles Coverdale*.

Young Church in Action, The, 1955. A paraphrase of the Acts of the Apostles by J.B. Phillips* subsequently incorporated into The New Testament in Modern English, 1958*. Published by Geoffrey Bles, London.

Young, Patrick (1584–1652). Biblical and Patristic scholar and Royal librarian when Codex Alexandrinus* was presented to Charles I*. Probably assisted James I* in preparing the Latin edition of his work, 1619. Prepared an edition of the entire Bible which was incorporated after his death in the London Polyglot*, 1657.

Young, Robert (1822–88). Scottish theologian and Orientalist. Born in Edinburgh and apprenticed to a printer, a job which he combined with bookselling and studying languages. Went to India as a literary missionary in 1856 and became superintendent of the mission press at Surat in 1861. A Calvinist in theology

who believed in literal inspiration, with an insatiable appetite for eastern languages, ancient and modern, and best known for his *Analytical Concordance to the Bible*, 1879, containing 118,000 references with each English word arranged under its own Hebrew or Greek original. The seventeenth edition was revised by W.B. Stevenson and the publishers were the Religious Tract Society, subsequently the United Society for Christian Literature and Lutterworth Press. His Literal Translation of the Bible is often referred to as Young's Translation*, 1862.

Young's Translation, 1862. The popular name given to Robert Young's* Literal Translation of the Bible. Almost a word-for-word rendering of the original texts into English and sometimes described as 'the most literal translation ever made'. A third edition appeared in 1898. Though affected in the OT also by Young's eccentric theory on Hebrew tenses, his objective was to put the English reader on a par with those who were able to read the Bible in their original languages.

BIBLIOGRAPHY

*Recommended for further reading.

Text

Driver, G.R., *Semitic Writing: From Pictograph to Alphabet* (The Schweich Lectures, 1944; London: Oxford University Press, 2nd rev. edn, 1954).

*Flack, E.E., *et al.*, *The Text, Canon and Principal Versions of the Bible* (1956).

*Kenyon, F.G., *Our Bible and the Ancient Manuscripts* (London: Eyre & Spottiswoode, 1958).

—*The Story of the Bible* (London: John Murray, 2nd edn, 1964).

—*The Text of the Greek Bible* (London: Gerald Duckworth, 1949).

Pritchard, James B. (ed), *The Ancient Near East: An Anthology of Texts and Pictures* (London: Oxford University Press, 1958).

Roberts, C.H., and T.C. Skeat, *The Birth of the Codex* (London: The British Academy, 1983).

Thomas, D. Winton (ed.), *Documents From Old Testament Times* (London: Thomas Nelson, 1958).

*VanderKam, James C., *The Dead Sea Scrolls Today* (Grand Rapids: Eerdmans, 1994).

*Vermes, Geza, *The Dead Sea Scrolls: Qumran in Perspective* (London: SCM Press, rev. edn, 1994).

Formation of the Canon

*Barton, John, *Making the Christian Bible* (London: Darton, Longman & Todd, 1997).

—*People of the Book* (London: SPCK, rev. edn, 1993).

*Baxter, Margaret, *The Formation of the Christian Scriptures* (NT Intro. 2. TEF Study Guide, 26; London: SPCK, 1988).

Beckwith, Roger, *The Old Testament Canon of the New Testament Church and its Background in Early Judaism* (Grand Rapids: Eerdmans, 1985).

Campenhausen, Hans von, *The Formation of the Christian Bible* (Philadelphia: Fortress Press, 1972).

*McDonald, Lee M., *The Formation of the Christian Biblical Canon* (Peabody, MA: Hendrikson, 1995).

Miller, John W., *The Origins of the Bible: Re-thinking Canon History* (New York: Paulist Press, 1994).

Old Testament

*Ap-Thomas, D.R., *A Primer of Old Testament Text Criticism* (London: Epworth Press, 1947).

Roberts, B.J., *The Old Testament Text and Versions* (Cardiff: University of Wales Press, 1951).

*Tov, Emanuel, *Textual Criticism of the Hebrew Bible* (Minneapolis: Fortress Press, 1992).

Wuerthwein, E., *The Text of the Old Testament* (ET of 1st edn [Stuttgart, 1952] by P.R. Ackroyd; Oxford: Basil Blackwell, 1957).

New Testament

*Comfort, Philip Wesley, *Early Manuscripts and Modern Translations of the New Testament* (Grand Rapids: Baker Book House, 1990).

*Grant, Robert M., *The Formation of the New Testament* (London: Hutchinson University Library, 1965).

*Metzger, B.M., *The Canon of the New Testament, its Origin, Development and Significance* (Oxford: Clarendon Press, 1987).

*—*The Early Versions of the New Testament* (Oxford: Clarendon Press, 1977).

*—*The Text of the New Testament* (Oxford: Clarendon Press, 1968).

*Parker, D., *The Living Text of the Gospels* (Cambridge: Cambridge University Press, 1997).

*Pattie, T.S., *Manuscripts of the Bible: Greek Bibles in the British Library* (London: The British Library, rev. edn, 1995).

*Patzia, Arthur G., *The Making of the New Testament: Origin, Collection, Text and Canon* (Downers Grove, IL: InterVarsity Press, 1995).

Non-Canonical

*Cameron, Ron (ed.), *The Other Gospels: Non-Canonical Biblical Texts* (London: Lutterworth Press, 1983).

*Dunkerley, Roderic, *Beyond the Gospels* (Harmondsworth: Penguin Books, 1957).

Grant, Robert M., and David Noel Freedman, *The Secret Sayings of Jesus* (London: Collins, 1960).

Hennecke, E., *New Testament Apocrypha* (2 vols.; London: Lutterworth Press, 1963–65).

James, M.R. (ed.), *The Apocryphal New Testament* (Oxford: Clarendon Press, 1924).

*Jeremias, Joachim, *Unknown Sayings of Jesus* (London: SCM Press, 1957).

*Koester, Helmut, *Ancient Christian Gospels: Their History and Development* (London: SCM Press, 1990).

English Bible

*Bailey, Lloyd R., *The Word of God: A Guide to English Versions of the Bible* (Atlanta: John Knox Press, 1982).

*Barrera, Julio Trebelle, *The Jewish Bible and the Christian Bible: An Introduction to the History of the Bible* (Grand Rapids: Eerdmans, 1998).

*Bruce, F.F., *The English Bible: A History of Translations from the Earliest English Versions to the New English Bible* (London: Lutterworth Press, 1961; New York: Oxford University Press, 3rd edn, 1978).

**Cambridge Bible Handbook* (Cambridge: Cambridge University Press, 1997).

Coleman, R., *New Light and Truth: The Making of the Revised English Bible* (Oxford: Oxford University Press; Cambridge: Cambridge University Press, 1989).

*Duthie, Alan S., *How to Choose your Bible Wisely* (Swindon: Bible Society, rev. edn, 1995).

*Hammond, G., *The Making of the English Bible* (Manchester: Carcanet, 1982).

Hills, Margaret T. (ed.), *The English Bible in America: A Bibliography of Editions of the Bible and the New Testament Published in America 1777–1957* (New York: American Bible Society, 1962).

Hunt, G., *About the New English Bible* (Oxford: Oxford University Press; Cambridge: Cambridge University Press, 1970).

Jones, G. Lloyd, *The Discovery of Hebrew in Tudor England* (Manchester: Manchester University Press, 1983).

Kubo, Sakae, and Walter Specht, *So Many Versions* (Grand Rapids: Zondervan, 1983).

Levi, P., *The English Bible 1534–1859* (London: Constable; Grand Rapids: Eerdmans, 1974).

Lewis, Jack P., *The English Bible, from KJV to NIV: A History and Evaluation* (Grand Rapids: Baker Book House, 1981).

*May, H.G., *Our English Bible in the Making* (Philadelphia: Westminster Press, rev. edn, 1965).

Metzger, Dentan, Harrelson, *The Making of the New RSV* (Grand Rapids: Eerdmans, 1991).

Moulton, W.F., *The History of the English Bible, 1835–98* (London: Epworth Press, 5th edn, 1937).

Mozley, J.F., *Coverdale and his Bibles* (London: Lutterworth Press, 1953).

—*William Tyndale* (London: ???, 1937).

Nineham, Dennis (ed.), *The New English Bible Reviewed* (London: Epworth Press, 1965).

Pope, Hugh, *English Versions of the Bible 1869–1946* (revised and amplified by Sebastian Bullough; London: Herder, 1952).

*Price, I.M., The Ancestry of our English Bible (repr.; ed. W.A. Irwin and Allen P. Wikgren; New York: Harper & Brothers, 2nd rev. edn, 1956 [1949]).

*Robertson, E.H., *Makers of the English Bible* (Cambridge: Lutterworth Press, 1990).

*—*The New Translations of the Bible* (London: SCM Press, 1959).

*—*Taking the Word to the World: 50 Years of the United Bible Societies* (London: Thomas Nelson, 1996).

Robinson, H.W. (ed.), *The Bible in its Ancient and English Versions* (London: Greenwood Press, 1970).

Sheehan, B., *Which Version Now?* (Haywards Heath, West Sussex: Carey, 1980).

Sheeley, Stephen M., and Robert N. Nash, *The Bible in English Translation: An Essential Guide* (Nashville: Abingdon Press, 1997).

Vance, Lawrence M., *A Brief History of English Bible Translations* (Pensacola, FL: Vance Publications, 1993).

Walden, W., *Guide to Bible Translations* (Boston, MA: Livingworks, rev. edn, 1991).

*Weigle, L.A., *The English New Testament from Tyndale to Revised Standard Version* (Edinburgh: Thomas Nelson, 1950).

Wonderly, William L., *Bible Translations for Popular Use* (London: United Bible Societies, 1968).

Translation Issues

*Hargreaves, Cecil, *A Translator's Freedom: Modern English Bibles and their Language* (BibSem, 22; Sheffield: JSOT Press, 1993).

Nida, Eugene A., and C.R. Taber, *The Theory and Practice of Translation* (Leiden: E.J. Brill, 1969).

General Reference

Blair, Edward P., *Abingdon Bible Handbook* (Nashville: Abingdon Press, 1975).

Bowden, John, *Who's Who in Theology* (London: SCM Press, 1990).

Brauer, Jerald C. (ed.), *The Westminster Dictionary of Church History* (Philadelphia: Westminster Press, 1971).

Cambridge History of the Bible. I. *From the Beginnings to Jerome* (ed. P.R. Ackroyd and C.F. Evans); II. *The West from the Fathers to the Reformation* (ed. G.W.H. Lampe); III. *The West from the Reformation to the Present Day* (ed. S.L. Greenslade; Cambridge: Cambridge University Press, 1970, 1969, 1963).

Coggins, R.J., and J.L. Houlden, *A Dictionary of Biblical Interpretation* (London: SCM Press, 1990).

Cross, F.L., and E.A. Livingstone (eds.), *The Oxford Dictionary of the Christian Church* (Oxford: Oxford University Press, rev. edn, 1974).

Douglas, J.D. (ed.), *The New International Dictionary of the Christian Church* (Exeter: Paternoster Press, 1974).

Kee, Howard Clark, (ed.), *Cambridge Annotated Study Bible* (Cambridge: Cambridge University Press, 1993).

Laymon, Charles M., *The Interpreter's One-Volume Commentary on the Bible* (Nashville: Abingdon Press, 1971).

Manson, T.W., *A Companion to the Bible* (ed. H.H. Rowley; Edinburgh: T & T Clark, 2nd edn, 1963).

Metzger, Bruce M., and Michael D. Coogan (eds.), *The Oxford Companion to the Bible* (Oxford: Oxford University Press, 1993).

Sæbø, Magne (ed.), *Hebrew Bible. Old Testament. The History of its Interpretation, From the Beginnings to the Middle Ages*. I. *Antiquity* (Göttingen: Vandenhoek & Ruprecht, 1996).

Soulen, Richard N., *Handbook of Biblical Criticism* (London: Lutterworth, 1977).